WEIMAR AND NOW:
GERMAN CULTURAL CRITICISM
Martin Jay and Anton Kaes, General Editors

CHRISTOPH ASENDORF

BATTERIES OF LIFE

ON THE HISTORY OF

THINGS AND THEIR

PERCEPTION IN

MODERNITY

TRANSLATED BY DON RENEAU

UNIVERSITY OF CALIFORNIA PRESS   BERKELEY   LOS ANGELES   LONDON

University of California Press

Berkeley and Los Angeles, California

University of California Press

London, England

Library of Congress Cataloging-in-Publication

Data

Asendorf, Christoph, 1955–

[Batterien der Lebenskraft. English]

Batteries of life : on the history of things and

their perception in modernity / Christoph

Asendorf ; translated by Don Reneau.

p.   cm.— (Weimar and now ; 4)

Translation of : Batterien der Lebenskraft.

Includes bibliographical references (p.   ) and

index.

ISBN 0-520-06573-5 (cloth)

1. Arts, Modern—19th century. 2. Aesthetics,

Modern—19th century. 3. Arts and society.

4. Social history—19th century.

I. Title. II. Series.

NX454.A7913   1993

700′.9′034—dc20   92-15011

                                                      CIP

Printed in the United States of America

1 2 3 4 5 6 7 8 9

The paper used in this publication meets the

minimum requirements of American National

Standard for Information Sciences—Permanence

of Paper for Printed Library Materials, ANSI

Z39.48–1984 ⊗

First published as Batterien der Lebenskraft: zur

Geschichte d. Dinge u. ihrer Wahrnehmung im

19. Jh. (Giessen : Anabas–Verlag, 1984).

The publisher gratefully acknowledges receipt of

a translation grant from Inter Nationes.

Reproductions of The Bicycle Wheel (1913),

The Bottle Dryer (1914), The Fountain (1917)

by Marcel Duchamp; Portrait of Eluard (1921),

The Elephant Celebes (1921), Deux filles se

promènent à travers le ciel (1929) by Max Ernst;

Portrait of Hans Tietze and Erika Tietze-Conrat

(1909) by Oskar Kokoschka; and Impression-

Rising Sun (1872), Gare Saint-Lazare (1872–

1873), Gare Saint-Lazare (1877), Cathedral at

Rouen (1894) by Claude Monet are Copyright ©

VG Bild-Kunst Bonn, 1990, and are reproduced

here by permission. All other images are

Copyright © Anabas–Verlag, Giessen and

Werkbund-Archiv, Berlin, and are reproduced

here by permission.

Excerpts on pages 2–5 from Robert Musil, ''Who

Made You, Oh Forest Fair . . . ?'' in Posthumous

Papers of a Living Author, translated by Peter

Wortsman, appear here by kind permission of

Eridanos Press, New York. Original text

Copyright © 1957, Rowohlt Verlag, Reinbek bei

Hamburg. English Translation © 1987 by Peter

Wortsman, first published by Eridanos Press,

New York.

Excerpts on pages 62–63 from Robert Musil, The

Man without Qualities, translated by E. Wilkins

and Ann E. Kaiser, appear here by kind

permission of Martin Secker and Warburg.

Robert Musil, Gesammelte Werke, edited by

Adolf Frise, Copyright © 1978 Rowohlt Verlag,

Reinbek bei Hamburg.

CONTENTS

"The crux of the matter," writes Karl Kraus, borrowing the language of the court case, "is that I would rather starve than eat Sternschuß eggs. Indeed, as long as such things exist, I consider death by starvation the only honorable way out of a hopelessly miserable situation." A catastrophe has been made of the enjoyment of an egg, a product of nature. The cause of the transformation is that the egg no longer appears on the market as an egg but as a Sternschuß egg: "A horrible state of affairs, which binds man and commodity into an indissoluble, disgusting union."[1] Sternschuß is accused of having delivered under his name eggs which were not Sternschuß eggs. Kraus turns the accusation around: what outrages him is not that Sternschuß delivered eggs that were not Sternschuß eggs, but that Sternschuß is allowed to put eggs on the market only as Sternschuß eggs. Eggs have been transformed from a product of nature into an article for the market, one which in turn assumes natural qualities, namely those derived from the nature of Mr. Sternschuß, or, as the case may be, of the chickens in his possession. Karl Kraus deciphers commodity exchange as an obscene erotic impertinence, refuses to allow the eggs into his mouth, and thereby presents in idiosyncratic miniature the metamorphosis to which things are subjected once released into circulation.

Who Made You, Oh Forest Fair . . . ? Oh, how you abhor everything out of the ordinary, everything that demands effort and ingenuity when you are sick, and how you long for the eternal, healthy mediocrity common to all men. Is there a problem in that? Let it wait! Sometimes it is a more pressing question, whether in an hour there will be chicken broth or something more invigorating on the table, and you sing to yourself: "Who made you, oh forest fair, rise so tall above the ground? . . . " Life seems bent so strangely straight; since, by the way, you never could keep a tune before.

But little by little your recovery proceeds, and with it the evil spirit of the intellect returns. You start observing things. Directly opposite your balcony that green canopy of trees still hugs the side of a mountain, and you still hum that grateful song to it, a habit which all of a sudden you can't seem to shake; but one day you realize that the forest does not consist only of a series of notes, but of trees, which before you couldn't tell for the forest. And if you look very closely, you can even recognize how these friendly giants struggle over light and ground with the envy of horses fighting over fodder. They stand quietly side by side, here perhaps a grove of spruce, there a grove of beech trees: It looks naturally dark and light as in a painting; and moralistically edifying as the touching togetherness of families. But, in fact, it is the eve of a thousand-year-long battle.

Are there not seasoned naturalists from whom we can learn that the stallwart oak, today a veritable epitomy of solitude, once spread in hoardes far and wide throughout Germany? That the spruce, which now supplants everything else, was a relatively recent interloper? That at some time in the past an era of the beech empire was established and, at another time, the imperialism of the alder dominated? There was a migration of the trees, just as there was a migration of the nations, and wherever you see a homogeneous native forest, it is in fact an army that established a stronghold on the embattled promontory; and where a variety of trees seem to conjure up an image of happy coexistence, they are really scattered combatants, the surviving remnants of enemy hoardes crowded

At the beginning of the nineteenth century, Hegel draws attention to the conditions of a differentiating mode of perception of things. The *Jenaer Realphilosophie*, a series of lectures Hegel delivered between 1803 and 1806 and first published in 1931–1932, includes far-reaching reflections on economics. Social stratification is explained by reference to the various forms of labor. The peasantry represents "immediate familiarity with raw, concrete labor" in nature. "Concrete labor is elementary labor, [the] material means of sustenance. . . . This materiality changes into the abstraction of labor and knowledge of the general: the class of commerce and law. The labor of the bourgeois class is the abstract trade of the individual; its disposition is uprightness. It took labor from nature and raised up out of unconsciousness the human capacity to lend form."[2] Materiality, immediacy, and concrete labor are confronted with abstraction and liberation from immediacy.

This differentiation is recapitulated within the bourgeois mode of production. The industrial mode of production is fundamentally distinct from handicraft manufacturing. The difference becomes visible in the workshop, which is historically situated between two major forms of production. Hegel's example is that of the pin factory, drawing on the description by Adam Smith: "In the same proportion as the quantity produced increases, the value of labor declines. Labor becomes deader as it becomes the labor of machines; the aptitude of the individual shrinks immeasurably and the consciousness of the factory worker declines to a state of utter apathy. And the connection between any specific type of labor and the whole infinite mass of needs [becomes] completely incalculable and turns into a blind dependency." The "assimilation of nature" transpires solely through the "interpolation of intermediary links."[3]

If the workshop initially unites independent craftsmen, over the course of time they nevertheless lose not only their economic but also their professional independence, since their exclusive production of specific parts causes them to lose their ability to manufacture the complete product. They become workers assigned quite specialized tasks within the division of labor. The objects are no longer in their hands from beginning to end, from raw

together, too tired and exhausted to continue battle!

This, at any rate, is still poetry, even if it isn't quite the poetry of peacefulness which we look for in the woods; real nature is above even that. Let nature revive your strength and—insofar as all the advantages of modern nature are put at your disposal—you will likewise make the second observation that a forest consists mostly of rows of boards bedecked by a little greenery. This is no discovery, but merely an avowal of the truth; I suspect that we could not even let our glance dip into the greenery, if all were not prearranged so that our glance was met by straight and even spaces. The sly foresters arrange for a little irregularity, for a tree that steps out of line to the rear of the columns just to catch our glance, for a diagonal branch or a toppled limb left lying there all summer. For they have a subtle sense of nature and know that we would not otherwise believe them. Virgin forests have something highly unnatural and degenerate about them. The unnatural, which has become a second nature in nature, recovers its natural aspect in woods like this. A German forest wouldn't do such a thing.

A German forest is conscious of its duty, that we might sing of it: "Who made you, oh forest fair, rise so tall above the ground? May our master's praise resound, as long as my voice fills the air!" That master is a master forester, a chief forester or forest commissioner, who built up the forest in such a way that he would by all rights be very angry if we did not immediately notice his expert handiwork. He provided for the light, the air, the selection of trees, access roads, the location of the lumber camps, and the removal of the tree stumps; and gave the trees that beautiful, perfectly aligned, well-kept appearance that so delights us when we come from the wild irregularity of the metropolis.

Behind this forest missionary, who with a simple heart preaches the gospel of the lumber business to the trees, there stands a grounds keeper, a land officer or princely apointee, who writes the rules. According to his ordinances, so many square feet of open space or young saplings are prescribed each year; he distributes the beautiful vistas and the cool shades. But it is not in his hands that the ultimate destiny of the forest lies. Still higher than this authority are the reigning

material to the finished product, but now only during a very specific phase of the production process. This change causes the relation between the producers and things to lose its basis in repetitive experience, continuity, and an overview of the entire process of production. The new relation that ensues, one already evident in the workshop, is based on partial experience. The essential characteristic of this mode of labor is the temporal and spatial separation of individual work steps from one another. The sequential character of the work process, the "and then," disappears—what follows is always the same. Experience formed from the coherence of the work steps taken together is obliterated. Labor with tools and machines removes the human being from the living connectedness of nature. This abstraction, Hegel concludes, rebounds in turn upon the human: "Labor is the immanent making of oneself into a thing."[4] The instrumentalization of nature makes the human individual into an instrument.

Along with this mode of production there arises a form of exchange that strips objects of their qualities; that is, the split between materiality and abstraction, already typical of the various class-specific forms of production, is recapitulated on the level of the perception of things. Hegel writes about the labor of the merchant class: "Exchange is movement, the spirit, the center, that which is liberated from use and needs, as well as from laboring and immediacy." The object is divided into the specific article of trade, on the one hand, and an abstraction—money—on the other. "The thing of need has become a merely imagined and unenjoyable one."[5] A relation to things that makes the latter accessible in their spatial and temporal particularity is just as little possible in the handicraft, later industrial, mode of production as in exchange, which is continually abstracting from the sensual nature of the product. Things are no longer experienced in a natural connection but in an indirect and fragmentary one.

The establishment of bourgeois society following the French Revolution coincides with the beginning of industrialization—the development of a complex of administrative procedures in the natural sciences, the humanities, and economics with one overriding characteristic: a stripping away of the qualities of the existing object world, its reordering into quantitative and abstract elements.

woodland deities, the lumber dealers and their clients, the sawmills, wood pulp plants, building contractors, shipyards, cardboard and paper mills . . . Here the connection dissolves in that nameless chaos, the spectral flow of goods and money which accords even the man whose poverty drives him to suicide the certainty that the consequences of his act will effect the economy; and promotes you to the status of superintendant of sheep and woods, all of which can go to hell, when in the sweltering big city summer your pants rub up against a wooden bench and the bench in turn rubs up against your pants.

Shall we then sing, "Who made you, oh lovely depot of technology and trade so fair, rise so tall above the ground? May our master's praise—of the termites sucking sustenance from your wood chips; but also, depending on the circumstances, other methods of your utilization—resound, as long as my voice fills the air!—?" To this question we will have to answer no, in principle. There still is the ozone that hangs over the trees, the forest's soft green substance, its coolness, its stillness, its depth and solitude. These are un-used by-products of the forester's technology and are as splendidly superfluous as man is on vacation, when he is nothing but himself. Herein lies a deep affinity. Nature's bosom may indeed be unnatural, but then man on vacation is likewise an artificial construct. He has resolved not to think about business, a resolve that constitutes a veritable inner ban of silence. After a short while everything grows unspeakably and delightfully still and empty in him.

How grateful he is, then, for the little signs, the quiet words that nature has in store for him! How lovely are those path markers, those inscriptions informing him that it is only another quarter hour's walk to the Welcome Wayfarers Inn, those benches and weathered plaques that reveal the ten commandments of the forestry commission; nature waxes eloquent! How happy is he who finds others in whose company he can tread closer to nature: partners for his card game on the lawn or a punch bowl at sunset! Through such tiny aids, nature acquires the salient qualities of a lithograph, and much of the confusion is filtered out. A mountain is then a mountain, a brook is a brook, green and blue lie with consummate clarity side by side, and

Paul Valéry, whose reflections are devoted to an analysis of modernity in its diverse forms, draws attention to the consequences for the natural sciences. About physics, he writes: "It is the end of the world. Finis imaginum. All the principles of physics have been discovered in opposition to immediate observation."[6] He continues more generally: "We have acquired a vast reservoir of indirect knowledge, which reaches us through relays and informs us through signals about events taking place in orders of magnitude so far removed from those having some relation to our senses, that all the notions by which we normally conceive of the world no longer hold good. . . . On the new scale of things, the concepts of particle, position, time, matter, energy, become virtually interchangeable. The very word *phenomenon* loses its meaning."[7] Immediate experience—that, for example, which the craftsman has of the product of his labor—no longer has any meaning; it has become obsolete in the face of the claims of scientific differentiation and social interdependencies.

What transpires in the natural sciences—the conversion of the immediate and naive perception of things into laws of universal applicability—has its analogue in the humanities: the removal of things and data from their context of origin for collecting and processing. One consequence is what Nietzsche regards as the "characteristic of modernity," defined more precisely in his critique of historicism and antiquarianism as "the ascendancy of dealers and middlemen." He takes as his examples the man of letters, the historian, but also the popular representative; and he proposes an excellent corrective: "In the city of antiquity . . . one put one's own foot forward, and had nothing to offer such modern representatives and middlemen, except, perhaps, a kick."[8]

Quite divergent names were invented, from the economic, scientific, cultural, or sociological points of view, for the same process. Hegel spoke of the making of oneself into a thing; Nietzsche of the ascendancy of middlemen and dealers; Valéry of the *relais*, those interpositions characteristic of physics as well as of knowledge of social life; and Musil put it succinctly, "life begins to become more and more abstract."[9]

The modern metropolis, inseparable in its origins from industrialization, is the place where new modes of perception arise out of abstraction. The city multiplies human contacts and at the

no ambiguities keep the observer from coming, by the quickest route, to the conviction that it is indeed a lovely thing that he possesses.

However, as soon as we have gotten this far, the so-called eternal values easily set in. Ask any man of today, not yet confused by critical chatter, what he prefers, a landscape painting or a lithograph, and he will answer without hesitation that he prefers a good lithograph. For the uncorrupted man loves clarity and idealism, and industry is infinitely better at both than art.

Such questions reveal the progressing convalescence of our patient. The doctor says to him: "Criticize as much as you like; bad temper is a sign of recovery."—"That makes perfect sense!" replied the distressed patient, returning to conciousness.

Robert Musil, *Posthumous Papers of a Living Author*, trans. Peter Wortsman (Hygiene, Colo.: Eridanos Press, 1987), pp. 91–96

same time removes from them the quality of persistence, which they had, for example, in the village community (*Gemeinschaft*). Continuity and individual characteristics disappear in the circulation of human beings and commodities. Nearly simultaneous and, although both under the influence of Georg Simmel's sociological investigations, completely independent of each other, Robert Musil and Walter Benjamin arrive at conceptually related analyses of the change in object relations and modes of perception in the city. Benjamin works with opposing concepts of experience, *Erfahrung* and *Erlebnis*. *Erfahrung*, grounded in the domain of the epic tale, the storyteller, and the craftsman, is bound to notions of continuity, habit, and sequence. Its opposite is *Erlebnis*, the discontinuous experience of the city, which is manifest as information (the form of communication corresponding to the industrial labor process), as sensation, or else as adventure.[10] Musil writes: "In the country . . . gods still come to mortal men. There one is something and experiences things. But in town, where there are a thousand times as many experiences, one is no longer capable of relating them to each other." One cause of this is the "system of 'indirectness,' developed to the point of virtuosity," which is characteristic of relations in the city, of those in financial affairs and in administration, where the one who orders a task done "does not directly take a hand in the execution of his directions." Ulrich, the man without qualities, calls that which no longer exists "the law . . . of narrative order," according to which one event follows the other along a "narrative thread."[11] He sees "a world of qualities without a man to them, of experiences without the one who experiences them."[12]

This affects the perception of things, now spatially displaced in generalized circulation or under the gaze of the natural sciences and pushed out of the domain of habitual experience. Things no longer inhabit a spatiotemporal continuum but exist only momentarily and in isolation. In Marx's analysis the commodity in circulation becomes a representative of the social continuum. The mysteriousness of the commodity form (Novalis speaks of a "theater of commodities"[13]) is the fetish character of the commodity itself; it consists in the circumstance that "the social character of men's labour appears to them as an objective character stamped upon the product of that labour: because the relation of the producers to the sum total of their own labour is presented to them as a social relation, existing not between themselves, but between the products of their labour. This is the reason why the products of labour become commodities, social things whose qualities are at the same time perceptible and imperceptible by the senses."[14] Commodities embody the abstract as materiality, as a natural quality of things. The form of perception of *Erlebnis*, which is in principle discontinuous, is characterized by the same ambivalence: on the one hand, it is a fleeting perception of fragments of reality; on the other, *Erlebnis* can, as for example in the view of Bergson or Dilthey, become the representative of an alleged totality, a "picture of the universe taken out of the explanatory context."[15] The isolated *Erlebnis* becomes a stand-in for a universal continuum, just as the commodity does in Marx.

The transformation of materiality into abstraction, and attempted reversals of the process, in a society devoted to commodity production is the subject of the following investigation. Its object is not so much the philosophical or sociological reflection of this dynamism, as its representations in literature, the arts, and in daily life.

THE BODY, THE ECONOMY,

AND THE WORLD OF THINGS

1. *L'HOMME MACHINE*   The question of the perception of things since industrialization leads to the question of the relation of people to things, of animate to inanimate. Descartes writes, in the fifth chapter of his *Discourse on Method* (1637), of the "*bête machine*," the animal machine. He draws a strict distinction between animals and people, to whom alone he attributes a soul and thereby the capacity for rational action. Yet Descartes identifies vital processes with the dynamic forms of an automaton, thus providing a point of departure for the adequation of the human world and the world of things,[1] that is to say, the meshing of organic and abstract processes, which was to occupy thought on various levels in the eighteenth century.

In 1748, a good century after Descartes and roughly contemporaneous with the mechanistic worldview of the Encyclopedists, La Mettrie publishes a work with the epoch-making title *L'homme machine*, in which he abolishes the distinction between people and animals emphasized by Descartes and attributes to human being the mere status of an especially complicated machine. When he was writing his controversial work, La Mettrie was familiar with the famous flute player Vaucanson presented to the Academy in 1738. The miraculous contrivance—an intricate mechnanism in which a set of bellows driven by a clockwork supplied air to a flute—caused an artificial flute player to produce tones just like a human flautist through the movements of fingers, lips, and tongue.

What happens here both theoretically and practically is a test run of the mechanics of the human body; it is the prelude to the mechanization that would emerge on a large scale a little later,

François Quesnay, *Tableau économique*, 1758.

after the invention of the steam engine in 1765 and the development of new techniques of production.

The identification of organic and abstract processes is also to be found in economics. Like La Mettrie (and Mandeville), François Quesnay is a doctor, and he also draws his theory from observations of the universal paradigm, the human body. In 1758, he drafted his *Tableau économique*, in which economic processes were derived from the model of the circulation of blood in the human body. The medical model of circulation is yet older, published by the English doctor William Harvey as early as 1628, at the time of Descartes. Novel, however, is Quesnay's transfer of the model of circulation to economic processes, which are thereby equated with the workings of nature: the (absolutist) state, conceived as a giant body, is kept alive by circulation.[2] Thus, the first logically comprehensive system of political economy to win a place among the human sciences develops as an analogue to the human body. That is also its great weakness. With economic life taken to be a natural process, with only land and soil, but not trade and industry, understood as productive forces, it cannot conceive such an important category as labor, nor the distinction between the natural price and the market price, that is, between use value and exchange value. Such a conceptualization presupposes the dissolution of the paradigm drawn from the natural and human worlds. Adam Smith, writing in the light of England's more advanced industrialization, accomplished the shift in 1776 with *The Wealth of Nations*. Smith is the first to grant recognition to the abstraction of economic processes, which had scarcely been imaginable in the rococo era, the transitional period between the baroque age and the Enlightenment and industrialization.

Benjamin Franklin's *Advice to a Young Tradesman* (1748), for Max Weber an illustration of the Protestant ethic, still conceives the circulation of money in the image of human procreation: "Remember, that money is of the prolific, generating nature. Money can beget money and its offspring can beget more and so on." In a peculiar analogy to the biblical doctrine of original sin, Franklin makes rejecting the specific procreative power of money a sin of nearly infinite consequence: "He that kills a breeding sow, destroys all her offspring to the thousandth generation. He that

Benjamin Franklin, armchair with folding library ladder, ca. 1780.

Illustration for de Sade, *Juliette*, 1797.

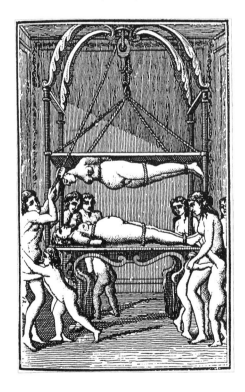

murders a crown, destroys all that it might have produced, even scores of pounds."[3]

Whether consciously or not, Franklin's choice of examples alludes to the fertility ritual of sacrificing a pig found, for example, in Roman mythology.[4] But, entirely in the spirit of the Protestant ethic, he turns this pointless waste into its opposite: it is not the sacrificial offering but its renunciation that promotes fertility.

The sacrifice left undone becomes the precondition of wealth, which, in the metaphor of family structure, is imagined as the blessing of an infinite number of children. Those who circulate money become omnipotent, uniting man and woman in one, or, to put it differently, they become the progenitors of a clan of "money children." Procreative drive and the economy unite as the power of creation itself, a thought which demonstrates that the Protestant ethic is acquiring a life of its own. Franklin, Quesnay's contemporary, also sees the body as the paradigm of the economy, though on the basis of different assumptions. There is as yet no mention of the abstraction that will accompany the development of money and commodity circulation under conditions of industrialization. These theorists see the economy as a natural process.

The association of the body and the economy also appears in Sade. The barter economy is key to the construction of the frame story of *The 120 Days of Sodom*, with Duclos delivering the stories in exchange for her continued safety.[5] She exchanges the charms

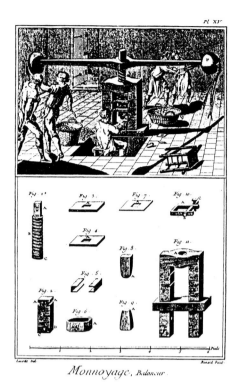

Minting coins and coin stamp.
From Diderot, *Encyclopedia,*
1751–1780.

of words for her life, since it is taken as a settled fact "that the sensations conveyed through the organ of speech are those which flatter more and whose impressions are the liveliest."[6] As a result of this identification of speech and eroticism the stories are the actual site of debauchery, and its practice serves solely as an intermission and for relaxation.[7] Duclos no longer makes use of her body; she produces lust with words. Her stories, the words of which multiply the body, are a medium of exchange like money; in the act of exchange, lust becomes free. Here Sade borders on Franklin, who represented the circulation of money (in Sade, words) as pleasurable procreation. The words have been separated off from Duclos's body and are, like money, freely disposable as a medium of exchange or pleasure. They are the bodiless representatives of lust.

The organization of the real, that is, orgies not narrated but practiced, is determined by methods derived from the division of labor as propagated by Adam Smith. The production of lust is subjected to rigorous calculation—the body becomes an object of which the most rational possible use is to be made. The principle of profitability is transferred to bodies, the systematic processing of which aims at increasing the wealth of lust. Like parts of a machine, people are integrated into a general mechanism. The individual parts of a machine are useless, and so, in Sade, are individual human beings. His groups are made up of particularized individuals acting in concert; lust is formed through a division of labor that leads to a mechanization of the body. The erotic is reified, but the "thing" so constituted consists of people.

The body, the economy, lust, and the machine enter into a close relationship; but in Sade it is still the body paradigm that determines the image of the division of labor, as it determines the image of the machine in La Mettrie and Vaucanson, and that of the economy in Quesnay and Franklin.

2.   *VATHEK*, OR DISINTEGRATION

Writing at the time of the first industrialization, William Beckford took the conflict between imagination and reality as the theme of *Vathek*, his novel in the form of an oriental fairy tale. It is organized around the ancient leitmotiv that the possession of something is possible only at the cost of the soul, shadow, heart,

From a handbook on silk
production, Neuchâtel, 1783.

or whatever might otherwise be the figuration of the self. This mythical–fairy-tale form of exchange sets a thing, a treasure or money, off against life. Mallarmé saw in Beckford's novel "one of the proudest games of the awakened modern imagination,"[8] and not without reason: it is concerned, after all, with the fascination of the world of things, which absorbs all available libidinal and social energies.

The story begins with the arrival in a city of a stranger bearing "extraordinary wares."[9] The supposed peddler is revealed as the possessor of wondrous utensils—slippers that assist the feet in walking, knives that cut without requiring a movement of the hand, etc. The goods, all of them adorned with precious gems, are therefore utopian machines that relieve human beings of labor; and all without the obtrusive mechanism of anything like a steam engine. The caliph Vathek is especially interested in a collection of sabers, "whose blades emitted an abiding shine," and on which are engraved apparently indecipherable foreign letters. Such are the wares that cast a spell on Vathek. And here begins a seduction by things whose quality is connoted doubly—the ware is a commodity and simultaneously a magical object; it materializes utopian possibilities, for which it is the reified substitute.

The message of the continually changing foreign letters is equivocal: if, on the one hand, they promise enticingly that the wares are only "the least of wonders of a place where all is wonderful," they threaten, on the other, misfortune for anyone who "seeks to know that of which he should remain ignorant."[10] In the novel, the possession of the ware and being delivered up to the oracle are identical—the boundary between the miracle-performing thing, comparable to a fairy-tale treasure where materiality is the least of its determinations, and the abstract ware is not fixed unambiguously: things are consequently not only purchasable[11] but at the same time carriers of imagination. The peddler is, as a magician, possessor of the wares; he promises the covetous caliph the fulfillment of his wishes in "a place no one knows,"[12] and disappears by turning himself into a ball and rolling into an abyss.

The form of the ball and the mobility of money stand in mutual relation: "the roundness of coins which makes them 'roll' symbolizes the rhythm of movement that money imparts to trans-

Architecture

I have a question for our honored artists. Why always nothing but pillars in architecture? Why always the same type of molding? Why this eternal repetition of the same designs? Good, these pillars are supposed to recall tree trunks, the moldings represent girders and the socles flowerpots full of plants—wonderful! But I have already seen it a thousand times. Could you not finally think up something new? Is architecture so limited—or is it the architects? Does every palace have to resemble another one somewhere else?

I herewith indict architecture for the crime of surpassing monotony and let it publicly be known that I am fed up with seeing pillars, pillars, and nothing but pillars wherever I look!

A bunch of pretty buildings, of which none resembles the other, of which every one is unmistakable, have recently come to line the city walls and beautify the outlying quarters. Their diversity proves that now and again architecture is quite capable of renouncing its accustomed rules to enchant and surprise the eye.

Architecture's true miracles, however, are accomplished by the Parisian architects in the interiors of their buildings. Using artful and sophisticated floor plans, they save ground space, indeed, even multiply the available surface, and they know how to endow what they gain in the most praiseworthy fashion with a comfort that would have caused our ancestors, who knew only how to build distressingly long, rectangular halls supported by gigantic crisscrossing rafters, no little astonishment. Our little dwellings today are equipped and turned like clean, well-rounded snail shells, and one can live agreeably of late in spaces that were scarcely to be used before on account of being dark and badly laid out. Would anyone have dared two hundred years ago to dream of rotating fireplaces that heat two different rooms, or of hidden, invisible staircases, of little closets concealed in corners where no one could suspect one, of false entrances that hide the real exits, of floors that could be raised or sunken, in short, of all of these labyrinths in whose hiding places one, sheltered from the curious gaze of the servants, can indulge one's inclinations? Could anyone have suspected back then that architecture would one

actions. . . . For centuries in the countries bordering on the Nile there even existed globular money composed of glass, wood, or agate—the differences in material used suggests that its form was the reason for its reputed popularity."[13] Beckford sets his novel in the era of spherical money of the Orient. The ball-shaped peddler-magician symbolizes the ideal form of money—the desire to possess becomes the dynamic energy that pulls Vathek and the entire population along with it: ". . . but no sooner did they catch a glimpse of the ball than . . . they . . . were incapable of resisting the attraction."[14] The desire for possession destroys the social fabric by progressively subordinating all activities to itself, which the novel manifests in the accumulative force of the balls. "Private property does not know how to change crude need into *human* need."[15]

From the underworld, the peddler-magician sets conditions as in an initiation rite; he demands "the blood of fifty of the most beautiful sons of thy viziers."[16] Possession can only be purchased through sacrifice. The historical predecessors of the circulation of money are the sacrificial altars of oriental temples, in which, after human sacrifices were done away with, their substitutes formed the basis for a developed commodity trade.[17] That is one aspect of the background to the only apparently bizarre demand; the other is that possession has a definite price under the conditions of private property: "Every person speculates on creating a *new* need in another, so as to drive him to a fresh sacrifice, to place him in a new dependence and to seduce him into a new mode of *gratification* and therefore economic ruin. Each tries to establish over the other an *alien power*, so as to find thereby satisfaction of his own selfish need. The increase in the quantity of objects is accompanied by an extension of the realm of the alien powers to which man is subjected."[18] To the "new needs" created by the "quantity of objects" correspond the "extraordinary wares" in the novel; to the "subjection to alien powers" corresponds the appearance of the peddler-magician, who lures the caliph into his powers and, having done so, demands a human sacrifice. Later, under conditions of commodity circulation, an outlay of money will suffice to achieve the same end. Deciphering the events in the novel thus becomes possible through the language of the economists.

John Martin, "Belshazzar's Feast," 1820.

The demand for a child sacrifice creates a connection between the repression of drives and possession, one that is formulated still more clearly elsewhere: Vathek's mother, Carathis, demands from him a clear decision between his beloved, Nuronihar, and the treasure. When Vathek loses sight of the other treasure because of his love, the mother storms up on horseback and, finding the couple locked in an embrace, reviles them: "Thou double-headed and four-legged monster! What means all this winding and writhing? Are thou not ashamed to be seen grasping this limber sapling in preference to the scepter of the Preadamite sultan?"[19] The son's love becomes a monstrosity in the face of the fabulous scepter, which, through the words of the mother, symbolizes the phallic-patriarchal, drive-repressing power principle. Possession is played off against the fleeting pleasures of love. Vathek arrives at a compromise: he travels with Nuronihar to the wonders of the promised kingdom, which turns out to be an underground palace.

In 1781 Beckford hosted a three-day Christmas party at his castle, Fonthill. The events there supplied the direct inspiration for the novel, which he purportedly wrote immediately afterward on a train, and the castle in particular inspired the representation of the palace. The painter and set designer Loutherbourg had drawn on the *Carcerci* series by Piranesi to lend the rooms of the palace the aura of hopelessness of reconstructed space character-

Philippe-Jacques de Loutherbourg, *Coalbrookdale by Night*, 1801.

John Martin, *The Flood*, 1826.

G. B. Piranesi, sheet VII from the second version of the *Carceri* series, etching.

istic of Piranesi's etchings and so important for the cultural history of the preromantic period. Beckford was quite familiar with Piranesi's work; the latter had, in fact, created a few of the *Vasi, Candelabri, Cippi . . .* (1778) etchings for Beckford's father.[20] The famous Piranesi series, valued especially by such representatives of so-called black romanticism as De Quincey and Baudelaire, bore, in the second, reworked version of 1761 (first edition, 1745), an ambiguous title: *Carceri d'Invenzione.* It could mean either "imaginary dungeon" or, on the other hand, "dungeon of the imagination." The site of the blasphemous Christmas party is redecorated as a dungeon, which leads Mario Praz to associate Beckford's diversions with those of another spirit of the times having a predilection for secluded and isolated castles—the Marquis de Sade. For Praz, the pleasures Beckford indulges "breathe the atmosphere of *Justine,* or at least of the *Liaisons dangereuses.*"[21]

Beckford, his beloved, and some friends walled themselves up in Fonthill for three days, as he recalls in 1838, nearly sixty years later: "The doors and windows were closed so tightly that neither daylight nor visitors could enter, let alone peer in."[22] The arrangement of the orgy presupposes complete isolation from the outside environment as the condition of undisturbed sensual pleasure. Inside the do-it-yourself dungeon an artificial counterworld arises, this one, unlike that in the novel, based in eroticism. Piranesi's unending rooms, reinterpreted hedonistically, present the spatial model of the experience: such an organization of space, the apparently endless interior perspectives, seems to guarantee the endlessness of sensual pleasure.

And likewise the presentation of the fabulous palace in the novel: "The moon dilated on a vast platform the shades of the lofty columns which reached from the terrace almost to the clouds; the gloomy watchtowers, whose numbers could not be counted, were veiled by no roof, and their capitals, of an architecture unknown in the records of the earth, served as an asylum for the birds of darkness which, alarmed at the approach of such visitants, fled away croaking."[23] Described here is a fantastic architecture of "monstrous" proportions, and one that is also completely devoid of people. This type of exaggerated scale, far beyond the dimensions intended for social intercourse, is characteristic not only of the fantastic architecture of Piranesi's ruins but also of the architectural designs of the French Revolution. With its "cosmic" dimensions, the abstract geometric design of the sphere of Boullée's cenotaph for Newton (1784) exceeds all human scale just as much as the palace Vathek finds in the novel. Beckford shares his preference for nocturnal illumination with Boullée and other revolutionary architects: Boullée sketches the cenotaph by moonlight, explaining that sharply delineated structures in the moonlight appear more monumental and enigmatic.[24] Gigantic cemetery architecture (aside from Boullée, Ledoux's 1784 design for the city of Chaux might be mentioned), like the ruins, designates the dark underside of architectural fantasies before and after the revolution; people appear minimalized, threatened by death and destruction. And the gigantic catastrophic works later designed by Piranesi's imitator, the painter John Martin, also provide a contrapuntal accompaniment to the restrained bourgeois classicism of the postrevolutionary period. It was also John Martin who, in 1820, painted views of the Fonthill castle for the aging Beckford.[25]

Next to the palace ruins in the novel stands a rocky cliff, where "a staircase of polished marble . . . seemed to approach the abyss."[26] Vathek and Nuronihar found themselves in a place "which though roofed, was so spacious and lofty that at first they took it for an immeasurable plain. . . . They went wandering on from chamber to chamber, hall to hall, and gallery to gallery, all without bounds and limits."[27] These interiors, as is evident from Beckford's letter of 1838 mentioned above, are inspired by the Christmas decorations in Fonthill, where Loutherbourg, following Piranesi's model, arranged infinite perspectives of stairs and passageways.[28] This architecture has no use value, but is, taken in itself, a symbol of the boundless depths of the imagination.

In the novel these halls are filled with enormous riches, among which there wanders a crowd of people who, like Vathek and Nuronihar, have arrived here at the goal of desire, apparently in possession of the fascinating wares. But their relations are like those of private property owners who sell things, thereby confronting one another as separate persons defined by their "reciprocal independence."[29] "They all avoided each other; and though surrounded by a multitude that no one could number each wandered at random."[30] This behavior anticipates that of the urban

E. L. Boullée, project for a cenotaph for Isaac Newton, 1784.

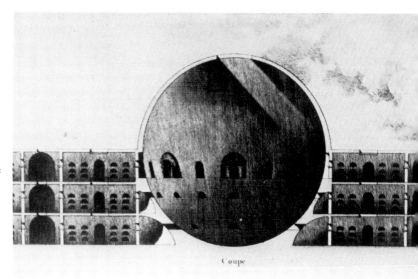

C. N. Ledoux, design of the cemetery for the industrial city of Chaux, after 1784, cross section.

crowd of the nineteenth century, as Poe, for example, describes it in the story, "The Man in the Crowd." People are under way not to communicate with one another but to take care of business, which reduces any other social contact to a nuisance. The people in Beckford's novel are isolated inside a crowd, are victims of their own search for treasures—their breasts are "transparent as a crystal," which affords a glimpse at a "heart enveloped in flames."[31] Petrifaction (or, alternately, burning) is the price of possession.

According to Marx's later claims, the creator of value under capitalist conditions of production is human labor "in a congealed state, when embodied in the form of some object," so that capital appears as "dead labor" and circulation as "the great social retort in which everything is thrown to come out again as a gold crystal." Beckford's treasure chamber anticipates symbolically the alchemical powers of capitalist transubstantiation, which moves things and petrifies man: the treasure chamber has become a tomb in which living-dead people are stored along with things.[32]

Proceeding from the boundless *Carceri d'Invenzione* of Piranesi, Beckford links the disintegration of space with the motif of the accumulation of commodities. In his plans for the salt-mining city of Chaux at about the same time, Ledoux became the first to take the labor process as the point of departure for city planning, but the construction of the project was halted in 1779 owing to lack of funds.[33] Architecture is the indicator of social changes; it

C. N. Ledoux, second project for the new city of Chaux, which was partially executed beginning in 1775.

appeals to the needs of the production process for its standard. The infinite *Carceri* recur in the form of the English industrial cities, as described by Schinkel in 1826: "It makes a terribly dismal, uncanny impression—enormous buildings erected wholly of red brick for utterly naked need by simple masters innocent of architectural knowledge."[34] The boundlessly fantastic architecture of Beckford, the space of the imagination petrified into a commodity, points toward the labyrinth of industrial civilization, in which people appear as nothing more than helpless, perishing worker ants.

3.   GERMAN ROMANTICISM: MONEY AND HAPPINESS, OR THE EROTICISM OF THE WORLD OF THINGS

a)   In his *Allgemeine Brouillon* of 1798–1799, Novalis writes: "The commercial spirit is the spirit of the world. It is the great spirit altogether. It sets everything in motion and ties everything together. . . . The historical commercial spirit—which conforms slavishly to given needs, to the circumstances of time and place— is only a bastard of the genuine, creative commercial spirit."[35] This, understood here in economic terms, is the romanticizing program of Novalis, a part of his concept of a "magical idealism." The world of things and the flow of commodities are not conceptualized as alienating but as something in which all-powerful subjectivity can embody itself. The world spirit is not comprehensible in itself but only as a concrete spirit—in the example given, as the commercial spirit. Novalis does not, as Tieck for example does in "Runenberg," see the metamorphosis of sensuousness into treasures as a danger. Quite the contrary, he sees in money a universal-utopian adhesive by which the subjectively guided romanticization of the world might be advanced. As a "relational schema" through which "every thing can be substituted," Fichte's theory of knowledge (the basis of all early romantic theories) is closely related to a "conception of money" for Novalis.[36]

If one reads just a little against the grain, it is also possible to understand from this point of view the program Novalis outlined in a letter of January 20, 1799, to Friedrich Schlegel: "Absolute abstraction—annihilation of the present—apotheosis of the future—of this actually better world, that is the core of the injunction of Christianity." The abstracting and annihilating power of money is an analogue to that of the romantic spirit, which, however, dreams in Novalis of the utopian mutability of the world. The sacrifice of existing subjectivity is the price it pays for its dreams, and, while in "Runenberg" Tieck's hero is negatively enchanted, Novalis is himself the enchanter who fantasizes "a golden age" into existence.

The novel *Heinrich von Ofterdingen* exemplifies this romantic worldview: in the desire for the blue blossom is incorporated the desire for a magical-animistic antiquity in which things spoke to people.[37] This nocturnal dream refers back to the enticing stories of the stranger who had spoken of a treasure and blue blossoms. This doubling of the goal gives Heinrich the opportunity to separate the sublime image from profane desire, which had been mixed together so perniciously in "Runenberg," and to decide for the blue blossom. The decision also results in the purification of desire, since the treasure in Novalis's utopia does not have the function of an end but at most of a means to a universal fusion—the one represented by the blue blossom. The romanticizing function of money in the service of the universal poetic fiction had, indeed, already become discernible in his remark on the commercial spirit, written roughly at the same time as the novel.

The old miner in *Ofterdingen* points to the principle of possessionlessness, claiming that the gleaming metals are only there to be observed, that "they lose their appeal once they become wares."[38] Novalis, who was a mining engineer, expresses a thought here that must appear odd given his profession; with it he shows that the transfiguration of the established commodity reality offers a basis for the romanticization strategy. Things only become freely mobile (like money) once they have been stripped of their actual character. Only under this condition is the metamorphosis of metals into people conceivable, as it is programmatically set out in Klingsohr's fairy tale and in the ninth chapter of the novel. Novalis elaborates Christian's mad system in Tieck's "Runenberg" into a utopian one, thereby eliminating the threatening power of abstract things. The nearly revolutionary liberation of nature and the indidvidual, which is abundantly developed in the novel, is only realizable as a romantic idea, through the use of the "magic wand of analogy."[39]

b)   The question at hand is this: how does the romantic consciousness react to the world of things? Novalis, relying on the magic of idealism, described the possibility of dissolving things, or, in the language of Fichte (to whom Novalis repeatedly refers), of establishing an equality between the "not I" and the "I." What appears here as a romantic unity is only a little later—in 1810, to be precise—redivided by Kleist in his essay "On the Marionette Theater" into the triad "consciousness" (that is, the no longer naive, but reflective person), "God," and "thing" (puppeteer and puppet). Consciousness no longer dissolves petrified reality, as in Novalis; rather, it is precisely consciousness that produces petrifaction. Either the eternal consciousness of God or the nonexistent consciousness of things is superior to human consciousness, which is responsible for an alienation from nature (from grace) due to the sin of reflection (Herr C. mentions the third book of Moses). Kleist uses the example of the dancer, inferior to the "antigravity" puppets because of the labor required for his reflection and movement, to depict the encumbering power of consciousness. Only God is capable of the weightlessness of the puppets in a marionette theater. Not the subject, but things offer here an image of utopian liberation, sketchily recast at the end of the text into a triadic model of history, in which paradise lost, after "knowledge has likewise gone through an infinity," is represented as a return.[40] Both Novalis and Kleist use the triadic model of the return of a golden age, but for Kleist it exists only as an intellectual game, while on the plane of action only the puppets (and the distant God) represent the utopian potential.

The first to recognize the puppet as the ideal counterpart is Nathaniel, in E. T. A. Hoffmann's story "The Sandman" (1815), and he ends up insane. He confuses an inanimate thing with the ideal woman of his longings, or, to put it in language of Kleist, the puppet and God have become one for him; it is precisely her dull-wittedness that seems to him the expression of a "heavenly" charm, as "a sacred language which imbues an inner world."[41] People are no longer animate—they appear, like Nathaniel's beloved Clara, as automatons; people are here the animators of

Lifting machine for planting full-grown trees. With the aid of this device the boulevard was lined with thirty-year-old trees in a single night.

C. D. Friedrich, *The Polar Sea* (the shipwrecked *Hope*), *ca.* 1823–1824.

things. Nathaniel animates the puppet: after his handshake, her ice-cold hand seems to him to glow with heat.[42]

Reversals of this sort are a common motif in E. T. A. Hoffmann. In the late story "Irrungen," a character knocks the nose off a statue, so that the "damned puppet . . . would not come alive and beat him."[43] The world of things becomes animated and takes over the position of nature, which has long since become the commodified thing described in a farcical passage in "Irrungen": "In the forest, my magician was seized by a sullen mood. As I extolled our walk, he replied sharply that I should not foolishly imagine that . . . they were real trees, that that was really growing grass, real fields and water: I could tell by the dull colors myself that it was all just stuff manufactured in fun. In the winter, claimed my magician, it all gets packed up and sent off to the city, some of it rented to the confectioners who needed it for their so-called exhibitions."[44] This remark refers back to the custom of the confectioners around 1820 of reproducing scenes in sugar frosting at Christmastime (photography had not yet been invented). It represents the general tendency in Hoffmann's work that fundamentally distinguishes him from the early romantics: the discovery of the loss of nature and, in response, the artificial animation of things—a reference to a split consciousness that also produces the type of the *Doppelgänger.* That which Novalis reinterpreted in affirmative terms, the apparent loss of secure relations to objects, Hoffmann regards as irreversible.

In the character of the goldsmith Cardillac in the story "The Young Lady of Scuderi," Hoffmann portrays the complications that arise when the subject continues cathecting objects that have long since become commodities. The goldsmith is incapable of parting with the goods he produces and, in order not to have to lose them forever, murders the buyers. Things that have become commodities are subject to the primacy of circulation—the behavior of the goldsmith is an obstructive anomaly in the otherwise solidly established mobility of goods. A personal relation to things is now only to be realized in the form of a criminal offense. Hoffmann thus marks a sarcastic end to the romantic concepts of unification: in relation to objects of commerce the romantic construction of perception turns out to be a life-threatening madness, one to which Cardillac falls victim by rebelling against the permanent separation of commodity exchange.

}

FROM THE "EGO CRYSTAL FOREST"[1]

TO THE CRYSTAL PALACE

"What! You have no colored glass, no pink,

no red, no blue! No magic panes, no panes

of Paradise? Scoundrel, what do you mean

by going into poor neighborhoods without a

single glass to make life beautiful!" And I

pushed him, stumbling and grumbling,

toward the stairs. . . . The shock knocked him

over and, falling on his back, he succeeded in

breaking the rest of his poor ambulatory

stock with a shattering noise as of lightning

striking a crystal palace.

Charles Baudelaire,

"The Bad Glazier"[2]

a)   A crystal is a regular solid body bounded by flat surfaces. Owing to its symmetrical nature, which effects a mathematical resolution in the very moment of petrifaction, it has been predestined from the start to be a carrier of notions of harmonious and ideal order. "Crystals," according to G. H. von Schubert in his *Ahndungen einer allgemeinen Geschichte des Lebens* of 1806, "represent the highest order of earthly perfection"; they are the "solid water of the earth, the water of primordial times."[3] In short, crystals are the stuff of creation.

In the golden age that Novalis anticipates in the fairy tale "Klingsohr," "crystal plants" and "jeweled blossoms" flourish in a city of transparent walls.[4] The petrifaction of lifeless matter is transcended so that matter can grow organically under the sign of an all-inclusive world harmony, taking on other forms and entering into combinations. In contrast with this crystalline utopia of Novalis, E. T. A. Hoffmann emphasizes the ambivalence of the crystal—petrifaction corresponds to metamorphosis, utopia congeals into an individual nightmare. Elis Fröbom fancies himself upon a sea, which on closer inspection turns out to be a solid "crystal floor." Even the sky is a "dome of darkly gleaming minerals." "Plants of glittering metal" rise up out of the ground, growing far below from the hearts of lovely virgins. Tormented by longing, the hero throws himself down upon the crystal floor, which yields beneath him, holding him afloat in the "shimmering air."[5] That which so far appears as the fulfillment of a wish—the lowering of the separating walls, the liquefaction of the petrified crystals in which the unattainable virgins had been enclosed (a triadic model, in which the dream water surpasses petrifaction to render the object of the wish accessible)—turns suddenly into fear. Hoffmann sees the regressive moment in the progressive development, namely, the danger of a dissolution of the ego: the virgins metamorphose into the threatening figure of a "powerful woman"; the crystalline transformation on the dark floor of the sea threatens to become a fatal birth in reverse, by which the independence gained is once again annihilated. The earth remains visible only through a "crack," while, for the hero, "his being dissolves into the shining minerals."[6] His awakening from the nightmare signals the end of this attempt at romantic synthesis, the desire to melt transformed into the fear of having melted. Here the crystal displays its ambivalent quality. It is ultimately the hero who is petrified by fear in the face of the possibility of a crystalline reverse liquefaction, a prospect which nonetheless entices him.

This schema is also found in somewhat accentuated form in Hoffmann's fairy tale "The Golden Pot." Here the ominous threat reads: "Run into the crystal which will soon be your down-fall."[7] The melodious "little crystal bells"[8] from an elder tree represent, on the one hand, erotic allure (the godfather to this sound image might well have been the glass-harmonica music favored by the romantics; until performances were restricted by law, it frequently caused nervous collapse in its listeners). But, on the other, the crystal, as "congealed ether," also stands for petrifaction in the form of a crystal bottle in which the protagonist is trapped, having been seduced by the voices. Inside he does indeed see the "hues of a beaming rainbow," but he is merely floating, after all, within a bottle, "devoid of motion and power."[9] Here, too, the crystal is the material onto which an eroticism energized by desires and images of transformation is projected, but Hoffmann allows this utopian quality to exist only at the cost of the imprisonment and destruction of the ego, thereby emphasizing, in contrast with Novalis, the deadly aspect of the crystal alongside its affinity with desire.

b)   Crystal is iridescent matter in a double sense, an attribution which can be traced back to a text that stamped the entire literary tradition since, the Book of Revelation in the New Testament, written on the isle of Patmos by Saint John on the basis of still

Sayings for the Glass House

1. Glassless joy—
   What a dumb ploy!

2. Bricks are soon past,
   Glass color lasts.

3. Glass in its color
   Puts an end to all rancor.

4. Happiness lasts
   In the culture of glass.

5. If you have no glass abode
   You will find that life's a load.

6. Fire is one thing no glass house knows;
   There's never a need for the fireman's hose.

7. A nasty bug is bad as sin,
   A house of glass it won't come in.

8. Burnable materialia
   Are genuine scandalia.

9. Greater than the diamond's flash
   Is the double wall of glass.

10. The universe is filled with light,
    And that's what makes the crystal bright.

11. But the prism is a wondrous shrine,
    And that's the reason glass is fine.

12. He who shuns what glass confers
    Sees nothing of the universe.

13. Glass brightens all the lot,
    Invest in it on the spot.

14. The time to come in glass is born,
    The past in brick just makes us mourn.

Paul Scheerbart, *Frühlicht*, 1920, no. 3

earlier sources. In the fourth chapter, God upon his throne is described as follows: "He sat there, and appeared like the stones jasper and sard, and a rainbow surrounded the crown like emerald. . . . And before the throne there was a glass sea, like crystal." It is evident from this tradition why the alchemists saw the sought-after lapis in the crystal, with which they hoped to achieve celibate (that is, self-) creation. The images—the rainbow, the glass sea—are still to be found in Hoffmann, no longer, however, as an expression of divine power and splendor, but as an ominous threat. In the twenty-first chapter of Revelation, the New Jerusalem appears as the crystalline city awaiting the visionary like a bride. The city is delivered directly from heaven; God and the crystal city are one, which makes of them a living stone. And all of this becomes possible through a transformation of the "first" earth into the "new" earth. Since the stone lives, because it is God, the opposition between solid and fluid, which is fundamental to the creation of crystal, no longer applies to it. This opposition is transcended in the paradox of the living stone, which signals victory over death.

The crystalline city is heralded as "woman," but it is nonetheless as regularly structured as a crystal grid: "the length and width and height of the city are equal." The foundation stones of the walls are adorned with precious gems; the city passages are "gold as pure as transparent glass"; the symmetrically arranged portals are each made of a single pearl. But then it is said that "nothing impure will enter" into this chaste crystal. The vision of the feminine crystal city is accordingly completely devoid of people; when the description arrives at the question of the inhabitants, the present tense changes into the future—this divine crystal is living and yet lacking in human life. People must first equal it and its purity; they become inhabitants only through a process of crystallization.

Ernst Bloch delivers an optimistic interpretation of this apocalyptic material, pointing out, in faithfulness to the prophecy that God is able to raise up children from stone (Matthew 3:9), that the inorganic images are to be understood as animate ones.[10] He sees the crystalline matter as an expression of the δυνάμει ὄν, of the "possibility of being," and not merely of a "reified lump." Utopia as the end of the world leads to a transformation, after which human being and the world (matter) are no longer alien

Glass Architecture . . . No material overcomes matter as much as glass. Glass is a completely new, pure material, into which matter is melted and transformed. Of all the substances at our disposal, it achieves the most elemental effect. It reflects the sky and the sun; it is like luminous water, and it possesses a wealth of possibilities in the way of color, shape, and character that is truly inexhaustible and can leave no one indifferent. . . .

If until now all human dwellings have merely represented soft buffers to movement, attempts to find rest in comfort and let everything go, then glass architecture will put us in spaces that continually prevent us from falling victim to the dullness of habit and coziness. And that despite the most refined and cultivated comfort of its furnishings. For glass architecture can respond to all justified longings for peacefulness and pleasure quite exquisitely. It is not by any means a Spartan institution, but it has the merit of never letting us languish along the habitual path. For it is indeed always new, always exquisite, always an occasion for admiration—not for people and their abilities, but because it transports us out into the infinite world and to this extent, even with all the exquisiteness and tenderness, is precisely "disagreeable." In a nearly confounding fashion, it remains ever primitive!

Its most profound effect, however, will be that it breaks the European of his rigidity along with his hardness. The European, where he is not responsible, is agreeable, but where he does bear responsibility, he is hard. Beneath an agonizing exterior he is dull and brutal. Glass will transform him. Glass is clear and sharp-cornered, but in its hidden wealth it is mild and tender. So will the new European also become: of clear determination and surpassing mildness.

Adolf Behne, *Die Wiederkehr der Kunst*
(Leipzig, 1919)

to each other.[11] The creation of living matter thus postulates a recasting of humanity.

Aside from the apocalyptics and romantics, it was above all the architectural utopians who felt themselves called to plan the New Jerusalem in the form of the ideal city. In the process, the annihilating quality of the crystal took its place alongside its transformative quality. It is not by accident that Hegel, in his *Aesthetics*, cites a claim of Friedrich Schlegel according to which architecture is "frozen music," because both art forms rest on a harmony of relations that can be traced back to numbers. A building, then, consists of "completely comprehensible crystalline forms," which, taken together in the ideal case, form a "secret eurhythmy" from which alone beauty derives.[12] Nor does this theory of architecture, nourished by apocalyptic and classical notions of harmony though not at all utopian in conception, make any mention of inhabitants.

What Hegel suggests becomes the central point for all architectural utopians preaching the moment of order and purity, in short, the pure crystalline character of their cities and thereby also of the latter's inhabitants. Whether Campanella's Sun City, Andreaes's Christianopolis, the ideal cities of Ledoux, architect of the revolution, or the phalansteries of Fourier—in the structure of all of these plans is that purified crystal from which any and all irregularity is banned. They aim at a regulation of the drives, and particularly clearly at the banishment (Fourier is a partial exception) of the one drive, the erotic, that stands in opposition to stereometric order. As Bloch notes in reference to Bruno Taut, subsequently the architect of suburban housing developments in Berlin, "the whole earth was ultimately to be converted into a crystal."[13] Alongside the utopian, the purifying and annihilating functions are always legible in these plans; they are implicit even in Scheerbart's apparently harmless rhymed slogans in *Frühlicht*. When they pronounce:

> A nasty bug is bad as sin,
> The house of glass it won't come in,[14]

then the meaning must be that only the pure will enter, a baffling repetition of Saint John's border control at the gates of the New Jerusalem.

Sketch by Bruno Taut (from
Frühlicht, 1920).

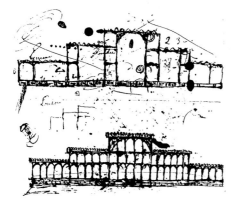

Paxton's original sketches for the
Crystal Palace, 1850.

Paxton's first draft sketch of the
Crystal Palace, 1850.

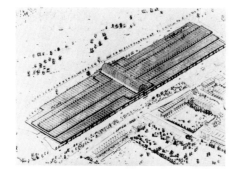

Final version of the Crystal
Palace, sketch.

c) On the occasion of the First World Exposition of 1851 in London, the commodity-producing society creates literally an enclosed superstructure that refers to the old utopia both in name and through the materials employed: Joseph Paxton's "Crystal Palace," the glittering shell of a gigantic commodity market. It crystallized the cherished dream of the capitalist bourgeoisie: to transform all needs into commodities and money.

The Crystal Palace is a symbol of the transformations undertaken by the nineteenth century, the first of which is the transformation of nature into interior space. Paxton solves the problem elegantly: he simply builds over nature by integrating a row of trees in Hyde Park under a heavenly awning made of glass. Nature and technology, exterior and *interieur* appear reconciled—nature has become interior and the *interieur,* mediated over the de-bounding of the windows, once again nature.

That is presumably not the least reason for the incredible fascination that the building must have evoked. Chroniclers attest to the presence of framed pictures on the walls in even the most out-of-the-way provinces—the Crystal Palace became an icon, a building met with nearly religious veneration. Julius Lessing reports as late as 1900 his first impression in 1862: he met the sight "with a shudder of reverence and in the purest rapture." The epithets running through his and others' texts repeatedly recall romantic writings. The trees and palms in the crystalline palace exert the effect of an "enchanted forest"; the sober economy of the space appears "magical," like "a bit of a summer night's dream in the midnight sun" (Lothar Bucher); and Lessing concludes, "What we imagined of old fairy tales, of the princess in a glass coffin, of the queens and elves living in crystal houses—that all seemed to us to have been embodied . . . and these feelings have endured over decades."[15] A. G. Meyer, in his study, *Eisenbauten,* discovers a further analogy in the history of design. The glass wall, which, as membrane and solid body in one, allows interior and exterior space to blend into one another, has a prototype in the Gothic church window.[16] Believers and their God are connected by light. According to the symbolism of the church building, "the glass windows correspond to the precious gems in the walls of heavenly Jerusalem."[17] The commodity market, as Crystal Palace, inspires romantic and religious associations.

From a contemporary memorial
album, *Crystal Palace View
Album*. On the top left, the view
from the southern transept to the
north. Top right, the view from
north to south.

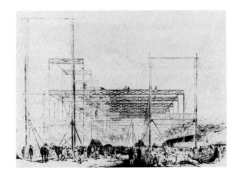

The Crystal Palace during construction.

View of the central nave.

The designation "crystal palace" lays an aura over the exposition hall, which thus becomes a piece of modern mythology with effects reaching into the present. The Seagram Building by Mies van der Rohe, completed in 1958, was still being apostrophized as a "cathedral of commerce."[18] Already his early plans for an office skyscraper, the projects for Friedrichstraße of 1920–1921, betray a crystalline structure, the effect of which derives from the carefully calculated reflections off the glass walls. He confirmed this intention in a 1922 essay for Bruno Taut's journal, *Frühlicht*, the organ of "The Glass Chain." Discussing his design studies, he wrote, "My experiments with a glass model showed me . . . that the use of glass depended, not on the effect of light and shadows, but on the rich play of reflections."[19] The goal is a dematerialization as it was realized in the glass walls of the Seagram Building, with the same minimization of supports as was attempted in the Gothic cathedrals. But now this transparency is vacuous, no longer signifying transcendence as it did in the Gothic cathedrals; rather "the vacant office building at night" radiates nothing "but its own emptiness."[20]

London's Crystal Palace occupies the exact midpoint between the cathedral and the Seagram Building—a precarious balance between a metaphysical cult on one side and capitalist rationality on the other. The cult is reduced to idolatry of the commodity. Precisely that which contemporary visitors to the exposition (as, for example, the German emigrant Bucher) praised so highly in the structure—its masslessness, the dissolution of the walls into metal grids in which glass was hung so that there scarcely remained a point of reference by which distances could be gauged and dimensions fixed, and especially the absence of shadows[21]—characterizes the profane-transcendental character of the Crystal Palace as well, in which the reality of the world, as exhibition, becomes dematerialized.

In the Crystal Palace, as an advanced iron and glass construction, a technologically brilliant solution to the problem of making larger and easier-to-assemble exhibition halls, the relation between force and mass shifts to the advantage of force, that is, in the direction of the greatest possible transparency of the solid structure. "As in a crystal, there no longer is any true interior or exterior," writes Richard Lucae, a contemporary observer. "If we

Mies van der Rohe, sketch for a high-rise on Friedrichstrasse, Berlin, 1921–1922.

imagine that air can be poured like a liquid, then it has, here, achieved a solid form after the removal of the mold into which it was poured. We find ourselves within a cutout segment of atmosphere."[22] Lucae provides here a description of a permeable solid structure, in which the solid and fluid, the structural masses and the effects of air and light, all seem to exist in a peculiar state of suspension.

In the Crystal Palace, the boundaries between interior and exterior space collapse. Likewise, in accord with the exhibition concept inspired by Saint-Simon, the boundaries between the countries unifying industry into a general spectacle fall away, as do those between animate and inanimate, between the human and the mechanical, which itself seems to have taken on life. According to one description of the Crystal Palace, machines worked "like crazy, while thousands around them in top hats and capotes sat quietly waiting, without grasping that the age of men on this planet was at an end."[23] Human intercourse is replaced by interaction among machines. This observation refers to the symbolic dimension of the transformation of all things, which is at the same time extremely real—the Crystal Palace represents circulation as "the great social retort into which everything is thrown, to come out again as a gold-crystal."[24] It is a space in which, for a brief historical moment, meanings appear to prevail; in it is realized the utopian-alchemistic transmutation of all things in the form of capitalist transformation.

Hearse in front of the Crystal Palace, photograph by Emile Zola.

]

ECONOMY AND METAMORPHOSIS

In a [certain] way, it is with man as with

commodities. Since he comes into the world

neither with a looking glass in his hand, nor

as a Fichtean philosopher, to whom "I am I"

is sufficient, man first sees and recognises

himself in other men. Peter only establishes

his own identity as a man by first comparing

himself with Paul as being of like kind. And

thereby Paul, just as he stands in his Pauline

personality, becomes to Peter the type of the

genus homo.

Karl Marx, *Capital*[1]

If Hegel, in the *Philosophie der Religion*, says "Our age has the outstanding characteristic of knowing of each and every thing, of an endless multitude of objects, just nothing of God," then Marx draws the appropriate conclusion: the objects themselves (the commodities which demand of buyers that they educate themselves, that they amass "encyclopaedic" knowledge[2]) take on a metaphysical quality. Their value now becomes a "non-natural property"; their physical form becomes the "incarnation" of all human labor; their transformation into money becomes "transubstantiation." The creation of use value is analogous to divine creation; "living labour" seizes hold of things in order to "rouse them from their death-sleep."[3]

The representation of commodity circulation in *Capital* teems with such physical-metaphysical metaphors—in that the commodity-producing society humanizes objects, it objectifies humans. The exchange of equivalents in *Capital* is the expression of a rationalized metamorphosis, that is, one supported by money: "circulation becomes the great social retort."[4] Money is the philosopher's stone the alchemists had sought in vain.

Goethe, in *Faust, Part II*, also emphasizes the power of money to mediate and create:

[it] will procure love's richest favors
far quicker than can wit or eloquence[5]

says Mephistopheles. Money, as the matchmaker between needs and objects,[6] demonstrates this power not only in the economic but also in the erotic sphere. As the binding agent in society, money is the objectified, or reified, form of sexual bonds. Therein consists its creative power. (An idea of the transformation of money into lust: "One imagines for a moment an impossible regression: an industrial phase in which the producers had the chance of demanding, instead of payment, objects of sensation from the consumers. These objects would then be living substances."[7]) After paper money has been passed out during Carnival proceedings, the treasurer reports:

> See how the town, so long half dead and mildewed,
> is full of life and teems with pleasure seekers![8]

People are able to circulate only once money has begun to do so. The circulation of money has a vitalizing effect on people, just as, vice versa, a standstill signifies decay. The equation of circulation and life—which is also that of standstill, the accumulation of wealth, and decay—will be repeated later by Marx.[9] The mobility of money and of life appear as one; money creates new life subject to its own laws.

Goethe is aiming at the ambivalent transformative power of (paper) money, which he distrusted, an idea that might have occurred to him because of the reports of Melchior Grimm. Grimm, editor of a literary correspondence known to Goethe, had suffered substantial losses in *assignats*, the notes issued at the time of the French Revolution and just as quickly devalued.[10] In his correspondence he reported an episode from the Regency bearing on the social effects of Law's paper money. This representation is quite obviously the model for the scene in *Faust, Part II*: Law[11] is for Grimm the "great magician" (like Mephistopheles for Goethe), whose issuance of paper money led to the revaluation of all values. The power of paper money caused "the treasures of the world alternately to appear and disappear. . . . In that time of turmoil and wanton ferment, the results of which were so lasting and pernicious, moral freedom also had its effect on the products of the spirit and taste."[12] Goethe, relying on Grimm's depiction of the "wanton ferment" of the incipient rococo period, relocates the transformative energy of paper money to Carnival festivities, thus seeming to relegate it to an ahistorical sphere. But precisely here Goethe also conceals his prediction of the revolutionizing power

Just as in the myths of antiquity, a man is changed to a stone or to a tree, and nature is peopled with creatures half horse, half man; half fish, half man; half snake, half man; so that there is no telling where the animal ends and the human begins, likewise in the singular creations known as patent-furniture it is almost impossible to tell where one category ends and where the next begins. They dissolve into one another. Multiformity and metamorphosis are part and parcel of their being. An armchair that changes into a couch, a couch that changes into a cradle, can justly be termed combination furniture, as can a bed that turns into a sofa, into a chair, into a table, into a railway seat.

Everything is collapsible, folding, revolving, telescopic, recombinable. Where does this part end and that part begin? No sooner have we reached a clean-cut verdict than all is shuffled afresh, leading to no end. The reason lies in the nature of this furniture. Part merges with part as, in the mermaid, fish and woman. They fuse into a new entity.

Sigfried Giedion, *Mechanization Takes Command*
(New York: Norton, 1969), p. 423

We have, Carlyle continues, thrown away the religiosity of the Middle Ages and gotten nothing in return: "we have forgotten God. . . . We have quietly closed our eyes to the eternal Substance of things, and opened them only to the Shews and Shams of things. we quietly believe this Universe to be intrinsically a great unintelligible perhaps; extrinsically, clear enough, it is a great, most extensive Cattlefold and Workhouse, with most extensive Kitchen-ranges, Dining-tables,—whereat he is wise who can find a place! All the Truth of this Universe is uncertain; only the profit and loss of it, the pudding and praise of it, are and remain very visible to the practical man.

"There is no longer any God for us! God's Laws are become a Greatest-Happiness Principle, a Parliamentary Expediency: the Heavens overarch us only as an Astronomical Time-keeper; a butt for Herschel-telescopes to shoot science at, to shoot sentimentalities at:—in our and old Jonson's dialect, man has lost the *soul* out of him; and now, after the due period,—begins to find the want of it! This is verily the plague-spot; centre of the universal Social Gangrene, threatening all modern things with frightful death. . . . There is no religion; there is no God; man has lost his soul, and vainly seeks antiseptic salt. Vainly: in killing Kings, in passing Reform Bills, in French Revolutions, Manchester Insurrections, is found no remedy. The foul elephantine leprosy, alleviated for an hour, reappears in new force and desperateness next hour."

Since, however, the position of the old religion could not remain entirely unoccupied, we have gotten a new gospel in its stead, a gospel fitting to the hollowness and emptiness of the age—the gospel of Mammon.

"Die Lage Englands," by Friedrich Engels, a review of *Past and Present* by Thomas Carlyle (London, 1843), in *Deutsch-Französische Jahrbücher* (Paris), ed. Arnold Ruge and Karl Marx, no. 1–2 (1844): 159–160

of later industrial capitalism, the incarnation of the magician in a new fashion.

Money transforms not only social relations but, as the standard of exchange value, commodities themselves. An abstraction from use value characterizes exchange value; the result is that the "existence [of the commodity] as a material thing" is "put out of sight." Remaining is its "unsubstantial reality," substance without form, as a "congelation of homogenous human labour."[13] In exchange, things crystallize into commodity values, independently of their material form. For it is precisely the stripping away of their "bodily shape" that makes it possible for commodities to carry out the operation of an exchange value.[14] Marx, then, also characterizes the process of a sale as a "metamorphosis"; it is recast as the "leap taken by value from the body of the commodity into the body of the gold . . . the *salto mortale* of the commodity."[15] With this transformation, commodities, as exchange values, are stripped of their identity as a commodity; a commodity is inter-(ex-) changeable with any other, either directly or by way of the detour of money.

The independence of the things meeting one another in the marketplace results from the appearance that they communicate with one another in exchange without human assistance. The human being is present only by virtue of the work that has assumed objective form in the things—thus relations between persons become social relations between things and things themselves become fetishes. The social relation between people has been transformed into the "fantastic form of a relation between things."[16] This relation arises out of the abstraction of work: commodity-things are congealed units of labor, which, on the market and independently of their producers, no longer appear as useful things, but much more as abstract things of value that are convertible into other things of value. The characteristics of the commodity have accordingly turned into completely different ones in the process separating production and sale. Labor is not directly convertible in society but only in the reified form of commodities—things then interact socially in the place of the laboring people. This apparent vitality of commodities, or, as Marx terms it, the "mystical character of the commodity,"[17] results because, in the units of congealed labor, social relations between people

. . . he even became quite accustomed to being hungry in the evening; on the other hand, he had spiritual nourishment, for he carried ever in his thoughts the idea of his future overcoat. His whole existence had in a sense become fuller, as though he had married, as though some other person were present with him, as though he were no longer alone but an agreeable companion had consented to walk the path of life hand in hand with him, and that companion was none other than the new overcoat with its thick padding and its strong, durable lining. He became, as it were, more alive, even more strong-willed, like a man who has set before himself a definite goal.

Nikolai Gogol, *The Overcoat*, in *The Complete Tales of Nikolai Gogol*, ed. with an introduction by Leonard J. Kent, trans. Constance Garnett and revised by the editor (Chicago: University of Chicago Press), pp. 316–317

. . . These Papers are delivered to a Set of Artists very dextrous in finding out the mysterious Meanings of Words, Syllables, and Letters. For Instance, they can decypher a Close-stool to signify a Privy-Council;

a Flock of Geese, a Senate;

a lame Dog, an Invader;

appear not as personal relations[18] but as relations that have gained independence from them.

Marx points to the *commodity as fetish* in developed capitalist society; Keller, in *Grüner Heinrich* (first published in 1854–1855), the memories of the adult hero of his distant youth, to the transformation of the *fetish into a commodity.*

In the novel, the business of Mrs. Margret bears mythical-matriarchal qualities; to the young Heinrich she takes the place of the "grandmother, rich in legends and traditions, and the wet nurse." She deals in "secondhand goods,"[19] that is, not in commodities that reach the consumer direct from the producer. With secondhand commodities, sometimes as much as a century or more of time has left its traces on the goods: thus is history sedimented into the pure bodies of the commodity, lending it an auratic dimension that is intensified still further by the temporal remove of Mrs. Margret's appearance. Her double role, as a businesswoman who is also steeped in legend, is manifest as well in her accounting system, in which numbers figure rather as magical ciphers, "like a magical script of ancient paganism." She knows only the four roman numerals one, five, ten, and one hundred, with which she, keeping no books, operates on the tabletop with chalk and a moist finger according to an opaque set of laws.[20] She sits motionless in her store like an oracle. Whenever possible she exchanges money for gold, that is, turns it into a natural substance; she does make loans, but they serve only to set in motion an extensive exchange of fruits of the soil, which is only vaguely reminiscent of modern money exchange. In addition, creditors behave toward her as toward "an old rural prefect or a rich abbess," that is, they treat the functions of commerce and those of the collective social life as interlaced. What creditors bring to her as gifts, she returns in the form of evening banquets. She behaves, that is, similarly to medieval feudal lords, who, following a method like that of the Indian potlatch, do not amass wealth according to the principles of capital accumulation but instead spend it lavishly, to gain in this way social influence that could not be obtained through money alone.[21]

Mrs. Margret's behavior is the exact opposite of that of a modern businessman: she squanders part of her income; and, on the other hand, she keeps a portion of her goods if they awaken her

the Plague, a standing Army;

a Buzard, a Minister;

the Gout, a High Priest;

a Gibbet, a Secretary of State;

a Chamber pot, a Committee of Grandees;

a Sieve, a Court Lady;

interest or she attributes to them "a remarkable history or even secret powers" that make them "sacred" to her.[22] Here the good is a fetish in an archaic sense, and in no way in the sense that Marx is considered to have discovered under the conditions of industrial commodity production. Moreover, there is the matriarchal motif of the nourishing mother, which is opposed to the social relations objectified in the good. For Mrs. Margret the goods are elements of a natural process in which she also takes her place as a person. From the point of view of modern economics, she is lacking in the capacity to abstract; she also takes the illustrations in her old books for "a real, living being." Everything is "significant" to her; she thinks in mythical categories of micro- and macrocosm, which allows the things to appear animated to her. She both broods the goods and possesses them.[23]

Yet this type of maternal commercial existence is nearly obsolete; her husband already calls her a "fantastic cow,"[24] thus heralding a transition to a rationalistic relation with the goods. This change is accomplished against the background of the replacement of the matriarchy by patriarchy. The last witch trials took place during the youth of the old commercial couple toward the end of the eighteenth century, and they indicate the historical triumph of the principle of male-dominated reason.

The husband, always excluded by his wife from joint dominion in business, now attempts to enforce this principle against Mrs. Margret. He demands "his share in the 'communally acquired' goods" and the courts decide for him. Separation is concealed in the word "share": the community of marriage ends in conflict, and the community of goods invested with meaning ends in pieces of gold, which the husband hoards by putting them in a suitcase and nailing it to the floor. Finally, at the end of the story, there is left the wife, mortally weakened by the separation, who "surrendered to weeping and praying," and the victorious husband who murmurs "fifty-one, fifty-one" to himself for hours at a time. According to Muschg's insightful observation, the principle of a just division ends at 51 percent, with which the advantage of one of the partners begins.[25] Following Mrs. Margret's death, the heirs, who come like "iconoclasts out of a plundered church," dissipate the community of magically laden goods, in

a Broom, a Revolution;

a Mouse-trap, an Employment;

a bottomless Pit, the Treasury;

a Sink, a C—t;

a Cap and Bells, a Favourite;

that the principal heir liquidates his share by turning it into money and, "without looking around," that is, without concerning himself for any nonmonetary meanings, leaves town with his "fat money pouch."[26]

This story marks the entry of magical things into circulation—the meaning of the things transforms itself into exchange value, from which magic was to arise in its modern form as the commodity fetish. In the commodity-exchange society, the goods are no longer, as they were for Mrs. Margret, representatives of human interrelations. On the contrary, the people exist "for each other only as representatives of commodities." The possessors of commodities, as the personifications of economic relations, now wear the masks of "the characters who appear on the economic stage."[27] The possessors of commodities transform themselves from members of a community into persons independent of one another who communicate in a state of "mutual alienation" solely by way of the exchange value of their goods. The statement, "the exchange of commodities, therefore, first begins on the boundaries of such communities," also means, therefore, "where the communities end."[28] On the social plane, commodity exchange occasions the dissociation of people in favor of the communication of things.

The commodity undergoes a "completed metamorphosis" in three phases: the commodity form; the stripping away of the commodity form (that is, the exchange of commodities through money); and the return to the commodity form.[29] This metamorphosis is reminiscent of the triadic models of romanticism, of the developmental path from the ego to the whole, from the whole back to the ego, or of the historical procession from the golden age through a period of alienation, the "great schism,"[30] toward a new golden age. The phases of the metamorphosis of commodities constitute, like the romantic metamorphosis, a circulating system. Marx makes use here of a cyclical model that conceives development only as the return to the point of departure. The romantics' progressive utopian implications, however, now disappear. Marx reifies the model into a phenomenology of commodities and thereby into a representation of the bad infinity of the eternal return of the ever-the-same. The commodity as

a broken Reed, a Court of Justice;

an empty Tun, a General;

a running Sore, the Administration.

Jonathan Swift, *Gulliver's Travels*, with the illustrations of J. J. Grandville, (Arlington, Virginia: Great Ocean Publishers, 1980), pp. 302–306

exchange value is conceived here as timeless, formless, and in constant transformation: while the goods are indeed active within social relations as if they were living, living social relations transform themselves into petrified, objective relations.

EXCURSUS: GRANDVILLE, OR

LAPUTA IN THE JULY MONARCHY

Grandville's gravestone epitaph, which he composed himself, unwittingly betrays the secret of the animated commodity that has become a fetish: "Here lies J. I. Grandville. He brought everything to life and, like God, made everything live, speak, or walk, while not understanding himself how to follow the path to his happiness."[31] Grandville's is the modern version of the archaic exchange that exacts the soul as the price of wealth. In Grandville's metamorphosis, the commodity is made demiurgically into nature, with nature (life) being delivered up to second nature (the commodity) in the process. The utopian-compulsive transformation is thereby Grandville's founding aesthetic principle, no longer, as in Andersen, within the frame of the fairy tale, but as a satire of the Beautiful New World. The title page of *Un autre monde* of 1844 indicated the tendency in its baroque extravagance. To be seen were: "Transformations, visions, incarnations, ascensions, locomotions, explorations, pérégrinations, excursions, stations, cosmogonies, phantasmagories, rêveries, folâteries, facéties, lubies, metamorphoses, zoomorphoses, lithomorphoses, métempsychoses, apothéoses et autres choses."

That is exactly the attitude which Baudelaire criticized in Grandville, namely, to breed such analogies without being able to infer consequences from them. His "rebuilding creation"[32] therefore could not be successful; Grandville ended up insane. What Baudelaire fails to mention, by revealing only the Grandville overwhelmed by commodities, is that the latter, in terms of

Grandville, *A Stroll on the Heavens*, steel engraving, 1874.

Grandville, *Fourier's System*, woodcut, 1844.

his intentions, took his place in a mythical and utopian-socialist tradition that found its way equally into Baudelaire's poetics—in the form of the doctrine of the "correspondances," derived in particular from the mystic Swedenborg. This theologian, dismissed by Kant as a "seer," saw conformities, analogies, and correspondences between the interior and exterior world, micro- and macrocosm, natural phenomena and spiritual meaning—a doctrine which, despite all its inherent obscurantism, would prove to have astounding historical influence into the modern period. In Grandville's time, aside from Baudelaire, Balzac concerned himself with the idea, as well as the American Ralph Waldo Emerson, through whose mediation Robert Musil would also quote Swedenborg in a prominent spot in *The Man without Qualities*.

The notion of permanent mutation, of a correspondence among all existing things, so that they are not divided into separate identities but always taking on new form like a kaleidoscope, was already at the basis of Ovid's *Metamorphoses*; the inspiration of the mystics is well acquainted with this state, in which the world of things and the subject melt into one. In the early socialist theory of Charles Fourier, this doctrine recurs as a utopian model of society. He writes, "Everything, from atoms to the stars, is an image of the particular characteristics of the human passions."[33] According to his student Flora Tristan, Fourier's model is based on Swedenborg's doctrine of correspondences; he planned the serial social harmony in the phalansteries in accord with this notion.

Baudelaire knew of the connection between Fourier and Swedenborg, but he came upon the experience of analogies and relationships from a completely different angle, namely through his analysis of hashish intoxication, a utopia subject to immediate reduction because it is limited to the individual. Intoxicated, it becomes possible to communicate with things—a reincarnation of animism, rather like that described by Emerson's nature mysticism.[34] Aside from this, however, what disclose themselves anew in the hashish illumination are the forms of language. An understanding of allegory, which can be viewed as the intellectual form of the mystical doctrine of correspondences, and that "which . . . incompetent painters have accustomed us to despise . . . regains, in an intellect enlightened by hashish, its legitimate dominion. . . . Even grammar, dry-as-dust grammar,

In 1832 Enfantin criticized the architecture of his time because of its alleged lack of "movement." He insisted that "durability, stability, and movement" were the three factors determining the quality of a building, and seems at times to have anticipated dynamic open-skeleton architecture. Such a bald statement, however, hardly suffices to give a picture of his soaring imagination, and it would be best to let Enfantin speak for himself: "The structure of a building should resemble the molecular structure of bodies. There must be solid areas allied with empty spaces. There must be flexibility, scope for movement. The various structural elements should be arranged as the molecules of a body are arranged." Iron, incidentally, is given the leading part in bringing into being the "architecture sacerdotale" of the future, which is quite remarkable in its way, since the use of iron in building had not at the time got beyond its modest beginnings. From construction in iron Enfantin expected to see wholly new "musical and optical" effects. Iron tubes were to serve both as supports and as organ pipes. "The whole temple could become a sonorous orchestra, a gigantic thermometer. The association of different metals, and the activities at the heart of things comprising the ceremonial, might lead to the most stupendous galvanic, chemical, and mechanical effects in a sanctuary having, by means of a lightning-conductor belfry, direct contact with the storm raging outside."

This vision of a musical-architectural composite work of art—already dimly conceived by Runge and afterwards followed up by Gaudí's Sagrada Familia—passes the limits of any normal man's imagination. It dreams of a temple of the electric generator, of a temple made of gigantic magnets. . . .

Werner Hoffmann, *The Earthly Paradise: Art in the Nineteenth Century*, translated by Brian Battershaw (New York: George Braziller, 1961), pp. 183–184

becomes something like a sorcerer's conjuration. The words are resurrected in flesh and bone."[35] In artificial paradises, it is not only objects but also language that takes on life.

In one of the poems in *Flowers of Evil*, Baudelaire depicted this experience, a "ritual" one, according to Benjamin. The poem is titled "Correspondences." Two central lines go as follows:

> Man wends his way through a forest of symbols
> Which look at him with their familiar
> glances.[36]

The distant, the exterior, the world of objects comes closer; nature begins to speak. This experience exceeds the synthetic one of which the romanticists spoke, in particular Hoffmann, who meant the translatability of one medium into another, for example, of sounds into colors. Baudelaire speaks of that too, but does not mean a virtuoso capacity for mingling perceptions, but the latter's own evocative powers. Benjamin emphasizes the way these experiences are lifted out of time: they "are not historical data, but data of prehistory."[37] The experience of ritual, as removed from time, appears to Benjamin to offer the only available alternative model to the collapse of experience among the moderns—appears, for he suspects that Baudelaire's poem is "devoted to something irretrievably lost."[38]

Grandville refers repeatedly to the doctrine of correspondences in Fourier's sense. A page from *Un autre monde*, entitled "Fourier's System" (according to the precepts of which forty-one communities were established in the United States at the time of Emerson and Thoreau, for example[39]), depicts, among other things, a circle of young women whose heads represent different phases of the moon, an expression of universal harmony, of the correspondence between heavenly and human bodies. But the equation turns into its opposite in Grandville: not only do objects become part of people—that is the path of mysticism—but the people become parts of the objects, and that is the path of alienation. The specific ambivalence of the metamorphosis becomes manifest here in the conditions of industrialization—it can mean either the removal of boundaries or the loss of the self. Grandville animates the machines and makes people into their dependents—the living machine produces mechanical life. The ambiguity in

Grandville, *Apocalypse of the Ballet*, wood engraving, 1844.

the expression, "to service a machine," contains something of the fright, long since become imperceptible, one might experience in the face of a machine that wants to be served like a guest.

In Grandville everything, whether person or thing, is transformable, every identity has become insecure. The filigree in his drawings evokes that of iron structures. The play of metamorphoses (like that of the analogies and correspondences) is characterized by an openness in principle, in contrast with logical-causal procedures aiming at a result or at progress. The latter is liquidated here; there remains only the incessant transformation of the always-the-same, the law of the commodity society. For the permanent turnover of commodities offers the image of a transformation the cosmic dimensions of which in Fourier are now taking over in advertising. In the 1860s the department store

"Les magasins du Louvre" solicited customers with the claim, "Les plus grands magasins de l'Univers."[40] In this *quid pro quo* the cosmic longings for transformation are replaced by the purchase of commodities. The always-the-same is sold as the completely-different. Grandville's paranoid world of living things illustrates this process, referred to by Benjamin in an inspired observation in "Planetenbrücke": "The World Exhibitions erected the universe of commodities. Grandville's fantasies transmitted the commodity-character onto the universe."[41] The moment the cosmic body, as that with which Grandville illustrated "Fourier's System," becomes a commodity, the commodity becomes a body, as demonstrated by the mechanical people in *Un autre monde*. Grandville, located in the no-man's-land between Ovid and Marx, portrays the industrialization of the metamorphosis, and proceeds from there to ruin.

4

ON THE PHYSIOGNOMY OF THE WORLD

OF THE COMMODITY AND THE MACHINE

1. THE MYTH OF THE LIVING

MACHINE

Unlike the eighteenth century, in which man became machine, in the nineteenth, the machine is assigned human characteristics. "Like steam engines, the men who submit to the work regiment all present the same aspect, with nothing individual about them."[1] What Balzac maintains here in an early novel is nearly a platitude in both the economic literature (Marx) and *belles lettres* of the time: the workers become "living appendages" of a "lifeless mechanism."[2] Two essential and interdependent moments come under Balzac's view here. The first is the homogenizing impact of labor discipline, reminiscent of the organizational forms of the military, in large-scale industrial operations arising at the time; the mechanization of production forbids all manner of individual behavior (for Balzac, the precondition of elegant life, with dandyism regarded as protest against mechanization). But the second moment is already becoming apparent in his reference to social leveling: the inversion of equality (*égalité*) not only into homogenization but into a new form of dependency. If the French Revolution had overcome the personal dependency of feudalism, then it did so only to have it replaced by a new dependency on the machine, which, in its impersonal abstraction (behind which was concealed the private ownership of the means of production), had become absolute and only indirectly accessible to perception.

Balzac sees that the human individual is transformed in the process into an "instrument of labor," that subjectivity not only is homogenized but, owing to technological development, is dissolved altogether. The machine has become a subject, the individual its object—"the workers are merely conscious organs, co-

Karl Friedrich Schinkel, *Epocha anni dom MDCCCXXXVI*, aquarelle, 1836.

ordinate with the unconscious organs of the automaton."[3] The economic literature begins to read like an excerpt from the literature of fantasy.

The classical schema of the master-slave dialectic suggests itself as an explanation of this *quid pro quo*, of this instrumentalization of human beings. In his fantastic-satirical novel *Erewhon* (1872), Samuel Butler transfers this relation, developed by Hegel in the fourth chapter of the *Phenomenology of Spirit*, onto the relation between the individual and the machine. As he puts it there, "the servant glides by imperceptible approaches into the master."[4] What reads here as a resumption of the Hegelian analysis is actually its perversion: Butler does not, like Hegel, refer to the interplay of human relations on the path to freedom, but to the ultimate defeat of the master by the slave, the machine.

The possible synthesis of master and slave in Hegel is out of the question for the individual and the machine. The working conception upon which Hegel bases the transformation of the master into the slave, whose objectification is succeeded by the transcendence of objectification, is a matter of consciousness and aims at knowledge, which makes change possible. Manual labor at a machine in the factory excludes this possibility, since it, as a result of its organizational form, is not a qualitative determination but aims quantitatively at the production of more goods and more surplus value. Given these premises, the transition of the servant

Gustave Doré, illustration for *Le chemin des écoliers*, Saintine, 1861.

"...and then everything is driven mechanically; Professor Lux is even occupied at present with the invention of a steam engine that understands French, English, and German; then people will not be necessary at all anymore. The factory is constituted as follows: in the courtyard behind is the paper mill, which makes **endless paper** that, already dried, is rolled into the bottom floor of the main building like a lava flow; there it is cut into sheets by a mechanism and conveyed into the print shop and then all the way to the presses. Fifteen presses are in operation, of which each makes twenty thousand impressions daily. Alongside is the drying apparatus and the bookbindery. It has been calculated that the paper pulp, which is still liquid at five in the morning, will be at eleven the next morning, that is, inside of thirty hours, an elegant little book."

Wilhelm Hauff, *Die Bücher und die Lesewelt*
(1826), chap. 3

into the master diagnosed by Butler no longer includes any transformation, but characterizes an ultimate condition in which the objective machines begin a life of their own as masters and the people are objectified as their slaves.[5] The life that seems to inhere in the machine, to which bodily characteristics—to the point of circulation and procreative capabilities[6]—are attributed, is founded in its exchange of roles with human beings.

The shock with which the rise of the new technology must have beset human self-consciousness is legible in its representation. A scene from an early German novel, E. A. Willkomm's *Weisse Sclaven; oder, Die Leiden des Volkes* of 1845, displays a representational strategy typical of the time, if in a somewhat curious fashion. An inheritance conflict is resolved by resort to a duel using steam-driven spinning wheels for weapons. The machine functions as a court, the economy of labor becomes the judge: the operation of the apparatus, that is, the amount of yarn produced in a specific period of time, is supposed to arbitrate the conflict. The representation of the battle demonstrates the psychological and ultimately physical effects of working at a machine. The monotony of this reified activity occasions the appearance of threatening visions that ultimately draw the death of the factory owner in their wake: the owner, overcome by an erotic hallucination, stretches out his arms toward his beloved, gets caught in the machine, and is torn to pieces.[7]

Max Ernst, *The Elephant Celebes*,
1921.

A thousand noises disturb this damp, dark labyrinth,
but they are not at all the ordinary sounds one hears in
great cities. The footsteps of a *busy* crowd, the
crunching wheels of machinery, the shriek of steam
from boilers, the regular beat of the looms, the heavy
rumble of carts, those are the noises from which you
can never escape in the sombre half-light of these
streets.

Alexis de Tocqueville, *Journeys to England and Ireland*
(1835)

The problem of objectifying labor is cast here in the form of a personal drama: the factory owner becomes the victim of a properly running machine. The machine produces commodities, which (according to Marx) replace human social interaction, and thereby annihilates its human operator. The uncomprehended character of commodity production results in the displacement of the machine into the realm of myth—the spinning wheel snips the thread of life, as once did Atropos, the goddess of fate. As so often in the literature of the nineteenth century, the machine, depicted mythologically and as threateningly feminine, is thereby excluded from the reality it was itself coming increasingly to determine.

In a second form of exclusion, the life-threatening and threateningly lively machine is styled—in this, the golden age of colonialism—as a monster. In the novel *Hard Times* (1854), Dickens describes an industrial city with the eloquent name of "Coketown," which, colored by ash and smoke, looks "like the painted face of a savage." The pistons of the steam engine move "like the head of an elephant in a state of melancholy madness." The uniformity of mechanical movements stamps itself upon the inhabitants of this industrial wilderness, who all walk "with the same sound upon the same pavements, to do the same work."[8]

It is precisely the most advanced technology, with its strict regimentation, that appears as contradictory and raw in the image of the savage and of the elephant run amok. The choice of such metaphors characterizes not only the representation of the machine world but also that of the big city arising at the same time. The modern, that which is noncontemporary with itself, appears as a jungle. Dickens's Coketown is a modern-mythical "labyrinth," of which no overview is possible and in which people are born in airless little nooks, to pass their lives without the possibility of escape, as "the Hands," that is, as tools.[9] Machines are the monstrous beings whom people, trapped in the labyrinth, serve with their labor.

In comparison with the eighteenth century, a shift in perspective has taken place. The body as a mechanical object has been replaced by the machine as a bodily object. If in the *homme-machine* the image of the machine was identical with that of the human body, then the consequences of this objectification become manifest in the image of the living machine: the separation of the body from the subject. In the description of the machine is to be seen the return of what was believed to have been lost—nature—in the form of a woman, a savage, or an animal. The rationality of the machine world is transformed into a mythology. The fear of reification becomes legible in this transformation.

2. THE COMMODITY SPECTACLE

CIRCA 1850

Relations between things replace relations between people. "The Human Comedy gave way before the comedy of cashmeres." People are no longer tolerated as anything but passive spectators—to be precise, as buyers. Balzac depicts in one of his studies[10] the transfer of the commodity character onto sellers and buyers. The organ that mediates contact between the buyer and the commodity is the eye. The impulse to buy is produced on this speechless level; the seductive manifold of things presented to view promises universal wish-fulfillment.

The glistening commodity-fetish—Balzac already describes it very precisely—acquires the function of a tempting signal. The methodical display of goods abstracts considerably from the use value of the individual commodities, which disappear into "the Babylonish luxury of galleries." The "piquant faces" of the saleswomen only add a further charm to the hoard of treasures. The eye mediates a frictionless sensuousness. E. T. A. Hoffmann's cousin with the telescope in the corner window was one of the first to derive pleasure from the colorful "variety"[11] of the commodity relations that had taken the place of personal relations.

The seller behaves as if in a theatrical performance, is in fact an actor who displays an item to the purchaser for the sole purpose of connecting the latter, whose money now lies on the counter, with the wishes embodied in the commodity. The buyer does not relate to the seller, person to person; rather, it is the speechless commodity that exerts its presence between the two of them. The seller merely brings the thing to speech by casting its advantages in the right light until the buyer finds his wishes confirmed by the commodity. Here, it is things that lend form to social relations between people.

The monopolization of commodities in the galleries of which Balzac speaks, that is, the concentration of the widest variety of

Paris, Palais Royal, Galerie d'Orleans.

items in arcades or bazaars, is the signature of the new commercial strategies designed to handle the manifold increase in product offerings of early industrialization. In comparison with the open, communicative structure of the marketplace, for example, this concentration represents the rise of a parallel to general changes taking place in sales: the greatest possible concentration of shops along with their simultaneous isolation from one another.

The buyer strolling through an arcade does not confront a relatively homogenous offering of goods, as in the marketplace where essentially only foodstuffs were sold, but a differentiated assortment of things. The arcade demands completely new perceptual maneuvers from the potential buyer, a readiness to shift continually between diffused and concentrated attention.

It is the age of the panorama. Paris, the city of arcades and museums (which also fall under this rubric), is, according to Ludwig Börne, a contemporary visitor, "the telegraph of the past, the microscope of the present, and the telescope of the future. It is a catalogue of world history in which one need know nothing but alphabetical order to find everything."[12] If Börne speaks in this way of an accumulation of knowledge and temptations, the point of which is to use them, then Poe's man in the crowd shows at

Galleria Vittorio Emanuele, Milan, constructed 1865–1867.

about the same time the other side of the encyclopedic offering, to which the only remaining reaction is nervous and apathetic: "He entered shop after shop, priced nothing, spoke no word, and looked at all objects with a wild and vacant stare."[13]

Concentration and diffusion—the encyclopedic offering is continued in the museums, and it is no surprise that Alexander von Humboldt would have the idea of setting up "Panorama Museums"[14] as spaces of universal illusion. These phenomena— the museum, the panorama, the commodity fetish built of embodied labor time in the arcades—have one thing in common: social or historical reality is recast in the form of things on exhibit, which, as Balzac indicates in this connection, trick the eye with the illusion of life. The *Encyclopedia of the Philosophical Sciences*, in Hegel's title, becomes that of the commodities in Balzac, becomes "the encyclopedias of carnival frippery." The catalogue of world history of which Börne spoke acquires a new catchword.

The shop becomes a site into which Balzac imagines his historical figures, to show that even a Talleyrand is vulnerable to the sophistications of a clever salesman. But this transformation of diplomatic strategies into sales strategies, their transfer into an apparently ahistorical realm beyond the compass of "culture," is simultaneously universal and circumscribed—the salesman remains on the boundaries of his business: "Take him away from his shop . . . he is like a collapsed balloon; only among his bales of merchandise do his faculties return, much as an actor is sublime only upon the boards." He merely plays a part in the social relations between things, relations which, indeed, absorb the rules of human social relations but can never themselves become real.

Balzac, who develops a typology of the salesman, sees that the latter become reproductions, are themselves modeled like the commodities into the differentiated images of the various wishes of the respective buyers. Thus are they "arms, as it were, directed by the head," integrated into an overall mechanism, like the individual machines in the factory. The salesman, who exacts a tax on the needs of his customers, is himself made by his art into an artifact.

As for the commodities—one thinks of Giedion's tidy maxim, "The sun is mirrored even in a coffee spoon"[15]—given the correct presentation, they become cult items; the seductive shine on a cashmere shawl appears as "a golden ray." The salesman, in perfected mimicry, "plays" on the shawl "as Liszt plays on the pianoforte keys." Art and history—the shawl is sold (an utter fabrication) as having come from the possessions of the empress Josephine, as Selim's gift to Napoleon—are combined in the service of a sale. The historical epoch, also the epoch of industry, arrives here at itself, in a general *quid pro quo*.

3. THE COLLECTOR AND HIS TREASURE: "AN ENTIRELY FURTIVE PRIVATE RELATIONSHIP"[16]

a) An imaginary conversation between Marx and Nietzsche could be developed around the figure of the collector. For the former, the miser is the "capitalist gone mad," who, instead of handing over his accumulated property to a new round of circulation, thereby increasing it further, withholds it.[17] The miser and the collector do not instrumentalize property as a means of increasing capital; rather possession itself is their goal. This latter implies the (nearly theological) motif of salvation in the face of the transience of modern life, that is to say, of commodity exchange, and sets self-assertion over against universal exchange. For Marx, the figure of the miser has long since become obsolete in contrast with the capitalist, but he refers in a note to the original ambiguity of the miser's activity: both the Greek σώζειν and the English "to save" have double meanings: hoarding and saving, but also saving in the sense of salvation.[18] The ambiguity touches on a central concern of the collector: he is, as is yet to be shown, one who attempts to overcome his social seclusion through the community he shares with the things he collects. Both the miser and the collector sacrifice personal gratification to the accumulation of treasures,[19] which are not for them a means of gratification, but objects (or money) that they gather as if in obedience to a compulsion. Because of their "passion for wealth as wealth," both the miser and the collector are closely related to the capitalist, but are distinct from the latter because theirs is a "mere idiosyncrasy"[20] that runs counter to circulation.

If, from the point of view of the rational use of capital, Marx regards the hoarding behavior of the collector as "sheer tomfoolery,"[21] this relationship is reversed in Nietzsche—capital utilization is tomfoolery and collecting a possible line of escape. For his interest in the analysis of the commercial spirit is precisely the idiosyncrasy of individuals, recast as a heroic attitude in opposition to the abstraction of all social relationships caused by now universal commodity exchange. In *Daybreak*, Nietzsche sees the rise of a culture for which "commerce . . . is the soul. . . . The man engaged in commerce understands how to appraise everything without having made it, and to appraise it according to the needs of the consumer, not according to his own needs. . . . This type of appraisal he then applies instinctively and all the time: he applies it to everything, and thus also to the productions of the arts and sciences."[22] Human social intercourse takes shape—and here Nietzsche's thought joins seamlessly with Marx's—in conformity with that between things whose individual qualities have been obliterated. The abstraction of human relationships in a commodity-producing society based on the division of labor appears to Nietzsche as "the ascendancy of dealers and middlemen, in the most intellectual pursuits as well"; examples are: "the man of letters, the 'popular representative,' the historian . . ."[23] Nietzsche's critique of commercialism merges here with his general critique of culture—of historicism, for example, which excludes all independent activity—for the exchange of commodities also enforces a general "virtue," in that exchange not only

After all, what is rubbish but the great storehouse of things multiplied to infinity by mass production? The fancy for collecting is altogether reactionary and out of date. It is in opposition to the process of production and consumption which is gaining momentum in our society—and whose end is the rubbish dump.

. . . The refuse dump is not an abyss in which the object is swallowed up but the repository where it finds a home after successfully passing through a thousand ordeals. Consumption is a selective process aimed at isolating the really new and indestructible aspect of production. The liquid in the bottle, the toothpaste in the tube, the pulp in the orange, the flesh of the chicken are all eliminated by the filter of consumption. What is left is the empty bottle, the squeezed tube, the orange peel, the chicken bones, the hard, durable parts of the product, the elements of the inheritance which our civilization will bequeath to the archaeologists of the future. It is my job to see to it that they are preserved indefinitely in a dry and sterile medium by means of controlled dumping. Not without getting my own excitement, before their inhumation, from the infinite repetition of these mass-produced objects—the copies of copies of copies of copies of copies of copies and so on.

Michel Tournier, *Gemini*, trans. Anne Carter (Garden City, N.Y.: Doubleday, 1981), pp. 75–76

presupposes an "equivalent concept of value" but requires in a related sense that the participants share an "equivalent character"[24] as well.

Commerce, like science, is characterized by the ascendancy of the necessarily uniform mediators. As a counter-model, Nietzsche produces the type of the great individual who refuses to submit to leveling. In his catalogue of answers to the question "What is noble?" he makes a principle of the refusal to conform to the laws of commodity circulation: noble is, among other things, "the slow gesture, and the slow look," and "the collecting of precious things."[25] Under the guise of a theory of nobility, Nietzsche promotes here a new relation to things, which is, in fact, very old; it is one in which things are not seen as commodities to be appraised but as objects with which one can communicate. The collector's frequently eccentric way of life is explicable by way of this double determination: he is both the greedy, self-sacrificing miser in the economic analysis of Marx and, beyond the gesture Nietzsche styles as noble, one who tries "to save" things and, in so doing, save himself. He preserves the things he has withdrawn from circulation as rudiments of the past.

b)   The social type of the collector is not a nineteenth-century invention; yet, for two reasons, it acquires a particular currency at that time. First is the proximity of the collector's peculiar occupation to the appropriating activity of the developing cultural sciences, leading to the establishment of various types of museums. Collecting is causally related to research, which interprets the collected objects, texts, or data. The unmediated connection of the two activities was manifest earlier in the Renaissance "wonder chambers" and in the affectations, for example, of Rudolph II of Prague or Della Porta in Naples: here were juxtaposed precise, modern natural scientific apparatuses and the most remarkable fetishes.[26] The preference for the *insolito*, the unusual, in these collections was not distinguished from empirical or historical interest. This indecisiveness, the interpenetration of magic and scientific precision, remains typical for the modern collector as well and distinguishes him from the positivism of the museums, although the collector often enough supplied the latter with their initial stock.

The second reason for the collector's prominence in the nineteenth century is the existence of capitalist society itself, the outstanding characteristic of which—wealth—Marx describes in the first sentence of *Capital* as an "immense accumulation of commodities." In this lies the potential both for satisfying the collector's needs, which are limitless in principle, and for continually creating new ones. The collector disdains all commodities that can be obtained easily on the market, and must therefore go wherever necessary to acquire that which, should it exist in quantity, he would not want to buy. He removes the mobile commodity things from circulation, not for the purpose of using them, but simply to possess them. He strips the things he buys on the commodity market of their commodity character by incorporating them into his collection. In doing so he cancels the alienation of things in commodity circulation, in which they exist not as themselves but as objects subject to arbitrary exchange independent of their sensuous nature, but does so without devoting them to their second function, namely, use. Collecting, taken in itself, is just as dequalifying as universal exchange—is, viewed abstractly, only the negation of the latter. The collector confronts the limitlessness of commodity circulation with his particular inertia, attempts to impose closure on the principled openness of commercial intercourse.

c)   The collector attempts to complete the uncompletable—a labor of Sisyphus, which is what best characterizes him. La Bruyère's description of the collector in his *Characters,* which was published around 1690 in the Paris of Louis XIV, already makes reference to this absurd trait. In regard to a coin collector, he writes: "all the drawers of his cabinet are full, and there is only room for one coin; this vacancy so shocks him that in reality he spends all his property and literally devotes his whole lifetime to fill it." Or, as an art collector relates, "I labour under a very serious affliction . . . which will one day or other cause me to give up collecting engravings; I have all Callot's etchings, except one, which, to tell the truth, so far from being the best, is the worst he ever did, but which would complete my collection; I have hunted after this print these twenty years, and now I despair of ever getting it; it is very trying."[27]

The intention of the collector is to create a complete alternative world in the area of his specialization, which supplies him with substitutes for all the pleasures of the real world. His passion has become displaced from people onto things, the gathering of which signifies to him psychological fulfillment. He strips the things of their exchange or use function and attempts to reproduce them in accord with his own private order. The single missing item is so valuable in this enterprise that all of the other objects in his collection, in comparison with this last missing one, lose their value. Should the last one be found, then he perhaps discovers a new one just appearing on the market, and the process of revaluation begins anew and continues into infinity. He attempts, through collecting, to escape incompletion, ultimately his own death, but succeeds only in anticipating the latter. To this extent he is related to the animal in Kafka's "Bau," whose protective measures serve only to acquaint it with the impossibility of protection. Indeed, the collector, by instituting these measures, by creating a defensive wall of things separating him from life, kills himself while still alive. Things promise the collector a magical defense against his own transience but only anticipate the latter in that they make him into a servant of things and, ultimately, into a thing himself.

d)   The relationship of the collector to death and decay is characteristic for the depictions drawn by Balzac and his contemporaries. In "The Wild Ass's Skin" (1831), Balzac confronts a collector, an old man in his antique shop, with a young man who seeks by visiting the shop, that is, by examining the things, to distract himself from his fantasies of death. In the shop there rests (in what is nearly a prototype of surrealist collage) "a kitchen jack leaned against a pyx. . . . The emperor Augustus remained unmoved and imperial with an air-pump thrust into one eye. . . . Instruments of death, poniards, curious pistols, and disguised weapons had been flung pell-mell among the paraphernalia [sic] of daily life; porcelain tureens, Dresden plates, translucent cups from China, old salt-cellars, comfit-boxes . . ."[28] The young man, under the impression of the life left behind in the things, experiences the sought-after distraction from his planned suicide as depersonalization: "He had left the real behind, and had climbed gradually up to an ideal world; he had attained to the enchanted palace of ecstasy."[29] Things for him become animated, allowing him to adopt an ecstatic overview, in which past becomes present and the present and his fear of death diminish.

The chaos of this collection is precisely what frees the imagination. The ecstasy combines the objects in such a way that they appear as "a poem without end."[30] This infinite poetic process distinguishes antiques from the inventory of things in a museum. It allows the observer to assume a completely different relation to this "gigantic bazaar of human insanity" than to the ordered space of the museum; in the former, he is so drawn to the things that boundaries collapse and he appears to himself "neither wholly alive nor dead."[31] Inherent in things, as in a fetish, is the power of transformation. They represent the past, which, through them, becomes the present, and appear to offer a means to escape the limits of one's own individual life. To the systematic coherence of things in a museum, Balzac juxtaposes in the antique shop "a panorama of the past,"[32] a dreamlike coherence that brings together the most disparate things. The visitor enters so completely into them that the self sinks away.

Balzac becomes aware of the central fantasy of the collector, namely, the achievement of a state beyond time, to which Marx gave a neat and precise formulation in a preliminary study for *Capital*: "The hoarder of money scorns the worldly, temporal and ephemeral enjoyments in order to chase after the eternal treasure which can be touched neither by moths nor by rust, and which is wholly celestial and wholly mundane."[33] (The behavior of the collector is related to the writing subject in Derrida's theory: writing as an attempt at immortality, as an enterprise by which the subject makes the self historical.[34])

To the overstepping of the boundaries of time corresponds a desire to stand still. When he falls mortally ill, the old usurer Gobseck begins to snatch things up for himself, without using them or relinquishing them to trade. The furniture in his apartment "seemed as if preserved under glass," his revenues in gold and silver he deposits in the oven. The sick room is full of commodities, art objects, and rotten foodstuff. That which Balzac terms here "covetousness . . . as an illogical instinct"[35] points precisely to the miserly tomfoolery of which Marx speaks. Death is here the driving force of collecting, the frailty of the body is denied through the accumulation of things—the transience of which in circulation appears as the image of personal transience and prompts defensive measures.

Pliushkin, the impoverished estate owner in Gogol's *Dead Souls* (1842), is not a capitalist but nevertheless resembles the usurer Gobseck living according to his version of the slogan "Enrich yourselves" under the July Monarchy. Both, if each in his own way, are hoarders, collectors motivated by greed. Gogol uses the condition of the estate to depict the anticirculation quality of its owner Pliushkin. The buildings have deteriorated and the gate through which the traffic of people and goods has to flow is covered by a green mold,[36] the symbol of decay and the absence of any kind of movement. Circulation knows no standstill; the noncirculating is made the equivalent of decay: Gobseck's rotting foodstuff corresponds to the moldy gate. Like Gobseck's, the estate owner's room is also a disorganized accumulation of things. Pliushkin—whose serfs have to continue supplying him—hoards the goods without selling them, until the flour turns to stone and cloth deteriorates into dust.

Unbounded economic passivity characterizes his behavior, but at the same time a compulsive drive to collect, which spurs him to extremes of activity. He "wandered about the streets of his village every day looking under the bridges, under the planks thrown over puddles, and everything he came across, an old sole, a bit of a peasant woman's rag, an iron nail, a piece of broken earthenware, he carried them all to his room and put them on the heap . . . in the corner."[37] He has been gathering things to himself since the life went out of his surroundings—ever since his wife died. Earlier: "Everything on his estate was done in a brisk fashion and took its proper course; his flour mills and fulling mills ran regularly . . . the master's sharp eye was everywhere, looking into everything, and like an industrious spider he used to run about busily from one end to another of his industrial web."[38] Only as a widower did he become a greedy collector, begin constructing an alternative world characterized not by functional connections but by a single mania for completion. Each thing, beyond any exchange or use value, exists for him only to enlarge his hoard, to fill the emptiness of his house. For Gobseck and Pliushkin, collecting is solely the expression of an insuperable lack; the individual things are devoid of meaning.

e)   What above all distinguishes the emphatic collector from the collector motivated by greed is the former's interest in the things themselves. He either eroticizes them or turns them into a fetish, into a substitute for missed opportunities, which, invested with libido, are transferred onto the things. In the novel *Cousin Pons* (1874), a portrayal of the classical collector, Balzac does indeed refer to the preconditions of the passion for collecting—for Pons his ugliness, which hinders his success with women, as well as his failure to achieve fame as a musician—that is, he establishes a deficiency that demands compensation. But the deficiency in this case produces its own attitude toward things, which regards the latter not as objects of exchange but as communicative partners. In the solicitude of his dealings with the things, which is closely related to that of a craftsman, lies the reason for Pons's professional failure as well: according to Adorno's interpretation, he is "also out of fashion because as a composer he has been left behind by the same industrial progress in instrumentation technique."[39] That which therefore causes him to fail professionally, his inability to conform to the laws of the music market and of the competitive struggle in the opera houses, his boundless naïveté, is at the same time the precondition for his particular view of things. Exchange value does not appear to him as immanent in the commodities (he does not even know the value of his collection, although he buys the individual items in principle for less than their full price) but as "lèse-bric-a-brac."[40]

The collector who is not in the position of selling himself is also uninterested in the purchase value of the things he collects; it is not their temporal value that interests him but their eternal value: "He kept his collection for his own ceaseless enjoyment. . . . Natures created to enjoy great works have the sublime faculty of true lovers: the pleasure is as great tomorrow as today, they never grow weary; and the masterpieces, luckily, are always young."[41] Things are the ideal romantic partner—always accessible and not subject to decay. Baudelaire wished to conserve his erotic reveries in a "Museum of Love"[42]—the melancholy refuge of erotic obsessions, for which the transfiguration of the objects is only to be had via the loss of reality.

While the baroque allegorist, to whom Benjamin refers as the polar opposite of the collector, makes decayed things into a symbol, the collector attempts to reproduce them. The Proustian procedure of the *mémoire involuntaire*, displaced onto the world of things, is his as well[43]—a condition of decay activates memory and thereby allows for the reconstruction of a past by means of which the subject finds his way to himself, that is, overcomes the deficiency. Characteristic of the collector is that his behavior, apparently animistic and at home only in the past, nevertheless belongs to the avant-garde, which draws the consequences of the experience of decay in conditions of modernity. Kurt Schwitters's "Merzbau" is one of the forms in which this avant-garde nature becomes manifest; that for which a longer practice of the commodity society was necessary becomes visible in him: "The true, quite unappreciated passion of the collector is always anarchic, destructive. For this is its dialectic: To conduct a stubborn, subversive protest against the typical, the classifiable, without betraying the thing, the particular within which it is sheltered."[44]

∫

CIRCULATION AS A WAY OF LIFE

a)   Circulation is the eternal idea of the commodity-producing society. Hobbes responds to the astronomers' discovery that the earth does not stand still but revolves about the sun by claiming mobility for persons and things as well: "Liberty, or Freedome, signifieth (properly) the absence of Opposition; (by Opposition, I mean externall impediments of motion;) and may be applyed no lesse to Irrationall, and Inanimate Creatures, than to Rationall."[1] Mobility is defined as freedom and freedom as mobility. At the beginning of industrialization, liberalism makes a program of commercial freedom; things are set in motion: "The continual movement in circuits of the two antithetical metamorphoses of commodities, or the never-ceasing alternation of sale and purchase, is reflected in the restless currency of money, or in the function that money performs of a *perpetuum mobile* of circulation."[2] To the continual turnover of commodities, to their absolute mobility, corresponds in the nineteenth century an ensemble of mechanical (railway) and communication technologies (newspaper, telegraph), which infinitely increase the capacities of people and information to move. The question here concerns the social and aesthetic consequences of circulation as βίων παραδείγματα.[3]

b)   Individuals, like cities, necessarily conform themselves to the newly developed forms of contact and interchange. And how they do that, how people change under the law of circulation, is depicted by Balzac in the physiognomical study with which he begins the story "The Girl with the Golden Eyes." Individual

Emile Zola, the moving sidewalk
at the World Exposition of 1900.

Honoré Daumier, *The Parliament
of the July Monarchy, 7 Prunelle,*
one of 36 bronze busts, 1832.

reasons to move are excluded: the people roll like a "cornfield,"[4] driven around the city by the power of money and enjoyments, which Balzac makes into a leitmotiv of the text. They are described as faceless, their faces mere masks. As in Marx, where the possessors of commodities as representatives of commodities are only the "characters who appear on the economic stage," since they are mere embodiments of economic relations, so, too, are Balzac's Parisians characterized solely by their greed for money or enjoyment.

Continual motion is their way of life, which is suited to the interchangeability of money and the fleeting nature of enjoyment. In this the city of Paris resembles its inhabitants: it is "social nature, forever in the crucible."[5] No part of the city has an immutable form, and the radical construction projects of Haussmann are no longer distant; both work their effects on emotional life: "In Paris no sentiment can stand against the swirling torrent of events; their onrush and the effort to swim against the current lessens the intensity of passion. Love is reduced to desire, hate to a whimsy. The one family link is with the thousand-franc note, one's only friend is the pawnbroker."[6] Exchange, the *quid pro quo*, now determines emotional life, makes possible fleeting ecstasies *en passant*, "A une Passante." The commodities, with their "lack [of] a sense of the concrete . . . always ready to exchange not only soul, but body, with any and every other commodity,"[7] offer the image of a structure of drives in which mobility has become the highest principle.

The various forms of mobility serve for Balzac as the class structure: The worker is "movement metamorphosed into man, space incarnate, the Proteus of civilization"[8] altogether. The mobility of the worker on the market, the compulsion to adapt—like a commodity to the buyer—to any available job, is reinterpreted sarcastically: the worker becomes none other than Proteus, the symbolic figure of an irony that always resists determination. His freedom of mobility consists in his ability to transform his person into labor power in ever-new reifying forms. That is the freedom of the commodity, whose bodily form, like that of the worker, is only the "incarnation" of human labor.[9] Business life offers a wholly different, and apparently substantially less multifaceted, image of mobility—it "bustles and stirs, as by some acrid and

Karl Eduard Ferdinand Blechen,
The Palm House near Potsdam,
painting, 1832–1834.

rancorous intestinal process."[10] Business activity simulates disorganized intestinal movements; constrained within the machinery of business, these doctors, lawyers, and business people live according to the rhythm of the advantages available to them. The business people alienate money, the workers alienate work, and the difference between them is that the workers do not receive adequate compensation. All are subject to the dictate of permanent motion. (In German, the word *Diktat* is also used to mean "command.")

This is how Balzac explains the ugliness of the average Parisian, while, at the same time, developing an escape fantasy that is extraordinarily typical for the nineteenth century. The age of colonialism was particularly adept in the invention (a protest against its own aggressive expansionism that destroys that which it desires) of fantasies of the Orient in which, so Balzac thinks, magnificent bodies thrive—an effect of "the undisturbed calm cultivated by those profound philosophers . . . who have nothing but scorn for perpetual motion."[11] In the large cities, people had to frequent the newly built palm houses to enjoy such peacefulness, and, through the fantasy of a scenic illustration, the harem ladies were included right along with the rest.

c)   The city of Paris is wholly governed by mobility, a fact that becomes evident in the priority placed on street construction at least since Baron Haussmann assumed his office in 1853. In the nineteenth-century network of streets lies a completely new motif in city structure. The planners and architects of the Renaissance or the baroque period concerned themselves with aesthetic and representational matters; their preference was to design single buildings and squares appropriate to an urban society still subject to an easy overview. The needs then were those of the pedestrian. The Second Empire had other ones; it required unhindered mobility.

The characteristic feature of the transformed Paris is the "cannonshot boulevard, seemingly without an end."[12] The odd image Giedion uses here is in no way pulled out of thin air, but stems from the time. Victor Hugo popularized it in his novel *1793*: "The ideal of architects is sometimes strange. The architect of the Rue de Rivoli had for his ideal the trajectory of a cannonball."[13] A remark of the brothers Goncourt indicates the general consequences in technical perceptual terms of this linear conception of city planning: "I am foreign to that which is to come, to that which is, and a stranger to these new boulevards that go straight on, without meandering, without the adventures of perspectives, implacably a straight line, without any of the atmosphere of Balzac's world, making one think of some American Babylon of the future."[14] The world of Balzac appears here inappropriately glorified, since what is now happening—the expansion of the Rue de Rivoli occurred in the period following 1848 under the administration of Haussmann and his predecessor, Rambuteau—is nothing more than the necessary consequence of urban circulation, as Balzac had already described it. Nevertheless, it is instructive that circulation is bound up here with the obsessive notion of a thoroughly rationalized America, a motif to be found in Tocqueville and Baudelaire as well. Balzac's emphasis gives way to an ambivalent approach to the same phenomena.

From the point of view of the rulers, however, there were good reasons for linear city planning: there had been, after all, battles at the barricades in the twisted city streets on nine separate occasions between 1827 and 1851. Haussmann presented the principles of his plans openly: 1) to clear the area around public buildings; 2) to improve sanitary conditions in the city; 3) the design of wide boulevards; 4) the connection of the train stations with the city center.[15] All of these principles have a twofold interest in common—the free circulation of people and goods and the secure supply of air and water, and, at the same time, the capacity to control them. The latter Haussmann declares openly. It includes the unencumbered mobility of troops and cannonballs arrayed against the threat of a popular movement.

The most astounding aspect of Haussmann's concept of city planning is the priority assigned to street construction, to which the building of apartments took second place. Haussmann worked—this too is completely new—with a thoroughly organized staff of technical experts, less so with architects. The latter, with their more artistic education, were not equal to the needs of urban development suited to circulation. Moreover, the individual configuration of buildings appeared superfluous. In view of the enormous volume of construction, Haussmann decreed the

Left: Boulevard Richard-Lenoir, 1861–1863. Below: Charles Meryon, *The Morgue*, etching, 1864.

uniformity of facades and, in doing so, of the interiors of the rental spaces as well.[16]

d)   Boulevards of this type present a novel experiential space. The concentrated and accelerated mobility of people and things demanded an assimilation of perceptual capacities. As film would later exercise a shocking effect through its initially confounding mass of images, so now the boulevard: given the multitude of contacts and encounters, the nervous system has to operate selectively and not simply collapse under the assault of impressions.

An episode in Poe's story, "The Man of the Crowd," conveys an impression of this new perceptual task. The people seem to find themselves in a state of extreme tension and a curious absence simultaneously; they are concentrated on pursuing their course and, at the same time, so absent that they bow "excessively" to those who are jostling them.[17] Consciousness seems to have become bifurcated: people move automatically in the crowd with their conscious perception diverted from the other people; amidst all the physical intercourse there occurs no social intercourse, with individuals isolated more than ever in the crowd and focused on their own private interests. The "unending stream of traffic" of which Kafka speaks later[18] reduces the flow of people to a fleeting exchange of glances. And this rapid shifting of perception has

For some time now such a social *idée fixe* has been a kind of super-American city where everyone rushes about, or stands still, with a stop-watch in his hand. Air and earth form an ant-hill, veined by channels of traffic, rising storey upon storey. Overhead-trains, overground-trains, underground-trains, pneumatic express-mails carrying consignments of human beings, chains of motor-vehicles all racing along horizontally, express lifts vertically pumping crowds from one traffic-level to another. . . . At the junctions one leaps from one means of transport to another, is instantly sucked in and snatched away by the rhythm of it, which makes a syncope, a pause, a little gap of twenty seconds between two roaring outbursts of speed, and in these intervals in the general rhythm one hastily exchanges a few words with others. Questions and answers click into each other like cogs of a machine. Each person has nothing but quite definite tasks. The various professions are concentrated at definite places. One eats while in motion. Amusements are concentrated in other parts of the city. And elsewhere again are the towers to which one returns and finds wife, family, gramophone, and soul. Tension and relaxation, activity and love are meticulously kept separate in time and are weighed out according to formulae arrived at in extensive laboratory work. If during any of these activities one runs up against a difficulty, one simply drops the whole thing; for one will find another thing or perhaps, later on, a better way, or someone else will find the way that one has missed. It does not matter in the least, but nothing wastes so much communal energy as the presumption that one is called upon not to let go of a definite personal aim. In a community with energies constantly flowing through it, every road leads to a good goal, if one does not spend too much time hesitating and thinking it over. The targets are set up at a short distance, but life is short too, and in this way one gets a maximum of achievement out of it. And man needs no more for his happiness; for what one achieves is what moulds the spirit, whereas what one wants, without fulfillment, only warps it. So far as happiness is concerned it matters very little what one wants; the main thing is that one should get it. Besides, zoology makes it clear that a sum of reduced individuals may very well form a totality of genius.

consequences for emotional life. The individual is delivered up impotent to the plethora of mobile stimuli—Benjamin speaks, in reference to Baudelaire's sonnet, "A une Passante," of "not so much love at first sight as love at last sight."[19] This remark characterizes, in the melancholy view of Baudelaire as well as Benjamin, the problem of perception: there is no longer any behavior appropriate to the ceaseless stream of stimuli.

The new form of perception, roughly contemporary with the development of the boulevard, found a training ground in travel by rail. The elderly Eichendorff, long past his prime as the poet of magical moonlit nights, described an experience around 1850 which corresponds to those of Poe and Baudelaire. He says about a railway trip: "These steam trips are ceaselessly jumbling up the world, which actually no longer consists of anything but train stations, like a kaleidoscope. The racing landscapes pass by, cutting ever new faces, before one has settled on any particular physiognomy, and the flying salon gives shape to ever different societies, before one has been able to master the old one."[20] The meaning is twofold: the physiognomy of the landscape changes as does that of the fellow passengers, who are replaced at every train station. Like the boulevardier, the traveler by train remains a stranger awash in the manifold. Later writers develop a very subjective form of dealing with this glittering stream of exterior perceptions: by means of it, by means of the eventually fatiguing stream of images or the monotony of mechanical noises, a state of interiority is produced in which the most personal reverie becomes possible:

> Puisque la douce voix pour moi murmure encore, . . .
> Au rhythme du wagon brutal, suavement.
>
> [As the sweet voice murmured once again for me, . . .
> With the rhythm of a railway car, harsh and bland.][21]

The rhythm of the train evokes that of sexual intercourse; the movement of the reverie and that of the machinery combine. The empathic projection of the self into the machinery corresponds to the same relation to circulating commodities.

e)   Baudelaire portrays a new type of artist: the flâneur. The figure of the flâneur is bound up extremely closely with urban cir-

It is by no means certain that things must turn out this way, but such imaginings are among the travel-fantasies that mirror our awareness of the unresting motion in which we are borne along. These fantasies are superficial, uneasy and short. God only knows how things are really going to turn out. One might think that we have the beginning in our hands at every instant and therefore ought to be making a plan for us all. If we don't like the high-speed thing, all right, then let's have something else! Something, for instance, in slow-motion, in a gauzily billowing, sea-sluggishly mysterious happiness and with that deep cow-eyed gaze that long ago so enraptured the Greeks. But that is far from being the way of it: we are in the hands of the thing. We travel in it day and night, and do everything else in it too: shaving, eating, making love, reading books, carrying out our professional duties, as though the four walls were standing still; and the uncanny thing about it is merely that the walls are travelling without our noticing it, throwing their rails out ahead like long, gropingly curving antennae, without our knowing where it is all going. And for all that, we like if possible to think of ourselves as being part of the forces controlling the train of events. That is a very vague role to play, and it sometimes happens, when one looks out of the window after a longish interval, that one sees the scene has changed. What is flying past flies past because it can't be otherwise, but for all our resignation we become more and more aware of an unpleasant feeling that we may have overshot our destination or have got on to the wrong line. And one day one suddenly has a wild craving: Get out! Jump clear! It is a nostalgic yearning to be brought to a standstill, to cease evolving, to get stuck, to turn back to a point that lies before the wrong fork. And in the good old days when there was still such a place as Imperial Austria, one could leave the train of events, get into an ordinary train on an ordinary railway-line, and travel back home.

Robert Musil, *The Man without Qualities*
trans. Eithne Wilkins and Ernst Kaiser
(London: Picador, 1979), 1:30–31

culation and therefore distinguished in principle from the *promeneur solitaire* as presented by Rousseau. He is a part (like the commodities) of a circulating crowd, moves entirely within the generality of circulation, but exists only in his distance from it—in that he observes, reflects on the accidental constellations in the crowd, preserves his seclusion. His way of life is independent of clearly regulated, utilitarian relationships; he has interest only in the infinity of potential events. All of this demands a mobile psychic disposition, the preconditions of which are "the love of masks and disguises, . . . the hate of home and the passion of travel."[22]

For the flâneur, whose behavior Baudelaire declares to be the equivalent of the poetic as such, the modern big city becomes a muse whose movements he studies. It is not primarily the transformation into a work of art that interests him, but the image of transformation the city offers. To enter into circulation, "to be at once himself and others," is the goal of the poet as flâneur—"Like those wandering souls that go about seeking bodies, he enters at will the personality of every man."[23] In this state of home- and egolessness, he is bound simultaneously to everything: "What men call love is small indeed, narrow and weak, compared with this ineffable orgy, this sacred prostitution of the soul which gives itself up wholly (poetry and charity!) to the unexpected as it occurs, to the stranger as he passes."[24] The flâneur's sense of transport remains dependent on offerings of the unknown into which he allows himself to melt: every transitory event becomes to him the promise of a moment, of deliverance from the bad infinity that is also his intoxication.

The series of passing moments he experiences as shocks. In the dedication of *Paris Spleen* to Arsène Houssaye, Baudelaire speaks of an ideal prose that is supposed to follow "the sudden leaps [*soubresauts*] of consciousness"—(in Benjamin's translation, *Chocks* [shocks];[25] older ones speak of "jibes," which describes the objective content in a richer image, though less precisely). Baudelaire feels himself inspired to this notion by the interweaving of countless urban relationships, which must be rendered artistically over and over anew. This thought is accentuated in the aphorism of "Rockets" in *My Heart Laid Bare*: "What are the perils of the jungle and the prairie compared to the daily shocks and conflicts of civilization?"[26] Its expression in another aphorism is therefore surprising: "Every engenderment of a sublime thought entails a nervous shock, which can be felt in the cerebellum."[27] But only in this way does Baudelaire produce the twofold structure of the concept of the shock, which founds the artistic sublime in circulation (of people, of the crowd).

This is also shown by the description of hashish intoxication, in which the intoxicated experiences himself as "the supernatural," as "merely the same man increased, the same number raised to a very high power."[28] He himself becomes the crowd; he intoxicates himself on its circulation, that is, transforms himself into a multiplicity that revolves within himself. In one of the aphorisms from "Rockets," which are in part sketches for *Les paradis artificiels*, this experience is referred directly back onto the big city: "The pleasure of being in a crowd is a mysterious expression of delight in the multiplication of number. Number is *all*, and in all. Number is within the individual. Intoxication is a number."[29] Circulation is an intoxication that multiplies the individual person.

Entering circulation corresponds in Baudelaire to the animation of things. The melting into the crowd of male and female others goes back to the erotic. A poem from *Flowers of Evil*, "Jewels" blends the attraction of the beloved together with that of the things she is wearing on her body:

> La très-chère était nue, et, connaissant mon coeur,
> Elle n'avait gardé que ses bijoux sonores . . .
> Quand il jette en dansant son bruif vif et moqueur,
> Ce monde rayonnant de métal et de pierre
> Me ravit en extase, et j'aime à la fureur
> Les choses où le son de mêle à la lumière.[30]

> [The darling one was naked and, knowing my wish,
> Had kept only the regalia of her jewelry . . .
> A world of dazzling stones and of precious metals
> Flinging, in its quick rhythm, glints of mockery
> Ravishes me into ecstasy, I love to madness
> The mingling of sounds and lights in one intricacy.]

The beloved stiffens in her dance, appears as a crystal being moved—and becomes thereby an illustration of the seeming vitality of circulating commodity-things. The body becomes stone, whose sparkles reflect desire, causing it to rebound back onto the enraptured spectator. (Compare the pictures of Gustave Moreau.) She "was naked and, knowing my wish"—this introduction shows the secret agreement of the two, to make love into a visual experience, into a spectacle of light reflexes. The sense of touch has retreated far behind that of sight, the light rays do not stroke the lover but cut through him with a shock. The gentle glimmer of the skin is not only disembodied in the reflection of the crystal but split up into a series of changing light rays. Thus is the thronging of the urban crowd transferred onto the body.

By acquiring a crystalline armor, the body is itself transformed into crystal. Not even the eye is excepted from this metamorphosis—the eyes of the beloved appear repeatedly in the poems, "Of mingled metal and agate," as "Your eyes . . . Are two chilly gems mingled of Iron and Gold."[31] The look, the sense of touch for the poet, has its desire return, reflected, having been subjected to manifold fragmentation and thereby made lifeless; "Her regard . . . Deep and cold, cuts and thrusts like a sword."[32] The animation of the dead, the erotic ecstasy of light in the brilliance of the jewels, the precondition of which was the killing of the living body, allows Baudelaire himself to appear in one passage as a "cemetery."[33]

It is not gratuitous that the figure of the prostitute, to Baudelaire a kindred spirit, appears frequently in his work. Her body is quite directly a commodity, which only becomes body again after it has been transformed into money. Her empathic involvement is a component part of the transaction. Empathy, the animation of the dead, which, as transport, Baudelaire pushes to the point of self-dissolution, lends things the appearance of subjectivity. The flâneur surrounds himself with the appearance of independence, but, as he is "the virtuoso of empathy," so is "his ultimate incarnation the sandwich-board man."[34]

The ambivalence constitutive of the flâneur as a type consists in the fact that empathy for the otherness of the commodity resembles artistic appropriation. A letter by Flaubert, to which Benjamin refers to illustrate the "*ivresse* of empathy in the flâneur,"[35] makes the parallel clear: "it is a delicious thing to write,

Gustave Doré, *A Sandwich-Board Man*, wood engraving.

to be no longer yourself. . . . Today, for instance, as man and woman, both lover and mistress, I rode in a forest . . . and I was also the horses, the leaves, the wind, the words my people uttered, even the red sun."[36] The capacity to give oneself up, behind which, in Baudelaire, there lurks the circulating mass and its impulse toward conformity, designates for Flaubert the pleasure of the poetic imagination.

Baudelaire delivers himself up to the shocks of contact with circulating things, which he processes with the precision of a seismograph. The poetic procedure of empathy is modernized here; it "comes into being through a *déclic*, a kind of switching. With it interior life provides a counterpart to the element of shock in sense perception."[37] Empathy thereby becomes a reaction to the attenuated external contacts of the commodity-producing society, an attempt to refer the social relations between things back onto people.

f)   In Benjamin's terms, the mode of apperception of the flâneur aims at *Erlebnis*, not at *Erfahrung*. "On the feuilleton: the point was to inject the poison of sensation right into *Erfahrung*; that means to perceive the *Erlebnis* character of common *Erfahrung*."[38] This remark contains *in nucleo* an epistemological theory of the flâneur's . . . activity as such. Benjamin's concept of *Erfahrung* (compare Benjamin's "Storyteller" essay) is implicitly based on the fundamental definition by Aristotle: "Now from memory experience is produced in men; for the several memories of the same thing produce finally the capacity for a single experience. And experience seems pretty much like science and art."[39] Experience in this sense is bound to the possibility of repetition, both in the arena of handicrafts and in the social sphere. Its subject is tied up in collective tradition. Factory work contributes to the atrophy of experiences: "The shock experience which the passer-by has in the crowd corresponds to what the worker 'experiences' at his machine,"[40] of which he has become a part. The division of labor impedes experience (*Erfahrung*) of the whole, which formed the basis of the handicraft mode of production and the simple exchange of products. The shock of *Erlebnis*[41] attacks these habitual customs; it is permanently episodic.

"*Erfahrung*" is bound to uninterrupted habits, to duration; Benjamin's counter-concept "*Erlebnis*" stems from the vitalist philosophy of the turn of the century, as developed theoretically by such figures as Bergson, Dilthey, and Simmel. An early version of it is to be found in the romantic theology of Schleiermacher, for whom every *Erlebnis* is "an element of eternal life."[42] This ties the exceptional character of the inspired moment emphatically to a continuum, makes it possible to experience the general in the particular—a subtle attempt to recognize the deterioration of *Erfahrung* and simultaneously annul it. Later this tradition will be joined by Proust, Joyce, and Musil.[43]

Benjamin removes his concept of *Erlebnis* of this quality of knowing, does not ground it in the concept of *Erfahrung*, as does vitalism, but separates the two. The reference of *Erlebnis* back onto totality, however conceived—*Erlebnis*, that is, as the experiential form (*Erfahrungsform*) of the cosmic (or as the form of knowledge in Dilthey that is suited solely to the humanities, for example to the understanding of poetry)—is replaced in Benjamin by a descriptive application of the concept as a representational means of the mode of apperception in the modern city. *Erlebnis* is grounded in the circulation of people and things. In the modern period, as Benjamin sees it, the exceptional no longer leads to the whole, rather the whole bears the character of the exceptional.

g)   In Baudelaire's theory of the modern, which he formulated especially clearly in the text about Constantin Guys ("The Painter of Modern Life," 1863), the principle of movement occupies the central position. He attempts to base the concept of beauty in the concept of change, which lends it the affect of opposition to the classical idea of eternal and absolute beauty. Baudelaire arrives at his definition of beauty by combining two elements: for one, an unchanging, eternal element, and, for the other, a relative, contingent element, "which will be, if you like . . . the age, its fashions, its morals, its emotions."[44] It is this modern element that primarily interests him. The transience of fashion, for example, thus becomes an expression of an unchanging beauty, which only momentarily assumes other masks.

R. B. Kitaj, *The Autumn of Central Paris (after Walter Benjamin)*, oil painting, 1972-1973.

This definintion leads him in turn to an interest in rapid artistic techniques like pastels, aquatints, and especially lithography (a process first discovered in 1798 by Senefelder), in which the fleetingness of impressions is captured better than in statuary painting. Constantin Guys, the "passionate lover of crowds and incognitos,"[45] is therefore presented by Baudelaire less as an artist in the traditional sense than as a man of the crowd in the sense of the story by Poe. (Only very few of Guys's drawings are signed; he worked during the Crimean War, for example, as a "picture reporter," whose drawings were taken every evening by a courier, transported to London, transferred to woodcuts, and printed in the newspaper.[46]) The point of departure in his artistic activity is curiosity. The curious person, who, like the child, "sees everything in a state of newness . . . [and] is always *drunk*,"[47] is the person most like inspiration itself.

This degree of openness in relation to continual changes, whereby the point was both to record them and forget them, predestined Guys "to become one flesh with the crowd. For the complete idler, the passionate observer, it is an enormous joy to set up house in the heart of the multitude, amid the ebb and flow of movement, in the midst of the fugitive and the infinite. To be away from home yet to feel oneself everywhere at home . . . to be at the centre of the world, and yet to remain hidden from the world."[48] Baudelaire ultimately compares him to "a kaleidoscope gifted with consciousness," thereby anticipating a formulation by Marx, who characterized the possessor of money as "capital . . . endowed with consciousness."[49] The ceaseless movements in the crowd are analagous to the ceaseless circulation of capital.

Baudelaire's artist as flâneur is therefore to be seen precisely within this tension: on the one hand, open to the point of abandon to all possible constellations, tied to no boundaries; on the other, a fleeting money soul. The whole comprises an attempt to extract a utopian quality from the alienation, the fleeting abstraction of relationships in the big city. Guys's journalistic illustrations surpass the classical notion of nature and beauty in that they discover them in the swarming of the city. With this the artist, in the religious topos found so frequently in Baudelaire, becomes a traveler "across the great human desert"[50] in search of modernity. In him, the desire to see everything, therefore to communicate *Erfahrungen* with the pictorial memory, is juxtaposed to the demands of changeable *Erlebnis.*[51]

The *Flowers of Evil,* on the other hand, connote movement and destruction. Conformity with the modern, which Baudelaire praises so emphatically in Guys, has long since disappeared in the poems. Circulation finds its concrete expression in *démolitions.* According to one *bon mot,* Haussmann characterized himself as an "*artiste démolisseur.*"[52] This movement seizes the imagination but simultaneously overwhelms it:

> Paris change ! mais rien dans ma mélancolie
> N'a bougé ! palais neufs, échafaudages, blocs,
> Vieux faubourgs, tout pour moi devient allègorie,
> Et mes chers souvenirs sont plus lourds que des rocs.[53]

> [Paris changes, but nothing of my melancholy
> Gives way. Foundations, scaffoldings, tackle and blocks,

And the old suburbs drift off into allegory,
While my frailest memories take on the weight of rocks.]

The last line of *Flowers of Evil* runs: "Through the unknown, we'll find the *new*."[54] The bad infinity of circulation appears here in images of melancholy and death. Its correlate is the petrifaction of the subject.

6

1. MANET Valéry once observed that the themes of the *Flowers of Evil* and those of Manet's paintings correspond to each other.[1] That would mean that impressionism, at least to the extent that it derives from Manet, draws a conclusion from the experience (*Erfahrung*) of the moderns as Baudelaire described it. The question is whether, besides the similarity of objects represented, the technique of impressionism, independent of subject matter, reflects a new mode of experience.

Valéry's observation can be grounded concretely in many examples; from the *Flowers of Evil*, Valéry himself mentions "Parisian Scenes," "The Jewels," "The Ragpicker's Wine," and, from Manet, *Olympia, Lola,* and *The Absinthe Drinker*. The reference to the latter in particular begins to suggest the entangled relations in the work of the two artists. Manet painted *The Absinthe Drinker* in 1858–1859. The subject matter supports the assumption that it was inspired by Baudelaire's "The Ragpicker's Wine." The ragpicker was a frequently encountered figure in Paris of those years; in the poem he is "the jumbled vomit of enormous Paris,"[2] and becomes a figure of identification for the poet. Manet, for his part, takes the identification literally, by lending the absinthe drinker Baudelaire's features.[3] The setting in which Baudelaire locates the ragpicker—

> . . .
>
> Au coeur d'un vieux faubourg, labyrinthe fangeux
> Où l'humanité grouille en ferments orageux[4]
>
> [In the muddy maze of some old neighborhood,
> Where human beings ferment in a stormy mass]

71

Edouard Manet, *The Old Musician*, 1862.

—is the part of Paris not yet touched by Haussmann's transformations, the part given over to decay. That is also the background for Manet's painting *The Old Musician* (1862),[5] in which the absinthe drinker reappears in the same clothing and pose. Manet found his model for the musician in the part of the city derogatorily designated "Petite Pologne," which Balzac had already described in "Aunt Lisabeth" and Sue in *Les mystères de Paris,* in precisely the period in which the slums had indeed been torn down, to make room for the Boulevard Malesherbes, but the old population not yet driven out.

The poeticization of urban renewal, which is also to be found in Baudelaire—for example, in the famous poem "Le cygne"—occupies the (not yet impressionistic) point of departure for Manet's work in the late 1850s. The picture therefore documents a transitional moment; amid allusions to Velazquez's painting *The Drinker* (Manet is often inspired by Spanish painting, especially by Goya; compare *The Balcony* and *The Execution of the Emperor Maximilian*), it gathers the Parisian lumpenproletariat together into a pastoral scene while their own part of the city is being demolished. The Boulevard Malesherbes that results appears to be populated by a crowd of people removed from time, in which

Garnier, *Main Staircase at the Paris Opera*, 1862.

only the absinthe drinker in his top hat (Baudelaire) refers to the present. It displays an ambivalent pictorial conception, and one rich in tensions, in which the instant of destruction frees the imagination to conceive an unforced, natural life.

With the two scandalous paintings of 1863, *Olympia* (inspired by Goya's *Nude Maja*) and the *Dejeuner sur l'herbe*, Manet once again employs the principle of grounding myth in modern daily life, for Manet a matter of targeted attacks on the mythological schematism of salon painting. The scandal that both pictures set off lie precisely in the realism of Manet's naked figures—Olympia coquettishly wearing a slipper—which is very distant from the figural decor. It deconcretizes and classicizes by virtue of its idealization, of, for example, the Paris Opera, the construction of which was just getting under way at nearly the same time (1862) in, according to the architect's intentions, the "style of Napoleon III."[6]

The composition of the *Dejeuner sur l'herbe* derives, as Aby Warburg proved systematically in a posthumous text,[7] from classical sarcophagi, mediated over Raphfael's *Heliodorus* of a group of river-gods with nymphs on Raimondi's engraving *The Judgment of Paris*. Manet's river-gods, however, are dressed in modern black frock coats. It was precisely these references to daily life, this proximity, that so alienated the scene to contemporary observers that they found it "immodest," in the commentary of Napoleon III.[8] The critics claimed that the ideal scene had been defaced "with the horrible, modern French costume."[9] The present was to remain banned from the realm of art. Manet committed a second sacrilege in the casualness of his technique, which violated the smooth style of painting of the salon. (Picasso, incidentally, retracted the first of Manet's offenses in his 1961 variation on *Dejeuner sur l'herbe*, by leaving all of the figures unclothed, thus reestablishing the classical ideal that Manet had opposed.) Manet worked with sketchy suggestions inside a general neglect of contour, and occasionally, as is particularly visible in the trees and the lawns, painted shapes exclusively through the use of contrasting colors.[10] He took a step on the technical plane, in a battle "for the human rights of the eye,"[11] in the direction of the dissolution of things characteristic of later, truly impressionist painting. The broken relation to tradition, already suggested in the

Manet, *Dejeuner sur l'herbe*, 1863.

Saw at the Auctioneer's a collection of 18th Century Clothing: sulfer flower, pigeon breast, rose rain, dolphin caca, and color of opal despair and flea belly in milk fever—with piles of pleasant glitter, gay to look at, gaudy, singing, dainty, joyous. The world, since it began, has never had to dress in black. The 19th Century invented this. The 18th Century climbed up and down the scale of colors; it dressed itself with sun, with springtime, with flowers. It played with life in the madness of color. From afar, the clothing laughed before the man.—That the world has become so old and sad and that a good many things have been buried is a serious symptom.

Idea of one man who had a collection of 18th century costumes and of servants whose only job consisted of laying them out and bringing them before the marquis to try on.

Edmond and Jules de Goncourt, 22 April 1857, *Journal memoires de la vie litteraire* (1856–1858), ed. Robert Ricatte, (Monaco: Les Editions de L'Imprimerie nationale de Monaco, 1956), 2:101

treatment of subject matter, finds a consistent extension on the level of technique.

Contrary to the impressionist painters, however, for Manet black was a color and he worked with it a great deal, in particular in the portrayal of contemporary clothing, which was what so shocked the critics in *Dejeuner*. The male figures in *Concert in the Tuileries* (1862), for example (among whom Baudelaire appears once more), or in *Ball at the Opera* and *The Balcony* are all dressed in black. Manet's choice here is not self-evident but reflects a change in men's fashion of the time, the specific quality of which Baudelaire exposed in 1846: "And observe that the black frock-coat and the tail-coat may boast not only their political beauty, which is the expression of universal equality, but also their poetic beauty, which is the expression of the public soul—an immense procession of undertakers' mutes, mutes in love, bourgeois mutes. All of us are attending some funeral or another."[12] It is not by accident that the arrangement of the black-clad gentlemen wearing top hats in the *Ball at the Opera* recalls that of the notables in Greco's *Burial*. The top hat comes into fashion only in the 1830s. Over the following years it becomes a symbol, if not of

Manet, *Concert in the Tuileries,*
1862.

reaction as in Germany after 1848,[13] then at least of the capitalist
bourgeoisie, as a glance at the paintings and photographs of the
time shows.

Warburg's interpretation of *Dejeuner sur l'herbe* aims at something else—Gombrich recalls the connection between the pose of
the reclining river-god, who lives on in the figure on the right in
Manet's painting, and that of the prisoners in mourning in Dü-
rer's *Melancholia.* He continues: "The ancient river-god, therefore, became for Warburg the embodiment of depression and
passivity, the very opposite of the striding 'Nympha' with her
fluttering garments and her affinity to the frantic maenad. . . .
This, then, is the original 'phobic' engram which Manet was ultimately to turn into an image of liberty-loving humanity."[14]

The individual steps in the metamorphosis of the classical
nymph into the female figure in Manet's painting should not
detain us here. The implicit reference to the tension between the
sexes, however, is important; it supplies the basis in domesticated
form for the composition of Manet's painting. The undressed
woman looks out of the picture with a vaguely suggestive smile.
In contrast with the men, she, now naked, was dressed colorfully.

The garments lie in front of her under a basket of fruit arranged like a still life. To her, therefore, is attributed color, fruit, and bodiliness, an earthbound sensuousness that contrasts with the men's black frock coats. Manet undertakes an equally pointed treatment of this contrast, which naturally reflects social conventions as well, in the *Concert in the Tuileries*, where the women's blue scarves correspond to the blue of the sky, and in *Ball at the Opera*. The color composition of both paintings lives from the tension between the black, monochrome surfaces of the men's clothing and the colorful clothes of the women. The connection established in 1861 by Friedrich Theodor Vischer, an aesthetic theorist and student of Hegel's, between political reaction after 1850 and the colorlessness of clothing[15] can, in view of the contemporary representations by Manet of men's clothing which also fail to "acknowledge colors," be carried over onto the petrifaction of relations between the sexes. Manet's early impressionism simultaneously describes the distance between the sexes and completes the emancipation of colors on the bodies of the women.

Manet is always being mentioned in connection with Baudelaire's essay "The Painter of Modern Life," although it is not he, but the relatively unknown artist Constantin Guys, who is named

Below: Claude Monet, *Rue Montorgeuil*, 1878.

Below, right: Manet, *Rue Mosnier, Paris, Decorated with Flags*, 1878.

in the essay as the one who developed adequate responses to the urban changes in Paris of the Second Empire.[16] The thesis is supported by the dating of the Guys essay—though not published until 1863, it was in fact written in 1859–1860. Manet's first work taking modern life as its content, "Concert," stems from the year 1862, a time, that is, in which Baudelaire had dealings with him on a nearly daily basis. If Baudelaire did not further revise the text about Guys, with whom he was also friends, he did attribute to Manet in the essay of 1862, "Painters and Etchers," the "vigorous taste for . . . modern reality,"[17] which he had conceived previously by way of Guys's example. In "The Widows" Baudelaire describes one of those concerts which are the subject of Manet's painting: "Gowns trail and gleam; glances are exchanged; idlers, weary of their idleness, loll about, pretending indolently to savour the music. Here are only wealth and happiness; nothing is here that does not breathe and inspire carelessness and the pleasure of floating idly on the stream of life,—unless we except the rabble . . . as it watches this shining furnace."[18] The text reads, although it contains no reference to it, like a description of Manet's painting, and thus suggests the similarity of the two artists' perceptions.

Manet, like Baudelaire and, later, Degas, represents the type of boulevardier or flâneur, and transforms this experience into his paintings. His perspective in doing so has an ambivalence similar to Baudelaire's—the unconditioned affirmation of modern circulation is contravened by the perception of destruction resulting from Haussmann's "démolitions." A relatively late painting, the *Rue Mosnier* of 1878,[19] serves particularly well as a key to this perceptual mode; it contains a distant echo of the mourning Baudelaire described in "The Swan" (1860):

> . . .
>
> Le vieux Paris n'est plus (la forme d'une ville
> Change plus vite, hélas ! que le coeur d'un mortel)[20]
>
> [The old Paris is gone (the face of a town
> Is more changeable than the heart of mortal man)].

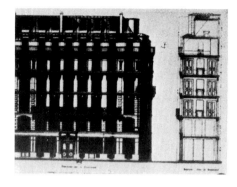

Building on the Boulvevard
Sébastopol, Paris, 1860. Façade
and cross section.

Manet, *The Balcony*, 1868.

The painting depicts a street decorated festively with flags for the World Exposition of 1878. It was the year in which the consolidation of relations following the Franco-Prussian War and the commune was to be celebrated. But if the flags, which are distributed loosely through the painting as the single (impressionist) dabs of color, and the treatment of the summer light, which causes all the contours to blur gently, also suggest the officially affirmed relaxation of tensions, the painting simultaneously contains confusing signs of failure. On one side of the street a couple of nicely dressed pedestrians stroll along a gallery of obviously new buildings; on the other side, a one-legged cripple, evidently a victim of the past conflicts, walks along a beaten-up fence at a construction site. He is relegated to the street, does not walk along the modern sidewalk like the pedestrians on the other side.

The people seem to be separated into different worlds by unbridgeable chasms. Manet emphasizes this impression through the emptiness of the street, which appears in the painting not as a site of circulation but as a no-man's-land dividing two social spheres. If one compares this picture with one painted by Monet for the same occasion,[21] the ambiguity of Manet's becomes even more evident: Monet shows a thick swarm of people—the new boulevards and the people are tied together in an **X**-shaped composition, which, perhaps not accidentally, recalls the iron structures of the buildings for the World Exposition. Where Monet dissolves the physiognomy of people and buildings, has them disappear into a single, if also compositionally domesticated stream of movement, Manet creates memory through pictorial structure, shows a side street in which the repressed preconditions of seamless circulation remain visible.

Yet another painting makes clear the indirect consequences of Haussmann's urban transformation: *The Balcony* of 1868–1869. The subsequently famous critic Albert Wolff wrote about it in *Figaro*: "Ask yourself why . . . a painter arrives at such an uncouth art where, as in the green blinds of his 'Balcony,' he degrades himself to the point of entering into a competition with house painters."[22] Hidden behind a technical remark, this is once again an outcry in the face of the unadorned representation of contemporary reality in the painting, as had already been heard in connection with *Dejeuner sur l'herbe*. The uniformity of the painted

Manet, *Bar in the Folies-Bergère*, 1882.

blinds is ultimately only the actual copying of an architectural detail on the typical apartment building: Haussmann spread, as Giedion writes, "simply and without discussion . . . a uniform facade over the whole of Paris. It featured high French windows, with accents provided by lines of cast-iron balconies like those used in the Rue de Rivoli by Napoleon I."[23] That is precisely what Manet brings into the picture, and at the same time he shows in the dissociation of the threesome the disappearance of communication among the inhabitants of the uniform buildings. The view from the "Balcony" goes in different directions into emptiness; nor does the external world seem able to offer any fixed point. That is the decisive distinction between Manet's painting and the subject matter of Goya's *Majas on the Balcony*. In a fashion similar to that in his painting *In the Winter Garden*, Manet sets his representation of alienation, especially erotic alienation, in typical contemporary architectural motifs.

The same applies to one of his last paintings as well, *Bar at the Folies-Bergère* of 1881–1882. Baudelaire had already described the organization of the new cafés, which also served as meeting places for artists: "The café glittered. The very gas-jet burned with the ardour of a beginner, and sturdily illuminated the blinding whiteness of the walls, the dazzling glass in the mirrors."[24] The cafés are arranged like optical illusions, made apparently limitless by the reflections (like, in another way, the Crystal Palace). The perfect organization of the operation stands in contrast with the absence of relationships among the visitors, which Baudelaire is already describing and which will become well known through the café paintings by Manet and Degas.[25]

In the case of *Bar at the Folies-Bergère*—whose operation Maupassant describes almost simultaneously in the opening chapter of *Bel-ami*—the abstractness of human relations is legible in the subtle composition: the barmaid looks into the emptiness, obviously somewhere into the crowd, which only becomes visible in the mirror hanging behind her. Between her and the crowd stand the goods, drinks and fruit, themselves arranged like an independent still life. The crowd appears as a multitude of white and black points in which, aside from a few faces, only the top hats become visible. The barmaid looks into the emptiness, while the reflected figure of a back that appears to be identical with her, but cannot be according to the laws of reflection, speaks with a guest. The room is without beginning and without end; it remains unclear whether the mirror on the wall offers a view of one or two floors of the establishment. The seller of "drinks and love," as Maupassant writes, is placed between these two poles, lost in a world of mirrors that endlessly reproduce but deny the viewer any possibility of securely fixing his position. The endlessness of the erotic as well as that of material circulation finds its representation in Manet's melancholy reflection.

2. DEGAS

a) Valéry, who writes that the figure of his "Monsieur Teste" is influenced by the person of Degas,[26] reports on a scene which the painter is supposed to have described to him one day: after his habit he was traveling through the city in the upper deck of a bus, to the last stop and back, when he observed a woman taking extraordinary pains to get herself "well arranged and comfortably seated." Following the completion of a series of adjustments her face took on the appearance of a person "whose task is done" and sat there for perhaps fifty seconds in "this state of total well-being." But after this period, which must have seemed unbearably long to her, she began to repeat the entire process: "A whole

Contemporary caricature of Manet's *Winter Garden*.

routine, intensely *personal*, followed by another apparently stable condition of equilibrium, which lasted only for a moment."[27]

The scene is significant for various reasons. Degas is observing a woman seeing to her toilet, a situation that was previously restricted to the boudoir. Manet unfolded at the same time in *Nana* a whole panorama of alienation between the sexes. With Degas the scene has become public; it arises not in connection with seduction, but is as lacking in purpose and reference to another object as Degas's bus trips. He does not tell a story, but conveys an impression that he had without communicating verbally. This is the perceptual mode of the flâneur, who intoxicates himself on anonymous movements. With Degas, however, this speechless unification with the crowd has transformed itself into a practice of observation which becomes the precondition of artistic work—"Ambulare, postea laborare" was his motto.[28]

The bus, which isolates a portion of the mobile urban crowd, transforms itself into *labor*, in which particular communicative conditions are dominant: "Social life in the big city as compared with the towns shows a great preponderance of occasions to *see* rather than to *hear* people. . . . Before the appearance of omnibuses, railroads, and streetcars in the nineteenth century, men were not in a situation where for periods of minutes or hours they could or must look at each other without talking to one another."[29] Modern urban mobility demands a kind of perception in which the perceiver and the perceived exist outside of a context of concrete interaction.

Degas's daily life experience reproduces precisely that defabulization which his early paintings already conveyed to the observer—as Max Liebermann noted in 1896: "No other modern painter has surpassed the novelistic as much as he."[30] What Benjamin later described as the end of narrative, its development to the point where information is delivered in fragmentary form, with individual facts rendered independently of context, Degas has already declared to be his artistic program: "Series about instruments and musicians—the external form—the bend of a hand, the bend of an arm, the neck of a violinist, for example, the puffed cheeks of a bassoonist or an oboist that then become hollow. . . ."[31] Where Manet had followed a more psychological path and analyzed the relations between people in classical-real-

Edgar Degas, *Opera Orchestra*, 1868.

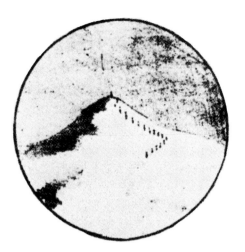

Having reached the summit of
Mont Blanc, we were so high up
that the spyglass could no longer
serve its purpose.

Then we made the descent by
sliding down on the snow.

But we hadn't realized that by
rolling down we would transform
ourselves into human snowballs.

Gustave Doré, *Desagréments
d'un voyage d'agrément*, Paris,
1851. (Shift in perspective;
observation of the ascent and fall
of a group of mountain climbers
through an opera glass.)

istic compositions, Degas is already making the change evident
in the perception of space; pursuing a snapshot technique, he
moves, in detail-like pictorial compositions, so close to the human
subjects' bodies that there is no room left for an impression of
the sort that Manet develops of the relationships between people
and things in space.

To find the beautiful today, wrote the Goncourt brothers in their
novel about artists, *Manette Salomon*, of 1866, "there is perhaps
need of . . . a magnifying glass, nearsighted vision, new psychological processes."[32] This nearly scientific, scapel-like view is the same
as that which Degas casts on his models. Whether the woman in
the bus, the horse, or ballerinas, everything is for him only a "pre-
text . . . for reproducing movements."[33] His paintings no more nar-
rate a story than the scenes he pantomimed for Valéry did; they
have no plot, but show a moment that is also isolated spatially.

b)   The pose of a woman, a moment's balance, points to the
problem of Degas's painting—to secure the moment and, at the
same time, remain thoroughly organized in compositional terms.
As Aaron Scharf has demonstrated,[34] Degas took inspiration from
photographic snapshots, from phase studies of movement like
those of the American photographer Muybridge, but at the same

time he surpassed them. "Upon closer inspection," Max Liebermann observed, "we discover the highest compositional art behind the apparent snapshots."[35] In saying so, Liebermann unconsciously verifies the program that Baudelaire had established for modern art in the essay on Guys: "to distil the eternal from the transitory."[36] According to Baudelaire, art exists within the tension between the transitory and the eternal; in other words, it delivers itself up to the moment, which has no reference to other units of time, but simultaneously creates for it a continuous temporal dimension by petrifying it and thereby rendering it accessible to memory.

The movement is held still and thereby lent duration, stripped of its transitory character—a fundamentally paradoxical procedure, but, according to Baudelaire, the only possibility of grounding art in the (mobile) present, of protecting it from the empty formulas of an abstract beauty. In the section "The Art of Memory," Baudelaire formulates the basic dilemma as follows: "a struggle is launched between the will to see all and forget nothing and the faculty of memory, which has formed the habit of a lively absorption of general colour and silhouette, the arabesque of contour."[37] The memory is always again assaulted by the "mob of details," that is, the shocks of modern daily life, and the artist has continuously to try to gain a new balance. In this he is in the same situation as the woman in the bus.

In a critique of the impressionists, who, in his opinion, gave themselves up to the accidents of unmediated perceptions of nature and light, Degas maintained that he needed not the "natural" but the "artificial" life. In fact, he was interested in movements only in their most developed form, as he could study them in ballerinas and racehorses, and he decreed: "It is very well to copy what one sees . . . it's much better to draw what one has retained in one's memory. It is a transformation in which imag-

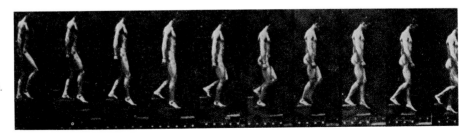

E. Muybridge, *Athlete Descending the Stairs, ca.* 1880.

Degas, *At the Ballet*, 1872.

ination collaborates with memory. One reproduces only that which is striking; that is to say, the necessary. Thus, one's recollections and invention are liberated from the tyranny which nature exerts."[38] That is an equally postimpressionist program—where the latter demanded liberation from the tyranny of mythological material in order to achieve a pure visual perception of nature, Degas goes beyond nature: with the help of memory he wants to fix the "necessary" (for Baudelaire, the eternal, immutable) in the moment.

The work on the moment becomes potentially impossible to complete—"work and distrust," in Valéry's formulation, go hand in hand in Degas. "For all his devotion to dancers, he *captures* rather than cajoles them." He defines not only the dancer by capturing the moment of movement, but, by losing himself to that extent in the ephemeral, whose laws he is pursuing, he also fixes himself—"from sheet to sheet, copy to copy, he continually revises his drawing, deepening, tightening, closing it up."[39] This behavior is the expression of that "fear" Baudelaire had already confirmed in Guys, namely, "the fear of not going fast enough, of letting the phantom escape before the synthesis has been extracted and pinned down."[40]

In his subtle considerations on the act of drawing, Valéry describes the problem on a technical plane: the cooperation of the eye, which follows the movement, and the hand, which, remembering the eye's perception, makes the mark on the paper, is not a simultaneous occurrence but includes a minimal temporal difference that raises the question of the relation of the two activities.[41] This difference determines the modernity of Degas, the attempt to transpose movement into duration. The subject thereby loses its meaning. A well-known painting by Degas, the *Place de la Concorde* of 1875, contains neither a depiction of the square nor one of the people occupying it, who can only be seen rudimentarily, but has ultimately for content only the—temporary—emptiness of the square in that moment in which people are leaving it. This aimless movement creates the empty space in which it also annihilates all statuary meanings.

c) Defabulization, and depsychologization as well, are the consequences of Degas's art, which now perceives reality only in its

Degas, *Place de la Concorde*, 1875.

fragmentary and petrified movement. Landscapes, still lifes, or coherent groupings of people appear scarcely at all in this perceptual mode, which is made to order for modern urban life and undertakes pictorial research of the human being as a mobile body. The picture of the person now arises only in a specific moment. This also imparts that coldness to the subject, whatever the eroticism otherwise present, which allows Giedion to write about one of Degas's dancers: "This painting exhibits in its field the impersonal, precise, and objective spirit which produced constructions like the Galerie des Machines."[42]

The ballerinas no longer appear as themselves but merely as the arbitrary personifications of functional mobility contexts. Degas's enterprise finds confirmation in the scientific researches of his time. While he was making use of the snapshots of the Californian photographer Muybridge, the French physiologist Marey was working on a systematic analysis of the nature of organic movements. In 1860 Marey invented an apparatus—"the Spygmograph . . . which inscribed on a smoke-blackened cylinder the form and frequency of the human pulse beat."[43] He researched movements, an aspect that also interested Degas, that escape the human eye, for example, the succession of a seagull's wing movements, the phases of which he could represent simultaneously. He thought it justified to call

"... you tonsured pigeons under my white dress in my pigeon rink, you will be richly rewarded. I will bring you a dozen tons of sugar. But don't touch my hair!"

Max Ernst, *Das Kamelienmädchen* (1930)

E. J. Marey: Photographic record of the flight of a seagull on three projection surfaces. Before 1890.

Around 1885 Marey pointed three cameras in such a way as to view the bird simultaneously from above, from the side, and from the fore. . . . At his laboratory in the Parc des Princes, Paris, he set up a vast hangar, before whose black walls and ceiling the sea gull flew over a black floor.

Giedion, *Mechanization Takes Command*, p. 22

the curves he gained in this fashion the "language of phenomena themselves."[44] This sentence from the physiologist, written in 1885, is confoundingly similar to Degas's artistic intention. Language will be lent to things by way of movement; in Degas, the language of movement becomes the carrier of pictorial content. In his work, communication is reduced to the language of gestures; his interest in the objects is mimetic. In this there lies a reflection of the communicational forms of the big city, in which countless meetings with unknown people demand a purely gestural, speechless way of reacting. There remains only the language of movements, which make people into speechless mobile bodies and therefore the equivalent of things.

Marey speaks of the movements he observed as "a luminous trail, an image without end, at once manifold and individual"[45]— a remark that reflects Baudelaire's thoughts on modern art from a scientific perspective. Degas's representations of the dance make the "language of phenomena" visible in human objects. (Valéry, too, would find inspiration in Marey's researches for his 1923 dialogue, "The Soul and the Dance."[46]) The dance provides the dematerialization of the body that Mallarmé captured in the paradoxical formulation, "a danseuse is not a woman dancing, because she is not a woman and she is not dancing."[47] Degas is not interested in the human figure but in the figure of movement in space. The body can be visualized only in movement. The eye registers the movements of persons, not the latter themselves; the objects are exchangeable like commodities in circulation. The dancers are doubly anonymous, as elements of the entertainment industry and as mobile bodies. Degas paints them in endless series.

3.   MONET

It is striking that, with few exceptions, there are no representations of people in the paintings of Claude Monet and, when people do appear, they are usually faceless and lacking individual definition. The contours of the human face disappear with those of things. Monet is more interested in atmospheric conditions than in objects. Already in 1902 Julius Meier-Graefe had found a nice formulation for this procedure: "For him the distinction between a tree stump in the morning and in the afternoon is greater than the difference between a male and a female being illuminated by the same sun."[48] Cézanne's remark, "Monet is only an eye—but what an eye!"[49] must be understood in accord with the premise of the fascination with changing light situations. Upon the death of his wife he registered involuntarily (to his own disgust) the various shimmers of light on her face[50]—which makes dramatically clear the relations between the human body and light.

Momentariness meant for him capturing the moment of a specific light effect. In this there lies an essential distinction between Monet and Degas, who thought precisely in the same unit of time: Monet is not interested in the most exact reproduction possible of an object but in the momentary light effect. The light makes for movement, not the object. This interest determines the choice of subject matter—it is rarely the fast-moving bodies in the big city, never ballerinas and racehorses, but static bodies (buildings) or things moving in slow natural rhythms like ships on the water, water lilies in the current, etc. The momentary effect of (day-) light is ultimately dependent only on the state of the sun and the clouds. Artificial light, which does appear in Degas's work, does not appear in Monet's.

After he had reached the age of fifty, Velasquez no longer painted anything concrete and precise. He drifted through the material world, penetrating it, as the air and the dusk. In the shimmering of the shadows, he caught unawares the nuances of colour which he transformed into the invisible heart of his symphony of silence. . . . Space reigned supreme. . . .

Jean-Luc Godard, *Pierrot Le Fou* (1965)

Monet, *Impression—Rising Sun,*
1872.

To shift from the movement of objects to the movement of
light signifies on the one hand an abstraction from the function
of things, which finally appear in this form only as still lifes, but,
on the other, allows reality to appear in a new coherence under
the primacy of light. The atmospheric light effect in which the
contours of the things disappear gathers together the dispersed
individual movements that allowed the world to decay into fragments in Degas and meld the objects together into an "impression." Thus, too, the title of the painting of 1872 that gave the
group exhibiting in the atelier of the photographer Nadar in 1874
its name. Monet chose the title because he "could hardly call it
'View of La Havre,' " as he put it himself.[51] The novelty of this
painting is demonstrated in this problem of titling the works; it
did not deliver realistic, recognizable views, but strove to recreate
the familiar, like the harbor in Le Havre. The objective interest
in the exact reproduction of light refraction coincides with the
interest in the expression of a subjective vision (impression) in
the unique moment of its representation.

The same interest determines depictions of modern life.
Monet's views of streets and train stations are painted from up
close. He does not choose a panoramic overview, like, for exam-

Manet, *Gare Saint-Lazare*, 1872–1873.

ple, the traditional painters of vedutas, but locates his focal point in the midst of the swarm. Thus it is that the city does not appear solidly structured, lying there in secure proportions, but in non-synoptic movement. Manet's *Gare Saint-Lazare* (1872–1873) offered yet another bewildering synthesis of two figures seen realistically in front of a black iron fence and the diffuse clouds of smoke from the railway operations behind it. (Compare the reversal of this pictorial structure in Manet's 1872 painting *Races in the Bois de Boulogne*:[52] the mobile bodies of the horses are sharply outlined, those of the static spectator become blurred.) This internally distinct combination of two perceptual modes falls away in Monet's Saint-Lazare series of 1877. The painter, who had obtained permission to work in the train station, dissolves Manet's expectant scenes in a "dynamic flux"[53] of movements, which includes equally people, machines, smoke, and the sunlight shining through the glass roof.

Beginning in the late 1880s, following the train stations, Monet painted the series of poplar trees, haystacks, water lilies, etc., in which he represented the objects not in themselves but as existing

Above: Monet, *Cathedral at Rouen*, 1894.

Right: Monet, *Gare Saint-Lazare*, 1877.

only among variations of light. The things, already stripped of their qualities by being placed in a series, arise only in the changing light conditions registered by the eye. ("Thing, body, matter, are nothing apart from combinations of the elements,—the colors, sounds, and so forth—nothing apart from their so-called attributes," writes Ernst Mach in 1885.[54]) It is striking in the series of the cathedral in Rouen that the narrow details chosen never deliver a view of the whole building, nor even the entire front. The paintings are strangely frameless (and devoid of people), and the sky merely lends them an additional color accent. The entry and the parts of the façade are hazily recognizable, but the overall impression is that of the highly differentiated shape of a surface. Space and perspective have disappeared; the panoramic view has turned into a microscopic one, which is concentrated not on the building but on the glittering nuances of the light. The spatial structure dissolves into the unit of time in which it is lit by a particular light. Kandinsky recognized, in 1895 in one of the haystacks exhibited in Moscow, that "the object was lacking in this picture."[55] The autonomy of the color impressions causes the things to disappear; the later water lilies show color perspectives that have become completely independent of the standpoint of things existing in space.

There is a description from Proust, whom Monet revered, of a nymph garden that seems to have been inspired by Monet's garden in Giverny and the water-lily paintings. The description can be read as a representation of Monet's de-realizing and highly aestheticized way of seeing: ". . . this skiey border also, for it set beneath the flowers a soil of a colour more precious, more moving than their own; and both in the afternoon, when it sparkled beneath the lilies in the kaleidoscope of a happiness silent, restless, and alert, and toward evening, when it was filled like a distant heaven with roseate dreams of the setting sun, incessantly changing and ever remaining in harmony, about the more permanent colour of the flowers themselves, with the utmost profundity, evanescence, and mystery—with a quiet suggestion of infinity; afternoon or evening, it seemed to have set them flowering in the heart of the sky."[56] That is the description of a mythical correspondence between color, light, and things distributed freely in space; fleetingness and duration collapse into one. Circulation has been retransformed back into the cycles of nature.

4.   ON THE HISTORICAL SITE OF THE IMPRESSIONIST WAY OF SEEING

That the things in the impressionists' paintings were not recognizable scandalized the first viewers. But the latter were only working through the shocks of reality, which only shocked them once they appeared in the paintings. Taken as a model of contemporary reception, the reaction of Strindberg to the representation of the phenomena of movement in impressionist painting and his reaction to the real process of mobility, namely, traveling in a train, demonstrate that the perceptual difficulties are identical.

Strindberg recalls his first experience of impressionist paintings before 1879: "I saw people swarming on a wharf, but I did not see the crowd itself; I saw a train rushing through a Norman landscape, the movement of wheels in the street, awful portraits of only ugly persons who hadn't known how to pose quietly."[57]

He did not see the things represented, but only the movement in which they disappeared. A few years later, in 1885, his perceptual capabilities have grown. The terrain is a different one, but the problem—to be able to recognize things in motion—has nonetheless been solved in the meantime. He writes, full of scorn for those who have not kept up: "It has become a superstition that one cannot see anything from a train window. The truth is that an uninterested eye recognizes nothing but a hedge or a row of telegraph poles. After having practiced for three years, however, I was able, from my compartment window, to 'report' and draw landscapes, flora, peasant houses, tools. . . ."[58]

As long as the eye remains fixed on things close by, like the telegraph poles, it will recognize nothing of the landscape. Only when it gains some distance, turns toward objects somewhat farther away, does it perceive details. It is the same procedure a viewer of impressionistic pictures has to employ: to take some distance from them so as to place the isolated spots of color into a context. (What is said here of spatial references, Proust, in an analogy to this characteristic of impressionist painting, transfers into the sphere of temporal references.[59])

Movement hinders clear and unambiguously defined relationships with objects. That it is possible to practice perception, as Strindberg did in the train (and, gradually, the visitors to impressionist exhibitions as well), is evident from a letter of January 10, 1775, by Lichtenberg: "It all seems like magic to the unaccustomed eye." He is referring to the movement of a crowd of people, which, as the rest of the letter clearly shows, is determined essentially by the needs of commodity circulation. Lichtenberg characterizes his description as a "fleeting painting." The specific quality of that which, remarkably, finds expression here in the categories of painting, namely the instability of perception, becomes apparent in a counterimage of the small city of Göttingen: There "one walks along and sees what is there at least forty paces in advance; here one is . . . happy to be able to save one's skin by waiting out the storm in a side alley."[60] The secure remove of distance is done away with by the crowd in the big city, and perception oriented to perspective is impossible—the eye must become accustomed to the speed and unintelligibility of movement, which it finds difficult to put in order. At issue here is a breakdown of visual habits; the big city appears as an unfamiliar image.

E. T. A. Hoffmann also makes use of expressions from painting—the description of the urban market in "Des Vetters Eck-fenster" of 1822 anticipates indirectly the technique of impressionism (which must be understood as stemming from the novel experiences of the city): "The view was in fact strange and surprising. . . . The most various colors glittered in the sunlight, and, indeed, in quite small dots."[61] What Benjamin says about the procedure of impressionist painting—"the picture is garnered in a riot of dabs of color"[62]—is already being practiced by the paralytic cousin in the corner window in Biedermeier Berlin.

The descriptions of the city of this time make this procedure their own; writers no longer offer overviews from an established point, but limit themselves to "fleeting remarks" (Kotzebue, 1804) or claim "to have recklessly written down immediate impressions" (Raumer, 1830). Perspective disappears: "what I noticed was perceived in the moment of the first impression, and only in this order is it presented" (Schaden, 1822).[63] The city has already turned into a series of momentary impressions.

Gogol writes in 1831–1832 about an annual fair: "everything is bright, gaudy, discordant, and rushing and bustling about before your eyes."[64] This mode of perception carries over onto nature: in the same text Gogol delivers a consistent impressionistic description of nature; trees are de-realized, appearing solely as the play of light: "the dazzling gleams of sunshine light up picturesque masses of leaves, casting on to others a shadow black as night, but flecked with gold when the wind blows. Like sparks of emerald, topaz, and ruby the insects of the air flit about the gay kitchen gardens topped by stately sunflowers."[65] Monet, the "priest of light"[66] and painter of big city crowds and reflections on water, has in Gogol an immediate predecessor. Already in the early nineteenth century, the image of the city (or nature) appears to the eye as fragmented into individual spots of color brought together into a momentary impression. The image can no longer be ordered according to the categories of homogenous time and spatial perspective, is no longer conceived as linear (compare the perspective of progress) but as a simultaneous multiplicity of particles.

Precisely the most advanced perceptual techniques, however, reach back—and this is evident from Hoffmann to Monet—to natural forms of movement for the representation of the endless particularities of urban motion. The isolated impressions, like a guarantee against general decomposition, are re-synthesized: the urban crowd appears as a fluctuation—corresponding water or wind metaphors[67] are to be found in Hoffmann[68] and Poe[69] as well as Gogol, who compares the activity at the annual fair to a waterfall and a whirlwind.[70] Individual things dissolve—but the isolated elements are put right back together as a stream of light reflections. (On this premise, Monet's cathedrals and his water lilies are interchangeable.) Thus arises a homogeneity of the unhomogenous.

"Monet's eye becomes the first instance of the modern." What a critic writes about Monet[71] applies, and it was said almost word for word of other painters, to impressionism as a whole. Social and historical experience is reflected in this unanimity. Interaction in the big city is characterized by consistent visualization and the retreat of verbal and tactile components; it does not admit of contacts other than visual ones devoid of touch. In an analogy to economic theory, one can speak here of the disappearance of individual, specific use value into abstract exchange value, according to the law of which the qualitative difference of one thing from the other disappears. It is not the objects, which cannot be fixed at all, that interest the painters. Their representation aims, in Monet's words, at that "which lives between me and the object."[72] This intermediary space is seen not in perspective but atmospherically.

In literature, as is demonstrated already by the descriptions of big cities in the early nineteenth century, the conceptual causal structure is given up; in painting, what is sacrificed is perspective; the result is the representation of "the autonomy of the visual."[73] The writers' impressions no longer round themselves out into a story, and in pictures there no longer appear volumes that are recognizable by the eye—they have metamorphosed into surfaces on which the things can no more be "grasped" than commodities behind a display window. On the vibrating surfaces of impressionist pictures the relationship among the individual particles remains undetermined and ambiguous.

This way of seeing is inseparable from the scientific researches of the time. Seurat studied the contemporary physical theory of color[74] in the early 1880s, Degas the photographs by Muybridge; and the researches into optical phenomena by the physicist Ernst Mach became, through the mediation of Hermann Bahr, the point of departure for the literary impressionism of Vienna. There are multiple points of contact between contemporary scientific and artistic production of the time, both of which are characterized by a sensitivity to the phenomena of movement and the dissolution of the anthropocentric image of the world. "The excessively praised exquisite sensibility of the artist makes him in a certain sense the complement of the natural scientist; it is as though his sensory apparatus enabled him to register smaller differences than those accessible to that of the scientist."[75] What Adorno refers to here as the sensitivity of modern romanticism is also the program of impressionism in painting, though among the impressionists it is a product not of nervousness but of the most precisely registered light stimuli. The demand for the sensitivity of the nerves has, in art-historical terms, a prelude in the demand for the sensitivity of the retina.

The impressionist painters had a rational optical orientation, or, according to Valéry's formulation, "the brain became nothing but retina."[76] The original synonymy between impressionism and naturalism, maintained in particular by Zola, confirms the realistic impulse; according to the definition of Castagnary, who coined the expression in 1863, naturalistic art "is the expression of life under all phases and on all levels," with the aim of reproducing the realities of modern life.[77] That applies, and to this extent Zola's use of the term is correct, to the contents of impressionist painting and the avoidance of symbolic or mythological drapings as was found in the salon painting; given, however, a look at the technique of painting, the remark is no longer appropriate. The critic G. Rivière, a friend of the painters, proposed in 1877 a definition centering not on the representation of reality but on a consideration of technique: "treating a subject in terms of the tone and not of the subject itself, this is what distinguishes the impressionists from other painters."[78] According to this definition, the sole attempt was to reproduce the impressions made by light on the retina, but precisely this precision led (in Monet, for example) to the disappearance of social reality, the representation of which the naturalists had demanded. Precisely in the most "naturalistic" possible treatment of the light, the visibility of the individual, clearly outlined things dissolved into a stream of color particles.

The impressionist technique in painting is characterized by processes that do not always match the representational intention of realism or naturalism: the use of bright colors, no dark shadows, sacrifice of the color in one particular area in favor of the general atmospheric effect, dissolving the sharp outlines of things, which are blended in to the surrounding area. The brushstrokes that remain visible serve to reproduce or suggest the movement of light and to capture rapidly changing moods.[79] Perspective becomes flat; solid objects, whose contours are blurred, become particles. The process of work runs parallel to this dissolution of the traditional notion of space: paintings, instead of being done one by one, often develop as simultaneous series. But neither are the individual pictures built up bit by bit; the point, according to Pissarro's advice to young painters, is to "paint everything at once by placing tones everywhere, with brush strokes of the right color and value, while noticing what is alongside. . . . The eye should not be fixed on one point, but should take in everything, while observing the reflections which the colors produce in their surroundings."[80] The process of painting itself acquires a peculiar dynamic; the look, which registers the smallest variations of light, thereby passes over the things in view. That which is isolated from everything else can be captured here as little as it can in the literary technique of stream of consciousness, which Adorno once termed "the truly modern Lethe."[81]

Ernst Mach is already drawing the portentous conclusion in 1885: "The primary fact is not the ego, but the elements (sensations). . . . The elements constitute the ego. . . . The ego is not a definite, unalterable, sharply-bounded unity."[82] Here too, things, as in impressionist painting, are being referred back to sensuous impressions[83] and, since they are without lasting substance, can only be fixed in the moment. As Max Raphael points out, however, things in the impressionist picture are not only analytically atomized, but simultaneously unified according to the laws of (Bergsonian) intuition[84]—that is, things become particles of color removed from their respective bodies, but the particles nevertheless combine harmoniously together into a picture. The isolated particles, brought together in a color continuum, only produce a likeness of reality in the interrelations in the picture as a whole. Outside the moment of the "impression" (which relates to the painter) and beyond a certain distance for the viewer, the picture changes immediately. It is a momentary continuum of relative contingency.

Eiffel and Boileau, Bon Marché, Paris—interior footbridges, 1876.

7

COMMODITIES AND THE EROTIC

1. PARADISE IN THE DEPARTMENT STORE

a) The architecture of the "Ladies' Paradise," a fictional Parisian department store modeled on the Bon Marché by Boileau and Eiffel (1876), appears in Zola's novel of the same name as a repetition of London's 1851 Crystal Palace. It seemed to contemporary visitors like a fairy-tale palace whose glass ceiling and walls, supported by iron girders, offered a view of infinity. So, too, did Zola describe his "cathedral of modern commerce": "all this iron formed, beneath the white light of the windows, an excessivly light architecture, a complicated lace-work through which the daylight penetrated, the modern realisation of a dreamed-of palace, of a Babel-like heaping up of the storeys, enlarging the rooms, opening up glimpses onto other floors and into other rooms without end."[1] In this description, however, the department store is transformed imperceptibly from a fairy-tale castle into a sinister creation. The boundless view from the Crystal Palace, where "the eye sweeps along an unending perspective,"[2] returns in Zola, with a decisive modification: in the department store, one has "glimpses onto other floors . . . without end." This cathedral begins to resemble Piranesi's *Carceri,* with the customer hostage to the endlessness of the universe of commodities. The architecture allows for "distant views illuminated by the rays of light from some glazed bay, and in which the crowd appeared nothing but a mass of human dust."[3]

Mirror tricks and the systematic arrangement of broken perspectives[4] strip the building of its actual volume and fragment it into an endless series of temptations and commodities. As in impressionist painting, the boundaries of the building disappear,

Eiffel and Boileau, Bon Marché, Paris—the glass roof over the skylight, which cannot be seen from the street, 1876.

Paris, Bon Marché, wood engraving, *ca.* 1880.

and the individual customers and goods dissolve into the flowing movement of the operation as a whole.[5] Iron staircases, bridges, and galleries cut through the space; the courtyards are transformed by the glass ceilings into halls in which light and air circulate as freely as the public.[6] The transparency of the architecture, still perceived in the Crystal Palace as a metaphysical quality, now has the purpose of expanding space with a view to sales, to induce in the public a belief in infinity, that is, in the inexhaustibility of the commodities offered for sale. If the American department store of the 1850s still followed the horizontal arrangement of floors set one atop the other, then the courtyards of light in Bon Marché, with a glass ceiling construction designed by Eiffel,[7] added a new element: they make the building permeable vertically as well. The visitor is met with a series of changing perspectives—the building, dematerialized like a Gothic cathedral, opens up a continually renewed view of the commodity universe.

It is a typical element of this architecture that the corners of the department store are designed as small pavilions—on the one hand, an element of the old representational architecture, a reminiscence of a castle's round towers,[8] and, on the other, an attempt to create little islands of calm in the middle of the teeming current, where the customers can prepare themselves for new excursions across the sea of commodities. The differentiated arrangement of space bundles and scatters perception in a well-calculated relation. In the construction of churches and palaces there is a comparable organization of space, only in this case it is oriented around a single point, altar, or throne, while the main thing in the department store is to put every commodity upon a throne for display to all customers. The centralized arrangement from a master perspective gives way to a network of overhead walkways and staircases cutting through the building in all directions. In Zola's description, the department store's passageways look like an entangled railway system. He repeatedly describes it as a steam engine.[9]

For his novel, completed in 1883, Zola availed himself of the revolutionary architecture of Bon Marché of 1876, and integrated into it a pathbreaking invention made only recently: if the "Ladies' Paradise" was lit during its design phases by gas lights, the new building itself shines in the light of electric lamps.[10] Thomas Alva Edison, as advertising strategist in no way inferior to his

Boileau, St. Eugene Church, Paris, 1854–1855. With iron pillars and costal arches.

imaginary contemporary and owner of the department store, Mouret, had long been busy with experiments in his Menlo Park laboratory (the myth of which, as well as that of its founder, was heralded in the 1886 novel, *The Eve of the Future*, by Villiers de L'Isle-Adam). Edison displayed his electric light bulb to three thousand (!) eager spectators on New Year's Eve in 1879. He demonstrated his invention with equally sensational success at the Electricity Exhibition in Paris in 1881, and afterward in London's Crystal Palace. The first installations were made in department stores and hotels, with general urban energy supplies introduced some time later.[11]

The wholly new type of light appears in Zola's department store in visionary glorification: amid the enchanted murmuring of the crowd the lamps shine as "illuminating moons," which lend the "magical glitter of an apotheosis" to the grand display of linens. The goods achieve transcendence, "become light." The courtyard of light becomes the sacred basilican "central nave," above which opens up a "dreamy firmament" affording a view of "the dazzling whiteness of a paradise."[12] Light, illumination, electricity: concepts of manifold significance that all make their way into the representation of the apparently prosaic light bulb. Illuminating them, the cathedral of modern commerce celebrated the first day in a new creation story. The building of iron and glass became definitively a sacred space, the commodities a fetish perfectly located in the scene.

b) What applies to architecture applies as well to the presentation of the commodities: there must be suggested a semblance of infinity. The department store at the same time redeems the promises that had been made since the 1840s in the satirical utopias of Grandville as well as in the advertisements of individual businesses, namely, that only the boundless universe could serve as the standard of the mass of commodities available for selection. The colossal increase, for example, in textile production brought on by steam-driven spinning machines, etc., caused the family operation of a cloth merchant under the handicraft mode of production (portrayed by Balzac for the Napoleonic period in the story "The House of the Ball-Playing Cat") to grow into a "magasin" requiring an image of the cosmos for representation, that is,

Statue of Liberty, New York—
mounting of the copper plates.
The design of the steel frame
comes from Eiffel.

Illuminated Magasin du
Printemps, Paris, 1883.

a store of dimensions exceeding the powers of the imagination. The advertisements of the fifties were expressive of the change: a department store claimed that it had purchased eleven million kilometers of material; another that it could span all of the railways in France with fabric; yet another promised it was able to place a canopy over the whole Seine Département. In their self-conception these "magasins" were, successively, the largest in the city, the country, Europe, the world, and—the universe.[13]

One of Villiers de L'Isle-Adam's stories of the 1880s that summarizes these aspirations satirically, "Advertisement on the Firmament," shows the pseudoreligious components of this boundless expansion in the production of goods. By using the methods of an inventor, commercial boasts are projected onto the heavens with electrical light beams, magnesium flames, reflectors, and lenses, so that the sky is raised "to the level of the times."[14] The particular finesse lies in the play of religious significations, according to the model: "Heavens, how delicious."[15] The heavens have become the carrier of literally universal advertisement. The expansion of the technological imagination into the cosmos is also manifest in some of the novels of Jules Verne (which Edison read with enthusiasm) or the caricatures by Albert Robida.

While the literary-technological imagination projects the apparently infinite possibilities of production onto the image of infinite cosmic space, the organizers of department stores go about choreographing the infinity of the commodity universe. Not only is the financial calculation explained in reference to the permanent turnover of limited reserves of operating capital,[16] but the commodities themselves are presented to the public as available in an apparently infinite mass. Illusory tricks assist the process. That which in the baroque period, for example in Bernini's architecture, served to represent the omnipotence of his client—the stretching of spaces through perspective—now intensifies the impressions of the ubiquity of goods: "mirrors, cleverly arranged on each side of the window, reflected and multiplied the forms without end."[17] The genealogy of the goods, their production in a factory, is veiled through the use of complicated arrangements— through their manner of presentation they seem to have sprung directly from the inexhaustible resources of nature: the silk scarves appear as a bouquet of flowers, muslin flows like the sea.[18] The department store offers up the whole of nature—everyone can enter the "paradise" in the middle of the city and, for a minimal price, take a piece of it away. That is a suggestion of omnipotence, pulled by the clever sales strategists from the heavens to the ground of the boulevard.

c)   In Charles Fourier's socialist utopia the "phalanstery" is the basic unit. Each is a community consisting of 1,620 persons, men and women, who are associated not only economically but erotically as well. The division of work and love is thereby transcended. Work is just as attractive as love, love ties are just as systematically organized as work. This organization makes possible the free unfolding of the personality in work as in love. Fourier's design is grounded in this ambivalence, in which regimentation supplies the guarantee of freedom—everyone can (and must) join the group that best suits his or her needs. The phalansteries, which were planned architecturally by Ledoux and others, have the effect of a mix of Versailles and ideal industrial cities—in the center, however, stands not the absolutist state or production but the cult of general gratification, that synthesis of libido and production which fascinated such varied thinkers as Emerson, Marx, and Benjamin.

Zola delivers an ambivalent contribution to the history of Fourier's influence in *Ladies' Paradise* when he repeatedly refers to the department store as a "phalanstery."[19] For it is precisely here that a strict prohibition on love rules the employees, whose possible erotic relationships are regarded as a hindrance to sales.[20] The employment of this concept must, then, aim at an "association" other than the erotic between man and woman, whose commonality is compared in strictly functional terms with the gears in a machine. This new form of association is that between the crowd and the commodities.

The department store accomplishes the perfect organization of passions, beginning with the configuration of the display windows. The goods are so arranged that they "enchant" and "captivate"—even the most modest stocking or glove is presented as if it is covering a tempting body, as if it were there only to lend expression to the beauty of every female shopper, a beauty that is completely untouched by the burdens of daily life. An ideal world

Caricature by A. Robida, Paris, *ca.* 1879.

is spread out behind the glass of the display window; the stocking appears to be lavishing the tender skin of a female leg, the glove the hands of a Byzantine madonna. The gently shining silk is "folded as if round a pretty figure"; in short, the goods are brought to life "by the clever fingers of the window dressers."[21] The commodities offer themselves to people as a second—and better—nature.

Zola uses the goods for sale in a clothing store to exhibit the erotic quality of consumption articles presented in the stylized form of a sensuous experience. This promise determines the exchange value of the commodities. The reaction of a young boy nestling against his sister, "as if wanting to be caressed, troubled and delighted at the sight of the beautiful ladies in the window,"[22] demonstrates the effect: the boy actually lives through that which Mouret's sales strategy is supposed to inspire in grown women as a desire to buy—the commodity as a "promise of happiness."

The presentation of commodities in the department store distinguishes itself essentially in one point from the strategy of exhibition for art or industrial products, in which the things are only visually perceptible. The World Expositions were, according to Benjamin, "the advanced school in which the masses excluded from consumption learned to participate emotionally in exchange value. 'Look at everything, but don't touch.' "[23] The department store put an end to this limitation—touching the goods, trying them on, the pleasure of rummaging about in the materials[24] bring to the visual a tactile component in the presentation of commodities, which minimizes the distance, necessary in the museum but disturbing in the department store, between people and the things. Touching allows for a provisional participation in the paradise of commodity plenitude, which only intensifies the desire for possession.

The power of this enticement is most evident in specific symptomatologies, like the appearance of "a new sort of nervous affection which a mad doctor had classed, proving the results of the temptation provided by the big shops."[25] At issue is kleptomania, and Zola offers a thorough depiction of its first obvious outbreak. He sees the connections between the pleasures of looking and touching and erotic lust, out of which, under certain conditions in the department store, there develops a dangerously sensual temptation. The attack on the nerves is well calculated; Mouret had broken with the traditional form of the symmetrical and harmonious presentation of goods to found, as it was so nicely put, the "brutal and colossal school in the science of displaying." Apparently unordered masses of material in the most glowing colors are supposed to shock and fascinate the customers—who, according to the founder's reasoning, "ought to have sore eyes on going out of the shop."[26] In the novel, this strategy achieves precisely the desired effect. The constant inundation of temptation weakens the self-control of the ladies visiting the shop and causes them, in "a rage of unsated desire," to make unnecessary purchases,[27] or, as the case may be, to become kleptomaniacs. The spectacle of commodities, now no longer as it was in Balzac's time, is choreographed as a powerful delirium.

Alongside the aggressive-seductive display of the goods is to be mentioned a second factor, the presence of which supplies the final determination of the department store: it is not only the goods that produce the fascination but also the libidinal quality of the crowds of people moving around in a narrow space. While psychologists of the masses, Canetti, for example, implicitly assume that the masses move in the open air, Zola insists on an interior space as the site of mass ecstasy. The masses of shoppers are the necessary complement to the turnover of the masses of goods on which the sales strategy is based—the limited reserve of operating capital is turned over more than once during the year, repeatedly transformed into commodities. The rapid turnover of goods and the equally abundant interest on capital combine a multitude of minimal profits into a considerable return, even given trifling profit margins, which means goods could be sold at a low price.[28] This operating method, which overthrows traditional mercantile practices, aims primarily at quantity rather than quality; it demands the continual supply of crowds of customers, compared in one place to the coal burned in a steam engine.[29]

Sales technique then resolves itself into finding an adequate procedure for having the "power of the goods intensified by mass"[30] work its effect on the masses of people. Therefore, for example, the theory of Mouret has it that crowds of people must be produced by bargain barkers right at the doors: "Noise, throngs, life should be present everywhere; for life, he says, attracts life, gives birth to new life and quickly multiplies itself." Thus is life transferred onto the things; through the excitement of even the passersby on the boulevard the goods "assumed a soul."[31] The movement of people has become a need (a function) of the traffic of commodities—through the traffic of people that they occasion, the commodities appear to come to life.

The process of selling is choreographed "so that the people in the street should mistake it for a riot."[32] The comparison reveals the calculus. A riot is a classical mass phenomenon. According to Canetti, "It is only in a crowd that man can become free of his fear of being touched. That is the only situation in which the fear changes into its opposite."[33] This process, this transcendence of distance between people, is simulated in the department store: it also allows the distance separating people from the goods to be reduced. The goal is to allow the "discharge" ("the most important occurrence within the crowd"[34]) to take place as a sale, as unification with the—living—things. In *Ladies' Paradise* two types of sensual appeal are combined: the appeal of the goods and that of the crowds of people, with the result of increased sales.

2.   THE EROTICISM OF MACHINES

Bereft of ornaments and comforts, under a simple coat

of red-lead paint, the machine exhibited without

modesty, almost with pride, its organs of propulsion.

Jarry,   *The Supermale*[35]

a)   In his analysis of commodity production, Marx came upon a phenomenon he designated as the fetish character of the commodity, meaning the substitution of things for social relations. It is not on the level of analysis, however, but on that of appearance that the seeming animation of things becomes visible in the steam engine, which, in the form of the locomotive, became the driving force of industrialization. Of the locomotive's three forms of motion—the up and down of the pistons, the circular motion of the wheels, and the movement forward through space—it was particularly the first whose up and down suggested the back and forth of the legs in human or animal mobility (and the thought of sexual intercourse). The machine appeared to be an organically animated figure. Before the invention of the locomotive running on wheels, there was an attempt to build a machine that "had two feet, which after the fashion of a horse, it raised alternately from the ground."[36] In the designations "iron horse" and "horsepower" lie the clearly visible remnants of this primary fantasy of natural-organic mobility, which failed to be repressed even later on as purely mechanical principles of mobility were developed.

The force that first made mobility possible, the energy produced by compressing steam from heated water, appeared in anthropomorphic images. Typical is a cartoon (a design sketch for a fresco) by Wilhelm von Kaulbach which depicted "The Production of Steam" as human copulation: Vulcan, spewing fire, ravishes a nymph and from this union comes the steam, while, alongside, an iron wheel begins rolling.[37] In the erotic image of the locomotive, the two motifs flow together—the driving force of steam and the visible movement of the piston out of the cylinder.

Mechanical motion could thus be described as an act of copulation: "Look at the machines, the action of the piston and the cylinder; Romeos of steel and Juliets of cast iron. Nor do the loftier expressions of the human intellect get away from the advance and withdrawal copied by the machines."[38] (Such metaphors are in no way confined to the late nineteenth century. In a 1951 book described by the publisher as a standard work in the modern science of sexuality, *Formen der Sexualität* by Ford and Beach, there is a comparison between coital thrusting motions and the movement of pistons and cylinder in an automobile engine—although, in an example of the de-organization of the machine, the suggestive movements in the latter case have long since been concealed beneath the hood.[39]) For Huysman's decadent des Esseintes, the openly displayed drive technology of machines lends them the status of a being far superior, in his eyes, to the natural beauty of women. The locomotive becomes an ambivalent masculine fantasy, the boiler "a shiny brass corset," into which "a smart golden blond" is squeezed; or "a monstrous creature with her dishevelled mane of black smoke" whose violent power "shakes the very earth."[40]

In his story "Bahnwärter Thiel" of 1887, Gerhard Hauptmann goes beyond the distanced observer's symbolic eroticization of the locomotive, as Huysman had proposed. He sets free the threatening eroticism, the "subliminal vampire connotation,"[41] of the machine, in that he couples it with the wife of the railway signalman. The machine bears organic traits: "panting and roaring," "the black, snorting monster" approaches;[42] while the woman has technological features: she digs in the fields "with the speed and endurance of a machine."[43] The mechanical being and the human

Hans Baluschek, cover art for the first edition of *Bahnwärter Thiel*, Berlin, 1982.

being are in one aspect identical: in the power to annihilate native to each. The body of the woman with full breasts and broad hips[44] appears to Thiel as desirable as it is threatening; torn between his fascination and his fear of her sudden suprise attacks of hate that hit him with a violence equal to a locomotive's,[45] he repeatedly withdraws into the dream world of his signal hut, until his wife's inattention allows his child from his former, now deceased wife to be run over by a train. This "novelistic study," as Hauptmann somewhat coquettishly called his product, is centered, in a way unusual up until that time, on the image world of the demonic machine, from which descriptions of human behavior are all but comprehensively developed. The machine is no longer anthropomorphized; rather, human processes are described in mechanical images and the plot is moved along by the machine.

Huysman and Hauptmann's texts originate in observations of the machine and not from considerations of its use. Zola shifts the view; alongside the poetic symbolic language of the novel *La bête humaine* (1890), there are descriptions of tactile-sensuous experiences on the locomotive: "Only on his engine did he live calm, happy, and away from the world. When she bore him along

Wilhelm Kaulbach, *The Production of Steam*, ca. 1859.

Anonymous, *In the Railway Compartment, ca.* 1880.

with the clatter of her wheels, at full speed, when he had his hand on the regulator and was wholly taken up with keeping an eye on the road, looking out for signals, he stopped thinking and took great gulps of pure, fresh air that always blew like a hurricane."[46] Here a new, contradictorily organized behavior is sketched, which is modulated in interplay with the machine—extreme concentration on the steering wheel and route signify simultaneously a lifting of psychological burdens, in which the "clatter," that is, the vibrations of continuous motion, produce a calm, happily abandoned state of mind. Ideal for the locomotive driver is this state in which the manifold factors of mobility raise themselves up into a stationary state—"maintaining regular speed without jerks and at the highest possible pressure."[47] This may well be one of the first descriptions of a delirium of speed, a phenomenon in which erotic lust and machinery are perhaps most clearly coupled within the frictionlessness of pure function.

If one credits a comment made by Freud in *Three Essays on the Theory of Sexuality*, there exists a connection between rhythmic, mechanical shaking, that is, the numbing "clatter" in Zola, and sexual stimulation. Rocking restless children to sleep, games of movement like swinging and tossing, are for Freud the predecessors of the enticing vibrations of a railway trip. What Freud denounces as the "compulsion" of connecting railway travel with sexuality, a lust that is often experienced only in repressed form, Zola describes as the experience of work.[48] Zola can depict the pleasurable character of feelings of motion so clearly in the example of the locomotive driver, because here the experience is immediate, without the twofold dampening characteristic of the bourgeois neurotic and travelers: psychologically through repression and mechanically through the suspension system outside and the padded upholstery inside the wagon.

b)   Still more clearly is the connection between machinery and the erotic manifest in the types of conveyances driven by bodily force. Here is it not the service of a machine that releases erotic associations, but the body itself becomes a machine, which conveys itself with the aid of mechanical limbs. The users of such machines do not touch the ground, but move forward through the connection of their hands and feet to grips and pedals trans-

Max Ernst, *Deux filles se promènent à travers le ciel*, 1929.

The Two-Screw-Sea-Rescue-Velocipede, Collection of F. Barathon, Paris, 1885.

ferring physical force to wheels, propellers, and such—"the masculine and the mechanism form an autarchic unity."[49]

Given the high and absurd degree of complexity of some of these vehicles, the demands of balance and the transfer of force from body to machine absorb the bulk of the rider's attention, so that a closed system is established whereby the goal—forward conveyance—appears to be utterly secondary. Inventions of this sort began to flood the popular scientific periodicals of the time, like *Le Magasin pittoresque*, *Scientific American*, or *La Nature*, from which Max Ernst was still drawing manifold inspiration for his collage novels. There were designs for "monocycles" and "unicycles," and vehicles like the one-wheeled velocipede of a California inventor: "To an outer hoop with a diameter of [approximately eight feet], the designer connected a smaller concentric hoop with forty spokes. The actual velocipede rolled in this inner ring on a wheel attached underneath the seat and two steering rolls disposed at head-level to the driver. As soon as the foot cranks were stepped on, the velocipede moved itself upward on the inner wheel-rim, thereby forcing the hoops into a rolling movement."[50] The users of these apparatuses—curious inventions that nevertheless reveal the imaginative background of mechanics—do not sit on the wheel, but within it or between two wheels, as if wanting to bring the machine into the closest possible contact with their bodies. The

H. Gray, poster, 1899.

wheel hub and the body's center of gravity are often arranged on a line—united into an organic-mechanical center of force.

These fantasies, which revolve not only about the wheel but also about the up-and-down movement of the pedals, conjuring up associations with pistons and cylinders in a steam engine, find their most concrete expression in the culture surrounding the bicycle. Bicycles and trains are the typical means of conveyance in the nineteenth century; since 1816, even before the railway, there was Freiherr von Drais's steerable walking wheel, later completed by the addition of a pedal mechanism. The industrial production of bicycles began about 1870, and only around 1890 did the low-wheeled cycle still common today begin to supersede the high-wheeled velocipede. Of interest here is not the bicycle as the affordable means of conveyance for the working class or its role as a vehicle of emancipation in the women's movement,[51] but the significance of the bicycle as a carrier of erotic fantasies.

Alfred Jarry's farce of 1902, *The Supermale*, depicts the subliminal erotic competition between the locomotive and the bicycle. Going up against the over-dimensional abstract machine of the locomotive in a thousand-mile race is a man-machine bicycle—a quintuplet (five-seated bicycle), with "ten legs joined on either side by aluminum rods."[52] The men become a machine, their body nourished on "perpetual-motion food." The perfection and stamina of the mechanized five-man unit causes it, after having achieved a dramatic increase in speed, to leave the ground. The technological body overcomes gravity in a mechanical triumph that becomes the tool of one of humanity's oldest dreams. The bicycle is the vehicle with which it becomes possible to translate bodily force into flight, considered by Freud an exquisitely sexual desire. Jarry's fantasy finds confirmation in the world of bicycle advertisement images of the 1890s—certain trademarks promise the users they will be lifted up into space or treated to a weightless flight with an unclothed beauty.[53] The pedal mechanism of the bicycle is also the basis of a whole series of inventions[54] meant to convey man, bound to his machine, securely through the water, in turn a feminine element in the old myths. The crank or pedal mechanism thus acquires a kind of (phallic) self-preservation function.

Above: The Opel brothers on their "Quintuplet," *ca.* 1897.

Right: Ferdinand Lunel, poster, *ca.* 1894.

The sex machines on a bicycle base—for example, Robert Müller's *Racer's Widow* of 1957 or other similarly designed apparatuses in Tomi Ungerer's *Fornicon*—as well as anonymous design sketches for masturbation machines[55] translate the symbolism of the pedal or piston motion identified in the bicycle and locomotive back into reality by making mechanical force concretely useful as sexual energy. The body and mechanics are blended together into a closed (bachelor's) system. Alongside the bicycle objects by Picabia (*Portrait of Marie Laurencin*), Picasso (*Bull's Head*), or Tinguely (*Cyclograveur*),[56] it is above all works of Marcel Duchamp—*Roue de bicyclette* of 1913, *Tu'm* of 1918, as well as parts of the bachelor machine—that complete the formulation of the "iconographic theme of the bicycle," namely, the reference "to *perpetuum mobile*, to the love machine, and to chronos."[57]

The locomotive and the bicycle, these machines that still function so "organically," offer verification of Arnold Gehlen's thesis that technology is a matter of "resonance phenomena." The mechanical motions evoke fascination as the repetition of the "automatic" human motions of the heartbeat, breathing, or walking.[58] The sight of the machine appears to guarantee to humans their status as *perpetuum mobile*, to release them from the fear of death. To the men describing machines, the organic machine conveys the vision of a permanent act of coitus.

8

THE DECAY OF THE WORLD OF THINGS

AND ITS RESTORATION IN ART

The mass product, produced quickly and intended for quick consumption, requires an abstract approach: commodities have become spaceless and timeless. Things are instilled with significance only artificially, by advertising. This happens in another way as well to seemingly animated things that suddenly appear in the literature and art of the 1880s. It is an attempt, by way of exaggerated symbolic investment, to reintegrate the now abstract world of things into subjective experience. Goethe could still describe things by reference to concrete social experiences: "From the goods I sent, you could tell where I was and how I was faring. From the wines uncle could certainly taste out my whereabouts; and the laces, the knick-knacks, the steel implements marked my path through Brabant to Paris to London for the ladies."[1] Rilke's description of van Gogh's *Chair* documents the new quality that things now acquire, as a substitute for interiority, in the absence of concrete social references: "a chair for instance, nothing but a chair, of the most ordinary kind: and yet, how much there is in all this that reminds one of the 'saints.' "[2] Van Gogh spoke of this himself, "to elevate the thing into the immortality of which the halo was once a sign."[3] This is a reaction to the desensualization that accompanies modern commodity production—things, no longer palpable in the experiential continuum of *Erfahrung*, are stylized into metaphysical *Erlebnis*.

Within German modernism, with Rilke in particular as a key mediating figure, there runs a line from van Gogh's presentation of things to the second observer of the "thingly character of things," Martin Heidegger, in his essay of 1935–1936, "The Origin of the Work of Art." Rilke's somewhat dramatic formulation returns here in more realistic and cautious form. On "The Shoes" by van Gogh: "A pair of peasant shoes and nothing more. And yet—"[4] The construction of the statement is identical—the assertion of the thing's usualness is followed by the qualification "and yet."

Heidegger's far-reaching argument aims at determining the "equipmental character of equipment," the "thingly character of a thing," and the "workly character of a work." The shoes are the equipment that, as a produced thing determined for practical use, takes an intermediate place between the mere thing and the work of art.[5] Heidegger distinguishes between the pictorial representation of the equipment and the "useful equipment in its use,"[6] namely, the shoes that will be worn in the field. It is only this usefulness of the equipment that shows in truth its equipmental character. The painting cannot reproduce this equipmental being of the equipment (which is tied to a practice); the where, what for, and whither is no longer visible in it. It remains—and this is a decisive formulation—"only an undefined space."[7] This absence of definition, however, is what Heidegger turns into definitiveness, in that he moves from the equipmental character of equipment to the "truth." It is the work of art that first allows the truth of the shoe equipment to be recognized.[8] The procedure is quite simple: the definition of that which a thing is is transferred from practice to reflection, which invests the undefined space of the work of art with significance.

What does this look at the shoes in the undefined space show? "From the dark opening of the worn insides of the shoes the toilsome tread of the worker stares forth. . . . Under the soles slides the loneliness of the field-path as evening falls. In the shoes vibrates the silent call of the earth, its quiet gift of the ripening grain and its unexplained self-refusal in the fallow desolation of the wintry field. This equipment is pervaded by uncomplaining anxiety as to the certainty of bread, the wordless joy of having once more withstood want, the trembling before the impending childbed and shivering at the surrounding menace of death."[9] Things have become demons, with something staring out from their dark openings; they whisper of earth, birth, and death. Hidden in this terminology is the assertion that things function as

Vincent van Gogh, *The Shoes*, 1886.

Now, I am degrading myself as much as possible. Why? I want to be a poet, and I am working to make myself a *seer*. You will not understand this, and I don't know how to explain it to you. It is a question of reaching the unknown by the derangement of *all the senses*. The sufferings are enormous, but one has to be strong, one has to be born a poet, and I know I am a poet. This is not at all my fault. It is wrong to say: I think. One ought to say: people think me. Pardon the pun [penser, "to think"; panser, "to groom"].

I is someone else. It is too bad for the wood which finds itself a violin and scorn for the heedless who argue over what they are totally ignorant of!

Arthur Rimbaud to Georges Izambard, 13 May 1871, *Rimbaud Complete Works, Selected Letters*, trans. by Wallace Fowlie (Chicago and London: University of Chicago Press, 1966), pp. 303, 305

. . . Our language denotes what a gathering *is* by an ancient word. That word is: thing. The jug's presencing is the pure, giving gathering of the onefold fourfold into a single time-space, a single stay. The jug presences as a thing. The jug is the jug as a thing. But how does the thing presence? The thing things. Thinging gathers. Appropriating the fourfold, it gathers the fourfold's stay, its while, into something that stays for a while: into this thing, that thing . . .

Science's knowledge, which is compelling within its own sphere, the sphere of objects, already had annihilated things as things long before the atom bomb exploded. The bomb's explosion is only the grossest of all gross confirmations of the long-since-accomplished annihilation of the thing: the confirmation that the thing as a thing remains nil. The thingness of the thing remains concealed, forgotten. . . .

Today everything present is equally near and equally far. The distanceless prevails. But no abridging or abolishing of distances brings nearness. What is nearness? To discover the nature of nearness, we gave thought to the jug near by. We have sought the nature of nearness and found the nature of the jug as a thing. But in this discovery we also catch sight of the nature of nearness. The thing things. In thinging, it stays earth and sky, divinities and mortals. Staying, the thing brings the four, in their remoteness, near to one another. This bringing-near is nearing. Nearing is the presencing of nearness. Nearness brings near—draws nigh to one another—the far and, indeed, *as* the far. Nearness preserves farness. Preserving farness, nearness presences nearness in nearing that farness. Bringing near in this way, nearness conceals its own self and remains, in its own way, nearest of all.

The thing is not "in" nearness, "in" proximity, as if nearness were a container. Nearness is at work in bringing near, as the thinging of the thing.

Martin Heidegger, "The Thing" (1950), in *Poetry, Language, Thought,* translated with an introduction by Albert Hofstadter (New York: Harper Colophon, 1975), pp. 174, 170, 177, 178

representatives of the context of nature. The latter reveals itself only in the painting. The unspoken consequence is that things in themselves, in practice, have no truth, that only art can disclose truth. In this hypertrophy of art is concealed the admission that things in themselves have no significance but only acquire it through the lonely contemplation of one who looks at the picture. Only it discloses truth; the work of art is "the reproduction of the thing's general essence."[10]

Heidegger reflects in his argument precisely on the decay of perception that Benjamin treated in the same year in his essay on the work of art. Where Heidegger artificially restores perception (and Musil in *The Man without Qualities* polemicizes against van Gogh's false aura[11]), Benjamin addresses its crisis. Heidegger's procedure, concentrated on interiority, bypasses the analysis of causes. It erects an exclave of truth in the middle of the operation that no longer knows the truth.

Attempts to reintroduce the significance of objects were already being made as impressionism was at its prime in dissolving things. The metaphysical speculation behind the expositions of Rilke and Heidegger derives directly from the aesthetic theory of those years, but is absolutized philosophically by Heidegger and thereby robbed of its historical site. Van Gogh describes in a letter the technique by which he produced the effect he sought. A portrait, for example, begun in fidelity to reality, is completed only through, as he said, arbitrary coloring: "Behind the head, instead of painting the ordinary wall of the mean room, I paint infinity, a plain background of the richest, intensest blue that I can contrive, and by this simple combination of the bright head against the rich blue background, I get a mysterious effect, like a star in the depths of an azure sky."[12] By way of the construction of analogies between the pictorial object and nature, here according to the pattern *head = star* and *background = sky*—a procedure frequently employed by the symbolists—the portrait is mystified and at the same time freed from the expressive value of color.

By placing expression above reproduction, van Gogh takes leave of the impressionists and, in particular, of neoimpressionists like Seurat et al. and their rational treatment of color and light effects. He writes, "for me . . . real artists . . . do not paint things as they are, traced in a dry, analytical way, but as *they* . . . feel them."[13] The medium for expressing this feeling is color. That reconnects him, despite his critique, with the impressionists, who were the first to liberate color from the object, even if they did so with other intentions. If the latter, however, pursued the representation of the atmospheric value of light, with substantial independence from subjectivity, whereby the contours and volume of the pictorial object also disappeared, then van Gogh made use of color freed from the object to seek something else, namely, to feel the "life of the things." Color is for him, as he often expressed it, the means by which this "suggestion" is achieved.[14] It is not the things, or, as the case may be, their images, that are meaningful, but their vitality, which they acquire only through the suggestive power of color and which is completely independent of the form and function of the things.

Impressionism renounced suggestion and expression; the goal was the reproduction of visual reality in objects other than the mythological motifs of salon painting. The reproduction of big-city reality brought impressionism near to naturalism. For van Gogh, who made repeated references back to Delacroix, something else slipped into his field of vision: "I still can find no better definition of the word art than this, 'L'art c'est l'homme ajouté à la nature' [art is man added to nature]—nature, reality, truth, but with a significance, a conception, a character, which the artist brings out in it."[15] The means to liberate nature and to become master of the excitations that seize the painter "before nature . . . to the point of unconsciousness"[16] are given in the suggestive color and not in the one that is optically correct.

Expression achieved in this way surrounds even the most profane thing with a halo. Things are simultaneously stripped of their qualities and elevated. Impressionism loosened the relationship between color and object to such an extent that color was treated as an independent visual phenomenon. Van Gogh goes one step farther and makes the color itself an object that expresses the movement of feeling.[17] Color dominates the object and vitalizes it. Van Gogh (and also Gauguin) come from impressionism; its treatment of color as an independent, rather than local, phenomenon leads them ultimately to a subjectivization of color.

The restitution of meaning to objects is the general issue taken up by the postimpressionist generation. They wanted to move

Odilon Redon, *The Eye as a Strange Balloon*, lithograph, 1882 (illustration for a text by E. A. Poe).

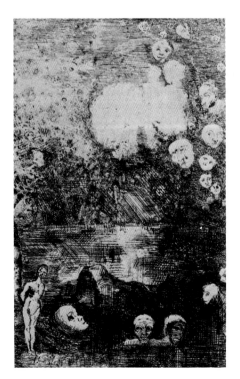

Odilon Redon, *Dream Vision*, ca. 1880.

beyond the external representation of reality—where van Gogh works with the suggestive power of color, Redon promotes, in decidedly anti-impressionistic manner, the shadow, the effects of contrast of the black graphic techniques: "The expression of life can appear differently only in light and shade." And, in opposition to the enlightened-bright light of plein-air painting: "Thinkers love shade."[18] The "blink-of-the-eye" of the impressionists turns into introspection.

Mallarmé, who was friends with Redon, formulated symbolism's program most clearly: "Poetry lies in the *contemplation* of things, in the image emanating from the reveries which things arouse in us. . . . An object must be gradually evoked in order to show a state of soul; or else, choose an object and from it elicit a state of soul by means of a series of decodings."[19] Things mean something other than what they mean in reality; they turn into subjective ciphers. Indisputably, early romantic motifs make themselves heard here, for example, the "magic wand of analogy" of which Novalis, who was translated by Maeterlinck, speaks in his programmatic text, *Christianity or Europe*. That, however, which is philosophical-historical speculation in the romantics, the symbolists make into a sublimely individual play with meanings in which things symbolize or suggest feelings or ideas.

Redon's symbolist procedure does not, as van Gogh's does, make use of color to bring things to expression; rather he achieves the desired effect of unreality in his drawings and lithographs through naturalistic means. In his puzzling combinational systematic of the quotidian, the concreteness of that represented stands in opposition to the darkness of meaning. Nonexistent objects are represented through a combination of existing ones—a head hangs like the moon in the sky; an eye with exposed nerve endings becomes a hot-air balloon floating freely over the landscape; a spider, which appears to fill up an entire room, has a nearly human face. In his novel *Against Nature*, the oft-cited bible of symbolism, Huysmans juxtaposes Redon's pictures with the "hallucinating effects" in Poe's texts;[20] the reference points precisely at the ambivalence in the representational mode of both artists, which lends appearance to the unreal, thereby alienating the real and turning it into a symbol. A look through the microscope of his friend, the biologist Clavaud, reveals to Redon an infinite

Gustave Moreau, *Oedipus and the Sphinx*, 1864.

Gustave Moreau, *The Apparition*, 1876.

space through which faces are floating.[21] The world of things stripped of their qualities becomes a boundless reservoir of the imagination.

The boundary between subject and object, between interiority and object, falls away. In his representations of Salomé, Moreau choreographs the interpenetation of organic and inorganic matter. In *Against Nature*, Huysmans describes one of the best-known works of Moreau, the aquarelle *The Apparition* of 1876. On the figure of Salomé represented there, he writes: "she is clad only in wrought metals and translucent gems. . . . Under the brilliant rays emanating from the Precursor's head, every facet of every jewel catches fire; the stones burn brightly, outlining the woman's figure in flaming colours."[22] The beauty of the stones is as important as that of the body; Moreau emphasizes the necessity of the luxuriant furnishings, "in order to create the reality of a metaphorical world in which the object is made sacred."[23] The price of this sacralization, however, is the petrifaction of the body. With the example of the striptease dancer, whose body is dressed up similarly to Salomé's in Moreau's painting, Roland Barthes suggests that the hard material that covers her body and, in particular, her sex, banishes the woman "into a mineral world."[24] Moreau's Salomé is simultaneously seductive and petrified; the interpenetration of body and thing mirrors the ambivalence of her fascinating and threatening appearance.

The poses of Moreau's models are frozen—aside from the rich furnishings as a representational tool, it was the expression of "beautiful motionlessness" for which the artist was striving.[25] The puzzle character of an animated objectivity determines his paintings—statuary people amid glistening jewels. The face of his *Sphinx* is taken from a children's doll popular at the time[26]—in the image of the puzzling fairy-tale being, the fetish character of the commodity is permeated by that of the doll. The mass product metamorphosizes into an esoteric-symbolic pictorial object.

9

THE *INTERIEUR*, OR THINGS IN THE

EVERYDAY LIFE OF THE BOURGEOISIE

The nineteenth century is the century of the *interieur*. The interieur developed as a protected, private space in opposition to the public sphere of social life and the world of work. It indicates a division of life into areas which, historically novel, is a characteristic of bourgeois-capitalist culture. The spheres of production and social exchange are excluded from the interieur, the living space of the bourgeois family. The two were integrated in earlier forms of social and familial life: the extended family, typical in rural areas in particular far into the nineteenth century, was characterized, contrary to the nuclear family triad, by the unity of production and consumption and of owning and laboring. Isolated cells of privacy were unnecessary. This applies just as much to the nobility. The center of courtly aristocratic sociability was formed by the salon (comparable to the central room in a peasant house). In the aristocratic palaces, there was scarcely such a thing as private life and the consequent intensification of subjectivity in the bourgeois sense. The salon was usually larger than all the private rooms combined.[2] There was no need even of shared quarters for married couples, who "sometimes met more often in the extra-familial sphere of the salon than in the circle of the family proper."[3] Social life did not take place within the sphere of the (nuclear) family; the question of the public sphere versus privacy did not arise.

The duke of Saint-Simon reports, and this can be regarded as typical for the time, that Louis XIV liked to take care of state business and audiences in bed. Public business of this sort in the boudoir becomes inconceivable in the nineteenth century—the bedroom has long since become part of the private sphere. Only in prostitution on a large scale, as Balzac and Zola describe it, does this public intimacy continue, with courtesans holding court like queens of earlier centuries. The sphere of social circulation is not separated off from that which manifests itself in the bourgeoisie as intimacy: kings and courtesans, as the unmoved movers, are simultaneously present in circulation as the eye of the needle through which the latter passes. The myth of the courtesan is to be seen in the nineteenth century against the backdrop of familial exclusivity, for which it supplies a counterimage.

The social life of commodity owners no longer finds its completion in public but in the movement of commodities regulated by the abstract medium of money. Advancing industrialization necessitates the division of labor—work becomes (in science as well) so specialized and abstract that it escapes the social continuum. The sphere of work and the private sphere, no longer subject to integration, begin to separate from each other. The division of labor corresponds to the division of society into mutually closed, intimate families. That leads to changes in the architecture of residential buildings. The large halls disappeared; there began the division of houses into clearly defined and separate areas. Kitchens and courtyards lost their function as sites of community life. A nineteenth-century historian of the family points quite distinctly to the tendency of these changes: "If we look into the interiors of our homes, what we find is that the 'family room,' the communal room for husband and wife and children and domestic servants, has become ever smaller or has completely disappeared. In contrast, the special rooms for the individual family members have become ever more numerous and more specifically furnished. The solitarization of the family members even within the house is held to be a sign of distinction."[4]

Family members are separated from each other as well as from the public sphere by the interior structure of the house. Individuals respond to the abstraction of social life outside by constructing a complete complementary world inside. The bourgeois creates for himself a second nature in the interieur.

1. MATERIALS: ARTIFICIAL NATURE

AND SYNTHETICS

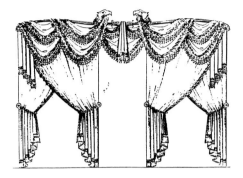

Drapery. Two croisées, 1810.

a)   This second nature is based in illusion. It can be created with the help of textiles: material is arranged in such a way as to suggest movement, splendor, and plenitude. In the course of time, all conceivable furnishings are upholstered or covered with material. This development begins to manifest itself even before the actual age of mass production in textiles. The architects and interior designers Percier and Fontaine, who were responsible for the improvements on the Rue de Rivoli, later the point of departure for Baron Haussmann's recasting of Paris, are taken to be the creators of this style characterized by the fine art of drapery. Large curtains, draped extravagantly with painterly grace over rods, were held together asymmetrically with cords. Valances and animal heads taken over from tapestries round out the picture, which stands in peculiar opposition to the strict contours of the furniture. Painted curtains are combined with genuine draperies and the decor completed with statuettes, flower vases, etc. Giedion finds here the key to the understanding of style in the nineteenth century.[5]

With arrangements such as these, the space becomes obscured; there begins "the devaluation of space. Furniture becomes a means of filling the room."[6] The arrangement of the furnishings expands more and more into the space and begins to stifle perception of the individual forms. If earlier ages had left the center of the room empty, now the decor begins to take up the whole space—the extreme contrary of the sparseness of furniture in, for example, medieval interior spaces. The furniture takes on non-functional aspects—in the hands of Percier and Fontaine, the strict bookshelf of English provenance becomes a monument in the form of an Egyptian temple gate covered over in hieroglyphs.[7] Furniture is decorated with all manner of motifs—tendentially the same process as that in which space is decorated with drapes of various materials.

Over the course of the century a new type of furniture appears, at least in Europe, for which the cover is constitutive: upholstered furniture stands for that which a French critic termed "La victoire de la garniture sur le bois," the victory of the wrapping over the wood. The profession of the tapestry maker, a man who originally dealt only with materials and ways of draping it, expands to

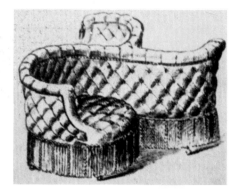

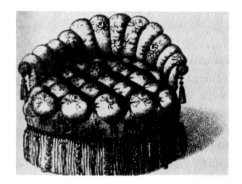

English and French sitting
furniture from the nineteenth
century.

include furniture dealer and interior designer. The meaning of
the carpenter in making furniture is devalued. He now delivers
only the substructure of the furniture and has nothing more to
do with its appearance. The tapestry maker's furniture no longer
has a structure, no more outlines, no form;[8] it is merely as big
and soft as possible.

Delacroix supplied models for this fashion in furniture, which
was inspired by the Orient, in such paintings as *The Death of
Sardanapal* or *Algerian Women in Their Harem*: the softly flowing
garments, the heavy red materials, and the naked skin of the harem
ladies combine to form an ensemble, a fairy-tale counterworld,
despite all the cruelty, to the melancholy daily life of Europe, where
men were beginning to walk around dressed in black. Only the
women and the furniture are sumptuous, soft, and beautifully decorated. Divans, cross-shaped sofas, fantastic furniture, as well as
large, heavy upholstered armchairs begin to make their way into
the interieurs.[9] These pieces of furniture are things out of a different, colorful oriental world, in which the inhabitants can sink as if
into a dream. Balzac lays bare this idea of the interieur in the

Delacroix, *The Women of Algiers in Their Chamber*, 1834.

example of the boudoir in "The Girl with the Golden Eyes." The soft carpet, the divan, and the pillows combine irretrievably with the "full glory of her feminine voluptuousness."[10]

The furniture of this time is covered in richly ornamented satin, velvet, and brocade materials, which demonstrate the expanding potential of the textile industry. The preconditions of mass production on this scale were the spinning machine and other mechanized forms of cloth manufacture, which made inexpensive production possible and therefore extensive distribution of the materials as well. Everything in the furniture that once referred to an internal structure is covered over with the fabrics—a procedure that parallels that of contemporary architecture, in which even advanced iron constructions were covered up by facade ornamentations.

b)   The universal compulsion for coverings is a material expression of industrial capacities and in no way limited to furniture production. In other areas, too, analogous procedures come into use. Typical is an example from England: "In less than ten years, from 1837 to 1846, the Office granted thirty-five patents for 'the coating and covering of non-metallic bodies,' 'coating surfaces of articles made of wrought iron which may be used *in substitution* of japanning and other modes now [1834] in use,' and 'mastic or cement which may be also applied as an artificial stone and for covering metals.' "[11] In addition, there are the techniques of galvanizing and electroplating, with which it became possible to lend plaster statues the appearance of bronze.

The path from a covering, in the first instance a drapery of cheaply produced textiles that soften the forms of furniture and spaces, to substitutions, which, in a *quid pro quo*, simulates one material with another, is not long at all: these techniques all combine the repression of design and original materials. India rubber, for example, a new material derived from the milky juice of tropical plants, manifests in its industrial applications since the 1840s a symptomatic end of the feel for materials that was the basis for handicraft processes grounded in long-term experience. India rubber is, according to Gottfried Semper in 1860, "the factotum of the industry," which "lends itself to all purposes . . . since its nearly unlimited sphere of application is imitation. This material is at the same time the ape among the utility materials."[12] India rubber is thus a precursor of plastic, which will determine the aesthetic of daily life in the twentieth century. With scarcely an object not manufactured of india rubber, the World Exposition in Paris of 1855 displays its nearly unlimited applications in the place of ebony and horn for buttons, knife handles, combs, machine parts, boxes, and furniture of all sorts: "There were shoes with clever vents, which do not let the water in, but do allow evaporation from the foot to get out . . . ; waterproof carpets . . . ; maps; tents; rings for hanging the carriage in the machine, instead of springs; picture frames; . . . book bindings; waterpots; . . . extraordinarily thin eyeglass frames. . . . Even the red velvet with which the cabinets are draped and the golden ties and tassels are made of rubber!"[13]

Here the relationship between thing and material, which was very close in traditional handicraft production, begins to break down. What things are made of is no longer evident from their appearance. The use of substitute materials to simulate the originals in the service of the rationalization of production initiates the process of perceptual deterioration that ultimately culminates in the interieur as an artificial second nature. Things, which are no longer what they appear to be, were spread about the interieur in plenty, as if to fill the vacuum left by the disappearance of the original materials, which were costly and difficult to process industrially. The more the natural sense of the material disappears from objects, the more strenuously must the fiction of nature be maintained. Characteristic is a patent velvet tapestry presented at the World Exposition of 1851 in London by the firm Pardoe, Hoomans and Pardoe: the artificial flowers on the machine-made carpet shine more gaudily than they ever could in nature.[14] Technical possibilities work their seductive power to the advantage of a gaudy surrogate nature that breaks the fundamental rule of carpet ornamentation, namely, the integrity of the surface that is to be walked on: what results overwhelms the furniture and seems to be well designed to keep the owner from walking on the dazzling flower garden.[15]

c) The interieur compensates for the loss of the connection to nature caused by industrialization. In *Mont Oriol* Maupassant describes an ensemble of furniture devised for therapeutic purposes: the effect of movement in open nature can be achieved inside the house. The story describes apparatuses (the chamber horse of 1793 by the English furniture builder Sheraton is the forerunner[16]) outfitted with complicated drive mechanisms activated by means of a hand crank for riding or going swimming without getting wet, for marching in sitting or standing position: "The engineer had fallen back into a rocking armchair, and he placed his legs in the wooden legs with movable joints attached to this seat. His thighs, calves, and ankles were strapped down in such a way that he was unable to make any voluntary movement; then, the man with the tucked-up sleeves, seizing the handle, turned it round with all his strength. The armchair, at first, swayed to and fro like a hammock; then, suddenly, the patient's legs went out, stretching forward and bending back, advancing and returning, with extreme speed."[17]

Expression is lent here to the tendency to create inside the house not only aesthetic but also physiological surrogates for the external world. Just like india rubber or the carpet, the medical instrument creates an artificial nature; the decline of authentic materials fol-

Apparatus for mechanical foot exercise.

American steam-bath bed, 1814.

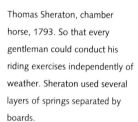

Thomas Sheraton, chamber horse, 1793. So that every gentleman could conduct his riding exercises independently of weather. Sheraton used several layers of springs separated by boards.

lows upon the deterioration of the capacity to perceive nature. The manifold reform movements of the period around 1850 arose in reaction; Rikli's "atmospheric baths" of 1855, which rediscovered something self-evident, namely contact with air and sun,[18] are directly related to the movement around Morris and Cole, as well as Semper, and their demand for artistic designs appropriate to the materials used by an industry gone astray.

2. THE PRODUCTION OF THE "FACULTY FOR DELUSION"

a) The interieur of the 1870s and 1880s was sunk in twilight. The first precondition for this was the cult of draperies practiced since the time of the Empire. The interieur was supposed to be shielded off from the external world, indeed was supposed to reproduce the latter indoors. Abundantly available houseplants brought nature inside, as they also blocked out the external world. With the aid of palms and creeping vines interior rooms were made into dim but temperate forests. But that was not enough. The windows still offered an image of the bothersome external world—according to Cornelius Gurlitt in 1888, "Our large windows deprive the space of its inner calm, relate it too closely to the outside world." The author follows his dream back into a preindustrial past, to the bull's-eye glass of medieval houses, and tries to imagine the mood in those rooms: "The entire room is twilit, snug. We feel alone here, whether with our thoughts or our friends. Whatever is happening outside is far away."[19] The bourgeois nuclear family—Gurlitt dedicates his book to his bride—with its intimate life cut off from the public sphere reaches for measures of defense even against the remaining opening offered by the windows: dull-milky bull's-eye windows or brightly colored panes of glass.

To this corresponds the ritualization of social interaction: just as daylight finds its way into the inside of the house only through a complicated sluice-work, it is equally difficult for visitors to make their way inside. In *The Man without Qualities* (set in 1913–1914), Musil depicts a human relic from this time, Professor Lindner. Usually at work behind his picture window, he has transposed the social system of waste removal onto his body: he washes himself in segments, every day of the week one-seventh, so that he begins anew each week. This system of separation is also applied to visitors. The housekeeper announces a young woman who wishes to see him; he withdraws from his ritualized midday meal with his son to collect himself internally in another room; and only then does he receive her.[20] The complicated path of light through the window glass, past the draperies, and beyond the plants reveals itself here as a metaphor for the social behavior of the inhabitants: protection against any direct confrontation.

The objects in the interior space are not allowed to cast any sharp reflections. Even a reflection in a polished metal surface, which might supply the unmediated image of objects or inhabitants, is forbidden. Sophisticated techniques are employed to break any direct rays of light. One such is the excessive use of light-absorbing materials, like velvet on the furniture. Gottfried Semper, in his book *Der Stil in den technischen und tektonischen Künsten*, an encyclopedic analysis of individual textiles and their effects and an appeal for applications appropriate to the materials, writes about the contrast between satin and velvet: "Just as the silk threads, observed lengthwise, [offer] the most lustrous weave, likewise is a surface so composed that an infinite number of silk threads cut transversely stand up next to each other, as in the case of cut velvet, absolutely lusterless, that is, light-absorbing or, more precisely, an impediment to the division of rays into absorbed and reflected light."[21]

What is expressed here in the sober language of a materials technician becomes in the hands of the theoreticians of old German coziness a program for the dull harmonization of even color contrasts and sharp reflections: "By making the brilliance 'matt' (i.e., smashing the neutral light reflections to such an extent that they yield no more sharp coherent mirror images and can be individually distinguished only by a microscope), we promote the more intimate fusion with the local color; this, essentially, is the basis for the splendid effect of the old pewter, the waxed or oiled wooden furniture, the satins, velvets, and brocades, etc."[22]

One can read this program as an apology for the patriarchal nuclear family—a reduction of the social body with its plenitude of contrasts to the family. In its intimate fusion, the family cultivates the values of an old, timeless community in which the individual members subordinate their independence to the true colors of the governing family. In Puritanical America, sharp reflections from a piano leg (not to mention its bare form) were sometimes regarded as ethically offensive; legs had to be covered up.[23]

The enormous indignation inspired by the first impressionist paintings is perhaps to be explained by its renunciation of color as it prevailed in the studio-brown, dully colored salon painting. The dissolution of things into a bodiless stream of color liberated from rules was a threatening act of opposition.

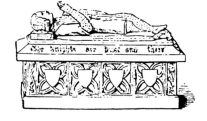

Matchbox in the form of a crusader's tomb, *ca.* 1850.

b)   Yet that which is affirmed there as a blurred unity, is, as far as the world of things is concerned, actually a collection of stage props that reorient the isolated nuclear family. Already around 1850, the age of ersatz materials, objects are being produced which evidence the close relationship between the new techniques of materials substitution and a corresponding superstructure, a thinking, that is, in ersatz materials. Various styles of matchboxes in the form of a crusader's tomb, for example, were available for purchase.[24] The match torn off by the smoker spreads the light of the eternal flame. But there is something else at issue here: the reconciliation of the bourgeois citizen in his interieur with the anonymous world of products, in that things appear with the decoration of a familiar cultural tradition. The purpose of such a historical reference lies in the repression of the industrial present, which can only be made acceptable in decorated form. Nietzsche's later critique of the remove of historical writing from life attacks this repression as it was found in educational institutions; to the uses of history he juxtaposes the disadvantage of the remove from reality.

The example of the matchbox is in no way an isolated instance, but an early symptom of a confusion of spheres that was to become typical of the historical age and the interieur associated with it. Friedell conveys an impression of the range of products involved: "A magnificent Gutenberg bible is discovered to be a work-box, and a carved cupboard an orchestrion; the butter knife is a Turkish dagger, the ashtray a Prussian helmet, the umbrella stand a knight's armor . . ."[25]—a list that could be continued *ad infinitum*. Things do not bear the meaning of what they appear to represent; the function is difficult to determine behind the decoration. These bits of "cultural jetsam"[26] recompose themselves into an ensemble only in the blurred mood of the interieur. Mood, still reflexively charged in romanticism, develops now solely through a remove from reality, work, and functionality. The individual fuses with a world he does not influence, a world that is perceived solely as an expression of interiority. The patriarchal nuclear family withdraws into the interieur and creates for itself a state of mind that takes the place of reality.

If Thomas Carlyle was speaking as early as 1850 of the "madness" of the plastic and graphic arts, which respond to industrial production by seeing their task as that of an arbitrary decor symbolism,[27] then it is precisely this moment upon which the apologists for the interieur of the *Gründerzeit* period seize for justification. In the words of Georg Hirth, "Indeed, this faculty for delusion, if I may say so, constitutes, for civilized man, an insurance against the inclemencies of fate, as necessary as insurance against the perils of fire and impoverishment. In this magic circle, in[to] which a good education can bring us and [in which] our own efforts can make us feel at home, the artistic design of our domesticity should, to a certain degree, form the center, the warming heart."[28] This is nothing other than a philistine's alphabet: the education of a civilized person aims at the creation of a capacity for delusion that is supposed to obscure the irrelevance of culture in a world functioning according to wholly different methods, namely those of a money economy. Only in a passing remark is the actual agent of this faculty of delusion expressed, namely the fear that the sheltered interior space cannot be protected from impoverishment. Behind this anxiety is concealed the unspoken recognition that between the inner cultivation of a civilized person and the external world in which he carries out his business there is an unbridgeable discrepancy, such that the interieur has to play the role of a transparently delusory life insurance. The nearly compulsive filling up of the interieur becomes a kind of magical defense.

The reason why the defense Hirth expects from the faculty for delusion cannot become truly effective lies in the growing differentiation of objects, which ultimately make of the interior space a mirror image of the world of commodities that the bourgeois citizen has tried vainly to flee. Through resort to the faculty for delusion he seeks to repress the fact that the system of circulation has long since been pulsing through his home—the "arterialization with gas pipes, water pipes, telephone wires, etc.,"[29] which got under way on a large scale in the 1880s, might be a contributing cause of the private citizen's fear of having been delivered up, even in the well-protected home, to anonymous-abstract forces that only the drapery can banish.

3. THE ROLE OF THINGS

a) There is nothing left to be felt of the cozy Biedermeier simplicity as Stifter depicted it in the opening pages of *Der Nachsommer.* In the second sentence of the novel he describes the house in which the narrator grew up as "moderately" large, thereby naming the central catchword of the epoch, whose dimensions were those of the nuclear family. The Biedermeier period, just as distant from the needs of representation and legitimation of the feudal epoch preceding it as from those of the later *Gründer*-bourgeoisie, "finds for the entirety of the arts a new unity, the center of which is the living room and home."[30] The living space of the nuclear family, marked off from society as a whole through its organizational form, is the interieur, in which the world is reproduced in doll's house format. Familial harmony animates the things inside the house—"Everything came together, to make both decor and cantata very enchanting. Our little hut was all the more an Elysium, the less pretentious everything appeared."[31] Family life is centered around a miniaturized version of the educational ideal with which the bourgeoisie made its appearance in the eighteenth century—the small statues, coin collections, and books are the form that history and the external world assume within its four walls.

The father becomes the center point of social life. In the household arrangements of the not-yet-industrialized society presented paradigmatically at the beginning of Stifter's novel, the general sphere of the house encompassed an area devoted to sales, an office, and a warehouse. The economy, still following the etymology of the word, is limited to the house in a fashion similar to that of the extended peasant family. But family life had already differentiated itself to such an extent that every child had an isolated "little room" in the house, "in which we had to devote ourselves to our occupations, already regularly inflicted upon us in childhood. . . . Mother looked in on us there and occasionally allowed us to be in the living room to amuse ourselves with games."[32] The family cosmos is parceled up and the children have their little occupations to pursue like the father his large ones.

The public sphere has shrunk to the dimensions of the familial, which, closed off from society, reproduces its order by glorifying it in the form of educational tasks. The interieur thereby becomes the guarantor of basic bourgeois values, of "property and education," as Musil will later term it satirically. It is repeatedly emphasized that the furniture and objects are "old," "antique," from "old times," or from "very old times."[33] These are not commodities acquired for a good price or as the newest fashion; rather the things are themselves statuary authorities the father brings to speech by relating their histories. These things are unique, embody experiences, which correspond exactly to the intentions of the paterfamilias: "Every thing and every person, he was fond of saying, can only be one, but that he must be completely."[34]

If the house still occupies the center point of social, convivial, and familial relations, then the novel nonetheless depicts the end of the Biedermeier domestic trinity: people are moving to the outlying districts, to single-family houses with yards. The family flees the loud and dirty city into the suburban fresh air, where they have the peace to go on working on their idyll. But along with this movement away from urban reality and the division of business and private life, there begins very quietly as well the process of disintegration and autonomy of the interieur, which reaches its temporary high point in the *Gründerzeit*. Disintegration means here that peculiar museumification of the house which shows that family life alone is no longer capable of filling it. The

Adolph von Menzel, *The Balcony Room*, 1845.

Nothing had changed since 1780 in my grandfather's house. There was still wallpaper with colossal gourds and Indians painted on it, faded tapestries, white-lacquered stools on rams' feet, cabinets with wooden mosaics, curtains of Chinese chintz, canopies decorated with copper engravings, pagodas over the fireplace, stuffed birds between statues of Dresden porcelain, and those heavy stuccowork ceilings from whose cold ornamentations the glass crystal chandeliers hang down like icicles. In these unfashionable rooms, still barren despite the abundant variety, colorful though pale from age, a dozen people moved around so punctually according to the clock that each, depending on his status in the house, made only the most necessary movements and fell silent whenever he did not have to talk; noise was forbidden; obedience here meant treading on noiseless soles. The children, too, were allowed to approach the parents only at certain times; the address was "your grace"! A deep bow put the seal on greetings and farewells, please and thank you. Before one entered here, one furrowed the brow in affirmation of earnestness, straightened the back, removed the glove from the right hand and probably took care, when one sat, not to lean back in the chair or cross the legs. A perplexed silence on the part of those present would have issued a sensitive admonition.

Friedrich Anton von Schönholz, *Traditionen zur Charakteristik Österreichs unter Franz dem Ersten* (Leipzig, 1844)

new house has special rooms for the various objects: book room, picture room, appliance room, a "little glass room" (a kind of winter garden). But not yet enough: "There was yet another little room, which [the father] had covered with the artistically sewn red silk materials he had purchased. Otherwise, however, no one yet knew what was to go in that room."[35] Here it is not the function that is important, but the draping of the empty space. In the father's stories, the monetary value of the furnishings begins to permeate the educational value of the old things, without, however, destroying it.[36]

In an analysis of the interieur around 1900, Georg Simmel distinguishes it from the interieur of the first decades of the nineteenth century through the "attachment" of people to things, possible in the earlier period owing to their durability and simplicity, which "appeals to the younger generation today as an eccentricity on the part of the grandparents." Simmel claims that this state of familiarity was brought to an end through "the sheer quantity of very specifically formed objects." What interests him here is not the rise of this multitude of things, due, for example, to industrial textile and furniture production or to ersatz materials, but the consequences of this development in the consciousness of the inhabitants. He regards a modest number of objects as assimilable, "while an abundance of different kinds almost form an antagonistic object to the individual self. . . . A woman could express her individuality more easily with a few undifferentiated objects than she could when confronted with the independence of a host of specialized objects."[37]

The differentiation of things and the differentiation of behaviors are related. Once-familiar things have become a multitude of commodities, about which there are no stories to tell because they have no histories. Money has made the things interchangeable: "Both material and intellectual objects today move independently, without personal representatives or transport. Objects and people have become separated from one another."[38] If this statement is referred back to one of Stifter's central statements ("Every thing and every person . . . can only be one, but that he must be completely"), the difference from the developed money and commodity society becomes obvious: where in the older text there prevails a strict, nearly lawlike principle of identity applicable to both persons and things, which binds them to the form they have assumed, this is now replaced by arbitrary exchangeability, its exact opposite.

In Simmel there is a light feeling of uncanniness in the face of the sheer "quantity" of things—he speaks of the "independence" of the things crowded around, of their service as fetishes, of a feeling that the things interfere with one's freedom, and thereby refers to the underground physiognomy of the interieur, which the surrealists were to be the first to lay bare. The things that are not needed begin slowly to appear as strange. The interieur of the *Gründerzeit* is mostly free of reference to the function of things, to their use value, which is often concealed as much as possible. Mass production was also responsible for vast quantities of nonetheless functionless decorative objects. Things simply sit there, like untouchable images of the divine in an imaginary cult of boredom. They are draped in coverings or packed in little boxes, which obscure the utter equivalence of their economic and psychological indifference (they are in both cases arbitrarily replaceable, possess no aura of uniqueness).

The slight uncanniness of the things amassed in the interieur might derive from the circumstance that they are not only not needed by people but that they make use of people—the simplest treatment of space given over to chains, curtains, cords, little boxes, and plants presupposes that people's movements conform most precisely to the given disposition of the world of things: movements must remain in the paths left open in the jungle of things. The smallest mistake, a small collision or some such, can set off a chain reaction in which the things begin behaving on their own according to the destructive laws of gravity. Friedrich Theodor Vischer, an aesthetic theorist and student of Hegel's, describes in his novel *Auch Einer*, which appeared in 1879, the high point of the *Gründerzeit* interieur, several such cases that demonstrate the "pranks of the object," a philsophical problem of his own invention. A gold repeater watch is smashed, a watch that, unlike the one offering functional, "honestly true," "modest," and "upright" service that the user subsequently obtained, constantly demanded service, repair, etc. "The quality of bias altogether inherent in the object" was revealed one night: the hook on the gold watch chain "slid . . . across the little table, on which

Count Robert de Montesquieu-Fezensac (in a painting by Boldini) was the model for Des Esseintes in Huysmans's *Against Nature*.

I had carefully laid the watch, quietly over the edge toward the bed, and attached itself to the seam on a pillowcase. I had no need of the pillow. I picked it up quickly and threw it onto the foot of the bed, the watch, naturally, along with it; it swung in a magnificent arc against the wall and fell with a shattered crystal to the floor."[39] Hook, chain, watch, and pillowcase enter into a combination with an inattentive user that only destruction can dissolve—a possible consequence of the "differentiation of objects" of which Simmel spoke.

b)   The existence of things is no longer grounded in their function. The private person, whose traces are obliterated in the anonymous urban center,[40] attempts to use things to create a substitute for lost social experiences. The containers, cases, and little boxes in which one packs one's things are the displacement of architecture inside the house. They form a simultaneous city out of thing-casings, among which the inhabitant can move without danger.

This is legible with particular clarity in Huysmans's novel of 1884, *Against Nature*. The hero Des Esseintes, whose actual model, Robert de Montesquieu, is supposed to have inspired Proust's Baron Charlus as well, is distinguished from the bourgeois of the 1880s by his extremely refined sensibility, but he nevertheless shares the intention of cultivating the interieur as "a box in the world-theatre,"[41] as a dream cabinet. The dandy-aesthete reveals perhaps most clearly the dream energy that also drove the bourgeois citizen. Des Esseintes's interieur is in many respects similar to that of the time. Walls covered in leather, furs on the floor, crackled windowpanes that allow light to enter only dimly and are draped with curtains, fire screens, and shimmering oriental rugs[42]—all of these are typical requisites of a time with such a predilection for covering things.

More important are Des Esseintes's principles of spatial arrangement: the world, which he has pulled together into an interieur, is then supposed to appear unlimited. Serving this purpose are opposing mirrors, which offer reflections into infinity, but above all it is the division of the space into multiple niches.[43] It is not only that fabric is used for the decor material, but that the space itself is folded like a piece of fabric—it is no longer

... As he sat down on the pouffe Piotr Ivanovich remembered how Ivan Ilyich had arranged this drawing-room and had consulted him about this very pink cretonne with the green leaves. The whole room was full of knicknacks and furniture, and on her way to the sofa the window caught the lace of her black fichu on the carved edge of the table. Piotr Ivanovich rose to detach it, and the pouffe, released from his weight, bobbed up and bumped him. The widow began detaching the lace herself, and Piotr Ivanovich sat down again, suppressing the mutinous springs of the pouffe under him. But the widow could not quite free herself and Piotr Ivanovich rose again, and again the pouffe rebelled and popped up with a positive snap. When this was all over she took out a clean cambric handkerchief and began to weep. But the episode with the lace and the struggle with the pouffe had put Piotr Ivanovich off, and he sat looking sullen. This awkward situation was interrupted by Sikolov, Ivan Ilyich's butler, who came in to report that the plot in the cemetery which Praskovya Fiodorovna had selected would cost two hundred roubles. She left off weeping and, looking at Piotr Ivanovich with the air of a victim, remarked in French that it was very terrible for her. Piotr Ivanovich made a silent gesture signifying his undoubted belief that it must indeed be so.

"Pray smoke," she said in a voice at once magnanimous and disconsolate, and began to discuss with the butler the question of the price of the plot for the grave.

Leo Tolstoy, "The Death of Ivan Ilyich," in *The Cossacks, Happy Ever After, The Death of Ivan Ilyich*, trans. Rosemary Edmonds (Harmondsworth: Penguin, 1960), p. 106

brightly and clearly structured as in the Biedermeier period, where every thing is positioned in accord with psychological and functional relationships, but such that the things disappear beneath upholstery and coverings, rendering the spatial construction invisible behind the draped niches. It is less a living space than a space for the imagination.

The dining room is a space within a space: "Like those Japanese boxes that fit one inside the other, this room had been inserted into a larger one, which was the real dining-room planned by the architect." The space between the window of the actual room in the house and the room that was made available for use is filled with an aquarium. In the internal space, furnished like a ship's cabin, "what daylight penetrated . . . had first to pass through the outer window, the panes of which had been replaced by a sheet of plate glass, then through the water, and finally through the fixed bull's-eye in the port-hole." The spatial containers layered over one another serve as a filter system that shuts off the inhabitant from the outside world and, at the same time, simulates another one in which he amuses himself with mechanical fish and the smell of pitch. "By these means he was able to enjoy quickly, almost simultaneously, all the sensations of a long sea voyage, without ever leaving home; the pleasure of moving from place to place."[44] The retreat into the interieur is a departure into the travels of the imagination. Des Esseintes takes literally the requisites the bourgeois citizen gathers around himself. Like the latter, he attempts to escape the abstract social interchange of commodity owners in the dream world of the interieur.

In a home fragmented and folded into niches, the individual seeks to preserve a form of autonomy that has become historically obsolete. The natural landscape—long since become a "monotonous store of meadows and trees . . . as if it were sprinkled with face-powder and smeared with cold cream"[45]—is replaced in the interieur with artificial scents that suggest an image of nature.[46] Extreme artificiality is the reflex of the experience that, in the face of now universal commodity production, "nothing wholesome"[47] is any longer to be found in nature, nor in bourgeois ideology, nor in religion. To Des Esseintes there remains only the retreat into the differentiated world of space and things of his interieur

Emile Zola in his study.

in which he treats himself to the spectacle of the outer world, which he believes is in reality lost.

While in Huysmans the home is a container, an interior place of retreat outfitted in the most beautiful colors, one of Chekhov's characters uses the protective uterus of the container as clothing. "The Man in a Case" (1898) always goes out, even in the summer, in galoshes, in a cotton coat, and with an umbrella, which, like his watch and his penknife, he always puts in a container. Dark glasses and ears stuffed with cotton round out the appearance of a person with "a perpetual and irresistible longing to wrap some covering around himself—one might call it a case—which would isolate him from external impressions."[48]

The container, which defines the bourgeois interieur in multiple forms, is related here directly to the person, who otherwise uses it only as decor—it has descended to the level of the body. The function, whether wrapped around persons or things (as clothing or a wall), is the same: shutting out the outside. The container is, and this becomes evident in Chekhov's text, a symbol of the private person shut off from the world, who packs up his privacy as he encases his things. Only here, in secret, beneath an impenetrable layer of protection, does it remain possible to have a private existence detached from the public sphere, from the sphere of circulation. Only under a protective layer do Des Esseintes's flowers bloom with artificial fragrances, does Chekhov's Greek teacher find it possible to experience that which he encapsulates in the exclamation "anthropos." The container stabilizes not only the freely fluctuating commodity things, but people as well.

c) The cabinet takes up a position between the container and the house. Using the example of the knight's cabinet, preferably with citations of Gothic and Renaissance forms and whose offspring were outfitted with bull's-eye panes and treasured in the *Gründerzeit,* Adolf Behne demonstrates that movable forms of property developed from immovables. The cabinet is based on the fortifications of a medieval castle: around the contents, drawer, or chamber, there is a massive external structure consisting either of a defensive installation or of ornamentation, meant to provide impenetrable protection.[49] Not only the knight's cabinets are immobile; in medieval and Renaissance interiors benches were often built into the wainscoting, and tables and chairs were often so heavy that they were immobile. Only later, writes Simmel in an inspired comparison, did "furniture, like capital . . . become mobile."[50] The inhabitant of the *Gründerzeit* interieur sought a fixed point amid the circulation of money and goods. Thus he created for himself the fiction of a static "property" in the form of immobile medieval furniture, which helped him endure the tension between necessary capital mobility and his desire for personal longevity: the interieur as the repression of permanent (ex)change.

Behne's attempt to trace the psychological implications of interior design in the *Gründerzeit* leads him to the question of the meaning of the arrangement of things. In exploring it, he proceeds from the observation that in many interior spaces things are arranged diagonally: with reference to the rectangle of the floor plan, the rug is positioned catercorner to the room's axis, as are the chairs; catercorner are the pillows and ornamental blankets on the upholstered furniture. The things are arranged "apart," in the familiar English expression of the time, that is, separated, set to the side. The knight, when he sensed an imminent attack, placed himself *a parte*, in an attack position to the right and left, catercorner, with a view to two sides. According to Behne this battle and defense position recurs in the interieur[51]—the *aparte* arrangement of frequently ornamented things is therefore doubled, satisfying a need for protection in both arrangement and form. That refers back to the container character of the dwellings.

The bourgeois need for protection is a consequence of a consciousness that is split into public (rational in money terms) and private (emotional) realms. The rationality of commodity producers is split off—to flee reification, which makes social relations into relations between things, they seek refuge in the interieur, where objects offer them consolation: the container that of the uterus, the knight's cabinet and the *aparte* positioning that of the "secure fortress," and the oriental rug that of the remote fairytale land. To the reduction of social experiences corresponds the expansion of inner experiences. Reification and fetishism stand in reciprocal relation.[52]

d)   Things are dressed like people, covered in fabric. The drapery clothes the naked volume of the space; the things inside are covered like people by their shirts. According to the evidence of Gottried Semper, textiles, which determine decor and clothing, stand historically in a close relationship with architecture: the "beginnings of building" coincide "with the beginnings of textiles." Various etymological pairings in German (*Gewand/Wand, Saum/Zaun*; the dual meaning of *Decke* as both ceiling and blanket) preserve reference to the mutual origins.[53]

Things are clothed not only in fabrics but also in styles and phantasmagorias. Benjamin, writing on the nineteenth-century interieur, retains the spatial metaphors of textiles: "The space veils itself, assumes the costumes of particular moods like an alluring being. . . . In the end the things are only mannequins and even the great world-historical moments are mere costumes, beneath which they exchange understanding looks with the void, the lowly and banal."[54] In the interieur the private person is enveloped in the wrappings of fabric and dreams, in which he clothes himself as if in a well-padded coat. Only in this way does he create the mood that makes bearable his isolation and superfluousness amid the commodity things.

The upholstery and slipcovers serve as protection against catastrophe. Thomas Mann, in his story "Railway Accident" (1908), cites the gratifications which a well-equipped interieur can offer in a train compartment. The traveler is secured "as if at home" from the threatening reality of movement, in which he is being conveyed just like commodities from one place to another, in the luxurious sleeper car complete with leather wall-coverings, protected as well by the organization of railway operations, which, in the form of the conductor (like the police for the home), promises peace and quiet—he is "the state, our father, authority, and security." But the security of the private person and his carefully protected private work, a precious manuscript, is maintained only so long as the traffic moves along the appointed tracks—upon leaving the habitual path (the accident), the sheltering armor is suddenly broken open, the private person thrown out of his container and among people, who appear to him as strange as

Atget: Interieurs. A merchant's bedroom.

"natives." Standing in front of his shattered housing, he sees a specter, "communism, . . . the great equalizer before the majesty of the accident."[55]

THE PRODUCTION OF "HOMOGENEOUS

AND EMPTY TIME"

Since my forebears had already had life well in hand for such a long time, it came to me, thank God, already in the form of a happily contrived watch, which is so perfectly in order that anyone who fails willingly to conform to its chains and cogs is chained and cogged himself. . . . Finally having matured into a mechanical member myself, I worked, in order to gain time, on watches, and in my leisure hours I sat on a tree branch, which I safely elevated behind me, so as not, in falling, to lose the branch and the time of climbing down. I always knew as well what it said on the watch, in order not to know how

a)   The mechanical measurement of time by means of a clock is an expression of an abstraction in the perception of time. The organic cycle of natural movements has been taken up into that of the mechanical clockwork. The contrary of this conception of time has become a favored topic of cultural criticism. Musil has his character Arnheim—the important writer behind whom is concealed Walther Rathenau, president of the Allgemeine Elektrizitäts-Gesellschaft—comment on "the clock" that it is "a compensation for the failure of our activities to follow each other any longer in a natural way."[2] The clock stands for mechanical unnature, to which the real Rathenau in his book *Zur Mechanik des Geistes* (which Musil reviewed with understanding sarcasm) opposes something concealed under the name of "soul." Rathenau's dichotomy represents a relapse to a position behind that achieved by Heinrich Heine, when the poet describes much more forthrightly than the industrialist how the end of the "idyllic calm" through industrialization has produced "philosophy and suffering." The epic conception of time is replaced by one derived from mechanical motion: "The railway's steam locomotive delivers a shivering shock to our spirit, whereby suffering can no longer dissipate."[3] Heine leaves no more room for the construction with which Rathenau/Arnheim would like to overcome the loss of nature in the organization of time.

The history of mechanically measured time began with the installation of clocks in the towers of the late medieval cities. This fact is an indicator of the shift of the center of gravity of social life from the countryside to the city, of the dissolution of agrarian-

The watchmaker Bogs. Illustration
from *Bogs der Uhrmacher*, 1st ed.
(Heidelberg, 1807).

cyclical time forms and the turn toward a mechanically measured linear time. With industrialization, that is, since the eighteenth century, and with the increasingly tight knit of the geographic fabric brought on by new forms of production and commerce, it became increasingly necessary to establish a division of time that could be conveyed from the individual clock towers into general applicability. Since the seventeenth century, the beginnings had been under way for dividing the day into equal hours independent of the position of the sun on the basis of its mean annual position in respective localities. This conventional day, which is to be distinguished from the natural day, became officially obligatory in Geneva in 1790, in London in 1792, in Berlin in 1810, and in Paris in 1816.[4]

This abstractly linear formulation of time coincides historically with the establishment of dimension and weight standards, in general the metric reforms, which were set in course by the French Revolution. At the time of the feudal discretionary powers over dimensions, there was for every product a basis for measurement specific to the concrete form of the object, like a span or a yard; this procedure was replaced with abstract and universally valid standards.[5] Thus in 1795 did the French National Assembly establish the meter as one forty-millionth of an earth meridian. (The original meter, made of platinum-iridium, is still preserved today in Paris, though since 1960 a new and, in comparision with the meridian, still less palpable paradigm has been in force, namely, 1,650,763.73 wavelengths of the red-orange spectrum of krypton.) Classical mechanics, in the form defined by Newton, became an additional factor in the dissolution of qualitative standards ("time of the event," etc.) in favor of abstract quantitative procedures. Experiments applying, for example, to the law of freely falling objects had to be repeatable in the same time.

Abstract linear time gained a hold on people only very slowly. The duration of the process, approximately five hundred years, demonstrates the complexity of internalizing an abstract standard: the mechanical clocks of the fourteenth century were perceived from a great distance, for they stood outside the sphere of social life on towers. In the sixteenth century the reduced form of the tower clock, the standing clock, made its way into the houses of the upper classes, and only in the nineteenth century did the

When I spoke in the previous chapter about the short sleepers, who awaken six hours before their antipodes, I did so, I think, quite likely because I did not want, in the 12th chapter, to shove the model of a clock made of human beings, long since my own invention, in among the rapid succession of events, but to save it for the 13th; into which I'm introducing it for display. I think Linne's flower clock in Upsala (**horologium florae**), whose cogs are the sun and the earth and whose pointers are the flowers, whereby one always awakens and blooms later than the other, supplied the secret occasion for me to hit upon my human clock. Otherwise I was living in Scheerau, right in the middle of the market square, in two rooms; in the front the whole square and the princely buildings looked in, in the back the botanical garden. Whoever is now living in both has a masterfully preset harmony between the flower clock in the garden and the human clock in the market.

Jean Paul, *Siebenkäs* (1796–97), chap. 13

clock, as pocket watch, become such a part of individual life that it was carried on one's person.[6]

The history of mechanical time measurement by means of a clock dovetails with the history of the economy. The tower clock of the late Middle Ages is, after all, no arbitrary technological innovation but a herald of the secular transformation of the "church's time" into the "merchant's time."[7] The regulation of working hours through the tower clock established an abstract metrical standard. Commercial activity as such, and long-distance commerce in particular, which began to prosper once again in the late medieval period, is tied to the time factor on several levels. The creation of reserves in the expectation of food shortages and taking note of conjunctural phenomena bind trade to various rhythms, some of which are independent of nature.

The protest of the church was directed in particular against the form of trade that made the time factor into the exclusive standard of profit: the credit system. It sensed an attack on an essential component of Christian doctrine, namely, the autonomy of creation and the time of divine providence, which the businessman's organization of credit, a mortgage on time, began to undermine. William of Auxerre (1160–1229), in the *Summa Aurea*, was the first to formulate the church's argument: "The usurer violates the universal law of nature, for he sells time, which is common to all creatures. Augustine says that every creature is obliged to give of itself; the sun is obliged to give of itself in order to give light; likewise is the earth obliged to give of itself all that it is capable of producing; likewise the water. But nothing gives of itself more naturally than time; for good or ill, every thing has its time. Now, since the usurer sells something that necessarily belongs to every creature, he offends against all creatures, even against the stones. From which it follows that, even if people were to remain silent, the stones would cry out, if they could; and that is one of the reasons why the church persecutes userers."[8]

If the church, in view of labor discipline controlled by the clock, suffered the conflict between *vita activa* and *vita contemplativa* to be decided in favor of *vita activa* in a fashion utterly contrary to the teaching in the Bible (Luke 10:38–42)—a question that extensively occupied the theologians of the late Middle Ages—then it also took a decided position against the credit system. William of Auxerre regards the selling of time as a fragmentation of the God-given unity of creation. Where "every thing has its time," the instrumentalization of time is impossible; indeed, it violates the nature of things by ripping them out of the continuum of creation. The subtle theological argumentation sees implicitly the abstraction of the world of things in which, following a lengthy period of development, precisely the instrumentalized thing, in its capacity as commodity, has to substitute for creation. Marx's theory of the fetishism of commodities reveals the answer of developed capitalism to the question of the instrumentalization of things through the mobilization of time that was beginning to appear on the medieval horizon.

That, however, which tormented the Scholastics became the categorical imperative of the Protestant ethic. Benjamin Franklin, for Max Weber the typical representative of this form of the "spirit of capitalism," makes a program of the *vita activa* precisely in reference to time. He writes in "Advice to a Young Tradesman" (1748): "Remember, that *time* is money. . . . Remember, that *credit* is money."[9] The instrumentalization of time and money in the form of work becomes the justification of a God-fearing existence.

b) The theological and ethical problem of time, the meaning of which completely changed in the period separating William of Auxerre and Franklin, was rendered definitively obsolete by the appearance of a new paradigm, of an artifact no longer in need of justification: the machine. From now on, things began to determine the rhythm of time. The steam engine made the production of energy independent of natural cycles and circumstances; the motions of this machine were carried out uniformly, that is, in a homogeneous and empty time in exclusive conformity to given technological conditions. The paradigm of mechanical motion is the uniform running of the clock; it is itself an automaton, just as the automatons of the baroque and rococo periods represent its playful application. Marx points to this connection in a letter to Engels of 1863: "The clock is the first automatic machine applied to practical purposes; the whole theory of production and regular motion was developed through it."[10]

I will attempt an *economic* justification of virtue.—Its function is to make the person as useful as possible and to approximate him, as far as is in any way feasible, to the infallible machine: to this end he must be equipped with *machine virtues* (—he must learn to perceive the conditions of his work in a mechanically useful fashion as the conditions most highly to be valued: for that it is necessary for *others* to be as spoiled for him, to be made as dangerous and disreputable as possible).

The initial step in this offense is boredom and uniformity, which accompany all mechanical activity. To learn to tolerate this—and not only to tolerate—to learn to see boredom as suspended in the play of a higher charm: that was previously the goal of the whole higher educational system. To learn something that has nothing to do with us; and to perceive precisely in this "objective" busy-ness his "duty"; to learn to evaluate desire and duty independently of each other—that is the invaluable goal and accomplishment of the higher educational system. That is why the philologist represented in former times the educator *in itself*: because his activity was itself the model of a monotony of activity taken to the point of nobility; under his flag the adolescent learned "to grind": the first precondition in those times of fitness for the mechanical fulfillment of duty (as a civil servant, bridegroom, office slave, newspaper reader, and soldier). Such an existence is perhaps in greater need of philosophical justification and glorification than any other: *pleasant* feelings must be devalued as altogether inferior by reference to some kind of infallible instance; "duty in itself," perhaps even the pathos of awe in reference to everything that is unpleasant—and this demand as speaking imperatively, beyond all utility, amusement, and expediency. . . . The mechanical form of existence as the highest, most worthy form of existence, self-idolizing (—Type: Kant as a fanatic of the formal concept "you should").

Friedrich Nietzsche, *Werke*, ed. Karl Schlechta (Munich, 1969), vol. 3, *Aus dem Nachlass der Achtziger Jahre*

The new, abstract, metric, mechanical time became palpable through the subordination required of workers to its uniform motion—otherwise than in handicrafts, where the worker made use of his tools, or in manufacture, where he is a part of a living organism, in the factory the worker serves the machine. The movements of the mechanical organism determine his own: "In the first place, in the form of machinery, the implements of labour become automatic, things moving and working independent of the workman. They are thenceforth an industrial *perpetuum mobile*, that would go on producing forever, did it not meet with certain natural obstructions in the weak bodies and the strong wills of its human attendants."[11] The cycle of the mechanical organism dispossesses that of the body; the heartbeat, one of the elementary experiences of time, loses its autonomy to the beat of the machine—the latter makes the body into a *perpetuum mobile* that has to move with the regularity of a clock.

The machine is the great transformer of time. The time for living (or "free time") that it is capable of liberating through the acceleration of work, it cashes in immediately under prevailing conditions of capitalist production by continuing to run and turning the time won into disposable labor time. It does not liberate time, as Aristotle, for example, dreamed it might,[12] but establishes through its potentially endless motion a standard of time that excludes interruptions, which would be a time of experiences and events.

Experiential time is now subjected to a threefold temporal check: the mechanical beat determines human motions; the labor time, which is maintained in the factory by a rigid discipline, determines the familial rhythm; and, third, the work time is doubly conditioned because piecework[13] represents the introduction of yet another standard of work intensity, that is, units of work per unit of time. The relation to things, to the products of labor, is thereby subjected to a process of progressive abstraction. The mechanical ordering of time cuts people off from sensuous perception unfolding freely in time; that is, it cuts them off from subjective time.

In the nineteenth century, industry becomes the dynamic multiplier of strategies of time scheduling that was begun in the late Middle Ages. At its point of inception is the time scheme devel-

Steam engine for the speedy and certain improvement of little girls and boys. Engraving from the end of the eighteenth century, from Michel Foucault, *Discipline and Punish*.

oped in the cloisters—the regulation of the course of the day, chores and prayers, gatherings, mealtimes, etc. But it is important to keep in mind, as one sees these techniques being taken over in military and educational regulations, later in factory discipline, that scheduling in the cloisters was relative: it maintained a reference to the time of redemption, the time of salvation, in which all manner of linear organization of time would be overcome. The linear was purely earthly time, a time of preparation for its transcendence. This essential relativism gradually disappeared through the secularization of the schemata of an abstract time first tried out in the cloister.

There is, however, a peculiar intermediary condition in this process, in which rudimentary references to divine time remain visible in the secular sphere. In the regulations of the large manufactories of the seventeenth century, the following example appears: "all persons shall wash their hands, offer up their work to God and make the sign of the cross."[14] The temporal organization of work, bodily hygiene, and religious practice enter into a combination in which, otherwise than in the cloister, the emphasis falls on paying heed to the discipline of labor. This combination did not persist as long in the factories—where it disappeared in the nineteenth century at the latest—as in the schools, where in some places it continues until today.

The annihilation of nonlinear time is more clearly legible in other programmatic points in the factory regulations. The story-teller's time and the time of narration is, with its free choice between various temporal forms (memory, present, fiction), in a certain respect related to the unregulated time of the divine. And the factory lords directed their disciplinary maneuvers against it: "It is expressly forbidden during work to amuse one's companions by gestures or in any other way, to play at any game whatsoever, to eat, to sleep, to tell stories and comedies," as it was also forbidden to bring wine to the factory and drink it in the workshops.[15] The prohibitions demonstrate how difficult it was before mechanization altogether to establish work discipline within a homogeneous and empty time. Everything mentioned here—gestures, games, sleeping, storytelling, drinking wine—upsets the linear order, since they all develop in their own time. Intoxication in particular is a form of experience that transcends a preordained temporal ordering. It might not be accidental that the nineteenth century is characterized by a multitude of apologetic texts on the question of intoxication; one need only recall the relevant texts by De Quincey, Poe, and Baudelaire. Artists thereby secure for themselves an autonomous experience of time, which is placed ever more in question by increasing temporal regimentation, of daily life as well.

Already in the eighteenth century, but then especially with the rise of scientific plant management, the forms of temporal regimentation underwent a qualitative change—the conditioning, one could say, moved into the body. If the old temporal schemata, in particular those in the military, were characterized by an abstract relation to the body, a study of natural bodily movements now yielded a more precise method of temporal organization bringing about a more intimate control of human motion in time and space. The body, previously a thing moved mechanically, regained its autonomy, but only to be reified on a higher level. The reference back to nature merely allowed for the more precise integration of an abstract total system. "If we studied the intention of nature and the construction of the human body, we would find the position and bearing that nature clearly prescribes for the soldier," according to a 1772 essay on tactics.[16]

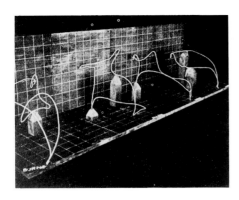

Frank B. Gilbreth, *Motion
Transposed onto a Wire Model*,
ca. 1912.

The considerations of F. W. Taylor or the Gilbreths toward the end of the nineteenth century aim in principle in the same direction: to transfer the linear time and movement of the machine onto the body by means of a stopwatch and motion analyses.[17] The point here is the systematic coordination of human and mechanical motion in an endless production process. Scientific plant management is composed in an important sense of the task of designing the human body: people have to be made into parts of a machine integrated seamlessly into the overall mechanism. Movement is developed in accord with the organic limitations of the body, then cut off from it and thereby objectified. The process of research had to discover movements characterized by the regularity of a machine, for which the body then became the motive power. The body was dispossessed of its immanent subjective (motion) time—with the latter not split off from the body so much as carried over in alien form into the production process.

c)   The mechanical time of the factory affects only those who are working there. The socialization in the community at large of this abstract, linear time was accomplished through another medium, the railway. An ensemble of the steam locomotive (the first machine to make its presence felt in bourgeois daily life), train cars, and an ever more complex coordination apparatus, the railway is the nineteenth-century phenomenon most responsible for totalizing homogeneous and empty time. Early on, writers described the temporal experience of this new means of transportation, an extraordinarily rapid one by the standards of coach travel; thus Heinrich Heine in "Lutetia": "What changes must now occur in our way of viewing things and in our imagination! Even the elementary concepts of time and space have begun to totter."[18]

Only thirty years after Heine's amazing premonition, the political economist and sociologist Gustav Schmoller could sketch a panorama, in an essay entitled, "The Influence of Contemporary Means of Transportation," in which the developments in question provide the backdrop for far-reaching social-historical changes. He regards the dominant factors in public life as having been changed by the railway. Associational life, the press, and public opinion had previously existed under different conditions—the exchange of news was slower; "Congresses, like the ones workers and manufacturers, political parties and religious groups now hold, were impossible."[19] The local press was dominant, while now, after the introduction of the railway, there is a transregional exchange of newspapers with many times more subscribers. With his reflection on the change in humor—"The tame, provincial bourgeois joke about flying pages is as characteristic of the forties as the bubbling foam and the humorously frivolous disdain of muddles are for our day"—Schmoller anticipates the insights Georg Simmel (who benefited from Schmoller's support) would develop thirty years later in his famous essay "The Metropolis and Mental Life."

The press supplies Schmoller's example of the change in the concept of education and the intellectual atmosphere: he saw the acceleration of information exchange as occasioning an acceleration of reading as well. "Intensive" study of "serious works" seemed to him to have become obsolete, a victim of the primacy of utility and the focus on the present, which were also expressed in the establishment of secondary, trade, and polytechnic schools.[20] It is a phenomenon of which Heine had already made suggestive mention. The dynamization, the acceleration of the exchange of knowledge necessarily brings with it a new formulation of the contents. Both journalistic sensations and scientific fact find themselves, as bits of information, in a linear temporal schema subject to conscious manipulation. Schmoller's conclusion as to the effect of the railway on intellectual life seems radical but scarcely exaggerated: "The whole of the imaginative material that fills the heads and hearts of the many . . . has changed."[21]

Homogeneous and empty time changes the structures of perception. In the large city and in industry, standardized time becomes the regulator of social life, which either fragments into a series of always equivalent moments or disintegrates into isolated temporal particles. Thus, for example, is a railway journey precisely determined temporally, with departure and arrival times fixed. The trip, as experiencing (under-going) the expanse of space, is reified by virtue of this fixity. In bourgeois daily life the role of the homogenizer of time is played by the railway (the role assumed by the machine in the life of work): standard time is a product of railway transportation. The first step on the path to

Mr. Rumpelmeier's journey on the centrifugal railway. *Leipziger Illustrierte Zeitung*, 1847.

standard times as we know them today was made by the so-called "railway times," whose point of reference was the time at a particular train station and whose validity was restricted to a particular section of the route. With each referring to the needs of the not yet unified railway lines, there were two or three different railway times in the train stations of many European cities. (In the United States, there were a total of seventy.) Local time and railway time, not at all identical with each other, coexisted.

In the regulations of the "King Christian VIII Baltic Sea Line" (Copenhagen, 1844), paragraph 23 reads: "Every signalman . . . must carry with him a properly running watch, which from time to time is to be adjusted by the stationmaster." This demonstrates the absence of a general temporal foundation—the time here is set, not by the church, but by the authority of the stationmaster, whose watch is supposed to be "adjusted to the time of the Altona Observatory" (par. 32). To organize time in this way was too complicated—the needs of railway traffic forced into being an internationally valid system of keeping time. The Time Convention of 1884, in which nearly all European countries participated, occurred in response to this demand. It foresaw the structuring of the world into time zones, each comprising 150 degrees longitude. National times, some of them already established (Great Britain, 1848; France, 1874), were absorbed into the system. The gain was obvious, for it had been necessary previously for a conductor, on the route between Ulm and Strasbourg, for example, to reset his watch four times. An imperial law of 1893 in Germany made the standard time initiated by the railway obligatory for the whole of civil life—the legal time was the median solar time, 15 degrees longitude east of Greenwich.[22]

The dictatorial quality of the new temporal order was revealed as early as 1848 by Charles Dickens: there is even a "train time," he writes, which clocks are required to follow, as if the sun itself had given way.[23] Not only clocks follow the new homogeneous time, which is independent of any local time, for it increasingly lays a grid over the whole of daily life. Out of the genesis of linear time there also resulted the apparatus-like character of social life. Through the modern means of conveyance people have indeed, according to Schmoller, "become masters of time and space like no previous species,"[24] but this mastery comes at the cost of an abstraction, of subordination to the regularity of traffic, which he characterizes as "a large apparatus," as "the apparatus of activity": "The virtue of precision has perhaps been promoted most of all. The railways have the effect, as has already been said, of great national clocks. Clearly, he who wants to keep up in life has to leave behind all individual desires, place himself at the disposal of the fast pace, of the general conditions of the long-distance race."[25]

Precision, the standardization of time, compels all to keep pace, and the image of the traveler who misses the train becomes the metaphor for the subordination of the individual to the abstract schema of the temporal order. Schmoller describes the time savings in terms of a paradox similar to that with which Marx described mechanization: the time gained is not liberated; rather schedules introduced for work and travel transform time into disposable units.[26] He draws the social-historical conclusion: homogenized time destroys family life and the "soul"-fulfilling work of the craftsman by sending individuals, like "a fluctuating population," off on the search for work in the large factories, in which they are nothing more than "a cog in the great machine."[27]

The introduction of homogeneous time as a result of industrialization and railway travel is equivalent to an acceleration of temporal processes. The time of a machine necessarily runs faster than the unstandardized time of agrarian or handicraft rhythms, because it divides the temporal stream into units and therefore renders it permanently present. The movement of streams of goods and people requires such an organizational schema, which ultimately restructures perception as well. Movement constantly changes the field of view, with the result that "we see, we experience a hundred times and more what our grandfathers saw."[28] The "stiff, slow gravity" of the traditional form of perception is dashed to pieces; what remains are isolated experiences, particles laden with meaning, which the linear-dynamic passing of time offers to individual perception as quickly as it withdraws them. Big cities offer "infinitely more pleasures and means of cultivation," a "variousness" of enticements. Schmoller describes this as a danger of shifting the view of "weak minds" away from what has "higher value,"[29] thereby threatening himself to relapse into a form of cultural critical argumentation inferior to his own insight into the typical structure of perception of homogenized time, which necessarily proceeds in step with de-subjectivization and the stripping of things of their qualities. What he describes as alienation is the signature of the new time—the "influence of contemporary means of transportation."

d)   The newly created "homogeneous and empty time" (in Walter Benjamin's term) finds its expression not only in the factories and the means of transportation but also in novel theorems in the philosophy of history. Homogeneous time runs linearly. This linearity is the precondition of a continual forward movement, that is, of progress. The Enlightenment (Perrault, Turgot, Condorcet) introduced a mechanical conception of progress, through which the course of history could be made manifest and conceived as an ascending development. The course of history corresponded to the motion of the wheel on a street covering the shortest distance from one point to another; the possibility of leaps or detours in the continuum of motion was denied. This kind of historical thinking means, in Foucault's nice formulation, that "the 'dynamics' of continuous evolutions tends to replace the 'dynastics' of solemn events." Analogously, "the administrative and economic techniques of control reveal a social time of a serial, orientated, cumulative type." Historical time is thereby rectified, and the " 'history-remembering' of the chronicles, genealogies, exploits, reigns and deeds"[30] becomes obsolete.

The idea of progress, in a dialectical variation, determines historical materialism and, in a naive version, also the intellectual stock of nineteenth-century social democracy. That "progressive steps in the mastery of nature" could also correspond to "regressive steps in society" escapes it. The social democratic idea of progress is indebted to the idea of "infinite perfectibility," as if there were a straight road—following the image of the railway. This thinking is as mechanical and additive as that of historicism, according to which the mass of facts in the forward movement of homogeneous time produced the advance of history.[31] The other, subjective time disappears in this mechanism.

It is no accident that there has been a protest against the hypertrophy of rational-mechanical time: the figure of the dandy and

Hermann Fürst of Pückler-Muskau drove with his team of reindeer down Unter den Linden to the Kranzler Café and sat for hours at a time reading in his carriage.

the cult of wasting time, of ostentatious indolence and cultivated boredom, are the clear signs of an (impotent) aesthetic protest against the binding of time to utility and linear progress.[32] The indifference of the dandy simultaneously personifies and is suffused by the formal equivalence of commodities as well as time. Vitalism also finds a point of departure here. For Bergson, for example, while space is homogeneous, time, on the contrary, is not. Real time, pure duration (*durée*), cannot be conceived by the faculty of understanding. A construction of time accessible to the understanding, according to Bergson, transfers an image of homogeneity corresponding to spatial mass onto time, which can be experienced solely by way of pure, unfragmented intuition. Despite its obscurantism, Bergson's thinking does do justice to the fact that the transformation of time into a linear phenomenon, its reification, has made the unfragmented experience of time impossible.

At the end of the first century of homogenized time, there therefore comes a renewed deterioration of the idea of time; subjective experiential time (*Erlebniszeit*) and mechanical time stand in irreconcilable opposition. The subjects, barred from mechanical time, begin the process of the "remembrance of things past." Marcel Proust was certainly the most radical—the *mémoire involontaire*, the sole guarantee of the memory of experiences, is hermetically sealed against serial social time. In the face of homogeneous and empty time, nothing but accident remains to offer an opportunity for subjective experience (*Erfahrung*), which the social homogenization of time excludes. Accident alone allows the subject to split open the continuum of time and create for himself his own time-space isolated from the others. The *mémoire involontaire* takes over the role of the originally sacred festivals, in which, prior to the totalization of homogeneous time, the social collective transcended the distinction between the present, memory, and anticipation.[33]

1. ON THE ROMANTIC IMAGE OF ELECTRICITY

When electricity begins to enter bourgeois daily life after 1880, it occasions confusion, which may have arisen out of the conflict between the profane technical utility, of a light bulb, for example, and the imaginative story of this invisibly flowing force. Only a bit more than fifty years had passed since Goethe's *Versuch einer Witterungslehre* (1825), in which he wrote, simultaneously concluding the romantic theory of electricity as part of a philosophy of nature, "Electricity is the pervading element that accompanies all material existence, even the atmospheric. It is to be thought of unabashedly as the soul of the world."[1] This "pervading element" is independent of gravity and the boundaries of things, through which it passes as in a dream. It moves silently and has nothing of the bulky cumbersomeness of mechanical appliances. That explains, perhaps, the fascination of the romantics, who allowed subjective-poetic and physical-electrical processes to intermingle, as in Novalis: "Is galvanism supposed to be something other than internal light? The trace of sensation in the inorganic realm."[2]

Things that flow (water, crowds of people, etc.) seem to move autonomously, to be without beginning and end. In the romantic subject sensations and cognitions flow together, are either fixed or continue flowing. A thought that is exchanged is tangible— and used up—like money. The romantic model of a flow of thoughts, in which there resonates the image of the self flowing, attempts to counter this type of quantification: everything flows; the (poetic) stream cannot be particularized—an idea of communication without end. A flow is the counterpart to reification.

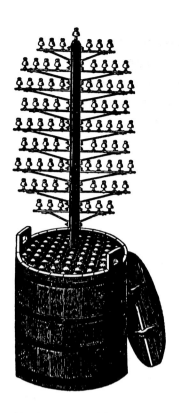

Max Ernst, *Portrait of Eluard*, 1921.

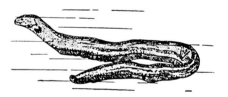

The electric eel, with a body two-fifths of which contains electrical organs, transmits bolts of currents up to 550 volts through the water. It was discovered by Humboldt around 1800 in Venezuela.

Flows dissolve petrifactions. That is the point of departure of "romantic medicine," which, in the person of Franz Anton Mesmer, received a theoretical, if occult, foundation. Mesmer thought that a force existed "which, carried by an aether, a very fine stream, pervades the universe and holds all of its parts together."[3] The problem was merely to gain control of this force for therapeutic purposes. The idea was based on the classical theory of aether, which states that the light-aether, in itself a static substance that fills the entire world, is the carrier of all electromagnetic waves. This hypothesis was not refuted until the second half of the nineteenth century by the experiments of Michelson. The romantic idea of aether, which set the image of medically useful electromagnetic forces, proceeded from the notion of an energy that, whether in the nature of a flow or radiation, influences people. It was applied in particular as a sedative to attenuate excessive agitation (hysteria). The peaceful music of Aeolian harp and musical glasses was employed to support magnetic therapies,[4] since they were attributed the capacity of channeling excessive flows, and at the same time to balance out the swings of hysteria.

Nervous disturbances were associated with uncontrolled, excessively rapid swings early on; thus Goethe in a letter of 1778: "I

Electrification as popular entertainment. Around 1800 in Hamburg one could subject oneself to an electric shock from this apparatus.

know that a mosquito can drive people with trembly nerves to distraction, and that no amount of talking is of any help against it."[5] "Nerves" is a word, like "nerve" and "nervousness," that derives from the French *nerveux*, which merely meant "sensitive" in the eighteenth century, but slowly underwent a change in meaning, of which Goethe's letter is evidence: from "sensitive" to "trembly," that is, from a mode of perception to an illness. The overly rapid buzz of insect wings is the example carefully chosen by Goethe as the trigger of nervous excitation; it will return as scintillation in the nervous aesthetic of the *fin de siècle*. Romantic medicine applies magnetic cures to excitations, hysteria, attacks of delirium, etc., in which the laying on of hands and hypnosis were supposed to lead to the calming of the flows of excitation.

Romanticism, thus, was already construing a connection between nervous life and (pretechnological) electricity. Nervous twitches were associated with the origins of life itself—here a path leads from Galvani's experiments with frog legs to the animation, in Mary Shelley's novel of 1818, of Frankenstein's artificial people, who announced their being through "convulsive motion" of their limbs.[6] Mesmerism provided (and Edgar Allen Poe was still an adherent; see "Mesmeric Revelation") the theory of an extrasensory, electromagnetic force that influences and steers the course of individual life. Marx demystifies the aether forces, this postrevolutionary bourgeois idea of the universal connectedness of all things, by naming the true "galvano-chemical power" holding society together: money[7] is the unmasked electrochemical aether.

2. POLARITY AND SEXUAL ATTRACTION

A part of the fascination with electricity might have arisen out of the closely related analogy to erotic attraction (or repulsion), so nicely characterized as tension between the sexes. Alongside the world aether, it is this idea of polarity that is already determining the image of electricity in the eighteenth century.[8] The somewhat macabre experiments conducted by the German physicist Georg Bose with the "electrica attractio" (in a title of Otto von Guericke of 1672) are thoroughly typical of the salon games of the rococo period, which were still very distant from the utilitarian technological application of electricity. Bose charged women, preferably pretty ones, wearing insulated shoes with electricity; the cavaliers from whom they demanded a kiss received a strong electric shock.[9]

Inspired by Benjamin Franklin (of whom d'Alembert said, "eripuit coelo fulmen sceptrumque tyrannis"—"he tore the lightning from heaven and the sceptre from the tyrants"[10]) and his experiments with electricity, the English quack Dr. James Graham undertook around 1780 to design a "heavenly bed" by means of which "children of extreme beauty" (his self-promoting characterization) could be conceived. An "electric fire" and magnets weighing fifteen hundred pounds were supposed to generate the optimal current for reproduction. Graham went bankrupt after transient public successes.[11]

E. T. A. Hoffmann's "Magnetiseur" is obsessed with the idea of exercising erotic power through the mastery of magnetic forces. He attempts "to capture all the rays from inside Marien as if in a reflector. . . . To draw Marien totally into my own self, to weave her whole existence so into mine that separation from me would have to destroy her, that was the thought . . ."[12] An interesting remark in passing in the same text reveals the relationship between magnetic rays and nerves. The Magnetiseur senses that he is being observed during one of his experiments: "Perhaps it was my eyes that betrayed me, for the body does indeed so confine the spirit that the stillest of its movements oscillates outward in the nerves and changes the face—at least the look in the eyes."[13] Nerves are the corporeal transformers of the immaterial spiritual-magnetic rays.

Even the old Goethe, in his conversations with Eckermann, formulated this idea of an erotic "electrica attractio," in which the Neoplatonic doctrine of universal symphathies comes into play: "We have all some electrical and magnetic forces within us; and we put forth, like the magnet itself, an attractive or repulsive power, as we come into contact with something similar or dissimilar. . . . With lovers this magnetic force is particularly strong and acts even at a distance."[14] Electricity or magnetism appears here as an identity principle, which, in the case mentioned, unites those who are separated.

"A magnet that falls in love with six pounds."

Lichtenberg, *Sudelbücher*

Goethe's point of departure is electromagnetic attraction or repulsion, that is, a force through which subjects possess a charge that is simultaneously fixed and bound to the personality and that produces correspondences between appropriately disposed bodies. Body and charge form a unity, and the attraction, or repulsion, occurs between two equal charges. Electromagnetic force is not abstract but is emitted by specific persons, is thus ultimately thought of as substantial.

In the *Phenomenology of Spirit* of 1807, Hegel, on the contrary, is already bringing another aspect into focus, which supersedes the romantic, panpsychic conception and leads to a specifically modern view of electricity. Hegel dissolves the connection between body and charge and describes electricity in an analogy to the abstractions of modern commodity and money circulation, which strips things of their qualities. The characteristic of positive or negative electricity is that "neither . . . is any longer attached to a particular kind of thing." Given a change in the charge, "these separated detached things have no actuality; the power which forces them apart cannot prevent them from at once entering again into a process, for they are only this relation." Thus are the things, as Musil would later demonstrate in the social sphere as well, without qualities; their relationship depends entirely on the state of the charge, which is completely independent of them, in which they happen to fall, or, as Hegel says: "They cannot, like a tooth or a claw, remain apart on their own and as such be pointed out. . . . The result of experiments . . . is to cancel the moments or activated sides as properties of specific things, and to free the predicates from their subjects."[15] Goethe's effort to merge positive and negative charges with the soul of the world or with human sympathies and antipathies is not even attempted by Hegel; the excitations are conceived exclusively as a principle of relation devoid of qualities.

Kleist, in his text "Über die allmähliche Verfertigung der Gedanken beim Reden," even makes an electrical excitation as Hegel had described it, that is, a sudden charge and discharge, into a possible cause of the French Revolution: Mirabeau's answer to the royal master of ceremonies, who is demanding the dissolution of the Estates General, was well known: "We have received the King's command," and, after a pause, "What right has anyone to issue commands to us. We are the representatives of the nation." For Kleist, the decisive moment, the instant in which a sudden "gush of enthusiasm," equivalent to the "discharge of a Kleist jar"[16] (which was invented by an ancestor of the writer in 1775, simultaneously with the Leyden jar and designed to produce the same effect), changed the speaker's opinion, is in the pause. The electrical discharge appears as the cunning of history; the abrupt excitation leaves things behind in another state.

These sudden charge states, since they seem to be independent of the identity of the persons in whom they appear, have a potentially ominous quality—the functioning of the accustomed ego is temporarily canceled by overwhelming energies. Where Kleist speaks of a "thunderbolt" of atmospheric discharge as rhetorical discharge, Balzac speaks of a bursting thunderbolt inside man that is willful and unpredictable. The excitation he describes is an anxious dream, the negative form of discharge. The anxious dream appears just as suddenly as the excitation, and the continuum of time is exploded—electrical epiphany. The momentary ecstasies[17] so important to modernist aesthetics first come to expression in the image of electricity. Electricity affects, as Balzac says, "human thinking power."[18] This energy model constitutes, once the romantic-panpsychic ideas have been removed, the background against which the deterioration of the consistent ego makes its appearance, in precisely the moment in which a practical application is beginning to be found for electricity. No longer distant is the point in time in which a child can be frightened and called to order with the threat: "She must be sent as a message by the telegraph."[19]

4. ANDERSEN: ELECTRICITY ON THE "ROMANTIC-TECHNOLOGICAL KNIFE-EDGE"

The technical-fantastic fairy tales of Hans Christian Andersen— for example, "The Galoshes of Fortune" or the tale of the nymphs at the World Exposition in Paris of 1869, "The Dryads"—are empirical historical sources in that they register the date on which romantic and fairy-tale sources of energy are taken into service by industry. Andersen, just like Grandville according to Bloch, is "on a romantic-technological knife-edge."[21] Wearing the "galoshes of fortune," the protagonist embarks upon a trip to the moon. But his "speed is as the crawling of the sloth . . . in comparison with the swiftness with which light travels. That flies nineteen million times quicker." The soul separated from the body flies "on the wings of electricity."[22]

Andersen's text sketches the metamorphosis of a dream energy into technology. If Heinrich Heine compares the charismatic radiance of Franz Liszt (Andersen was acquainted with both) to "magnetism, galvanism, electricity, . . . histrionic epilepsy, . . . the phenomenon of titillation . . . musical Spanish fly . . . and other scabrous things that have reference to the mysteries of the *bona dea*,"[23] in doing so he delivers a whole phenomenology of the romantic understanding of electricity, which was no longer taken entirely seriously by 1844. Andersen's text aims likewise at the technical applications of electricity, still subject to experimental realization in the 1830s and 1840s: Faraday discovered the phenomenon of induction in 1831; Morse designed the electrical telegraph writer in 1837; in 1846 Siemens the needle telegraph; Goebel the carbon-filament lamp in 1854—to name only a few examples.

The metamorphosis of the "treasure" into the commodity finds its counterpart here—a phenomenon of secularization that is just as easily legible in the changing conception of chemistry: the title of Goethe's novel *Elective Affinities* is merely the translation of the title *De Attractionibus Electivis* given by the Swedish chemist Torbern Olof Bergman to one of his works, in which he describes the type of attraction between elements that splits naturally occurring compounds. Goethe transposes it by way of analogy onto human relationships. And in doing so he understands the elements and the people explicitly as "one nature,"[24] thereby taking up certain of the thoughts of the early romantics. Thus did Friedrich Schlegel speak in the Athenäum fragments of a "logical" and "moral chemistry,"[25] advancing the claim that "revolutions are universal, not organic but chemical movements."[26] Novalis spoke similarly, long before Goethe's *Elective Affinities*, about the "theory of sensual pleasure": "The actual function of sensual pleasure (sympathy) is that of pressing toward the totality (a compound) of unification—the chemical function."[27] This universal conception of chemistry on the part of the romantics

Cup with "Brunshausen"— souvenir of Morse's telegraph, *ca.* 1855 (Altonaer Museum).

was taken up and realized in the 1840s in the first chemistry laboratories of Justus Liebig. Aniline, with which dirt, that is, coal tar, could be transformed into the most magnificent colors, now became the real redemption of the alchemists' dreams of the retort.

5. SIEMENS, EDISON, AND THE HISTORY OF MENTALITIES OF ELECTRIC LIGHT. ORNAMENT AND PSYCHIC STREAMS

"Technology has currently acquired the means of producing electrical currents of unlimited force cheaply and comfortably wherever labor power is available. This fact will come to be of equally considerable significance in several areas." These are the closing words of an address delivered by Werner von Siemens to the Prussian Academy of Sciences in 1867. The prophecy was not exaggerated; Siemens's dynamoelectric machine, dynamo for short, is the precondition of high-voltage technology and thereby of the industrial use of electric current as well. The current produced by the generator could be transported over large distances, with the effect, for example, that factory operations were no longer dependent on the central steam engine, whose kinetic energy had to be transmitted over a complicated apparatus to workplaces located as near as possible to it. As of 1882 Edison was able to supply power to the light bulbs in private homes from an "electricity central."

Here begins the empirical history of electricity, which would have enormous effects on daily life. Edison proclaimed what was supposed to happen with the invisible flows of electric current: "Cables will be laid through all the streets and lead into each house, where they will conduct not only light but heat and the energy of motors. It will be possible to run sewing machines, washing machines, shoe-polishing machines, indeed, even to cook with electricity."[28] The distinguishing characteristic of electricity is its silent omnipresence. The application possibilities are, unlike those of gas, nearly limitless. Electricity is "a pure, odourless, and immaterial form of energy."[29] Its technological potential was presented to the astonished public at the Paris Electricity Exposition of 1881: dynamos by Siemens and Edison, cables, telephones, the first streetcar with overhead power supply, and electric lamps (the sensation) en masse. The 1880s saw the application in industry and daily life—and in the literary imagination—of the new source of energy. Its effect on the spirit was ambivalent.

The new "Colossus of Rhodes" astride the whole of Africa, from Capetown to Cairo, after the completion of the English telegraph network.
Punch, December 10, 1892

Electric torchlight procession, New York, 1884.

The most visible effect was electric light. The revolutionizing innovation was not centralized energy supply, which had already existed for a long time in gas and water, but the special quality of electric lights in interior spaces. To judge by contemporary descriptions, the specific quality particular to electric light was that it was everywhere present, and did not, like the gas light, illuminate only a point in the darkness. Into "the distant depths of the departments," writes Zola in his department-store novel, *Ladies' Paradise*, penetrated "a white brightness of a blinding fixity. . . . There was nothing now but this blinding white light."[30]

Proust's ironic remark, "when electric lighting had been everywhere installed, it became possible, merely by fingering a switch, to cut off all the supply of light from a house,"[31] shows the other side of artificial light—its permanent availability also transformed the non-light, darkness, into disposable dimensions. The electric light also made it possible to switch the darkness on and off.

Contemporary reports speak of the "powerful electric light [that] enlivens the whole quarter."[32] The light is hard and glaring, leaves no dusky corners. Pedestrians on the street felt as if they were being drilled through by the hard rays of the arc lights. According to one report from 1855, the light was so strong "that ladies opened up their umbrellas . . . to protect themselves from the rays of this mysterious new sun."[33]

The electric light is stiff and uniform like homogeneous time—the flickering of a candle and the gas light's variations of intensity yield to a uniform flow of light, in which the constant light source obliterates shadows and perspective, at the same time dematerializing people and things. In electric light, unlike the differentiated light of day, or of candles or gas, things are disembodied; spatial volumes offered to the eye in a play of light and shadow are obliterated in the uniform brightness. This light is, in Bachelard's expression, "administered light"[34] of a generally abstract character in contrast with the individual lighting fixtures of the past. The centralized supply of energy and the application potential of electric light over a large area determine each other.

The illusionless electric brightness knows just as little of dark shadows as impressionistic painting, which arose at the same time. The description given by the art historian Wilhelm Hausenstein of his experience with candlelight during nighttime air raids in the Second World War, when the electric lighting was down, outlines the problem of perception. He writes, "We have noticed that in the 'weaker' light of a candle, objects have a different, a more marked profile—it gives them a quality of 'reality.' This is something that is lost in electric light: objects (seemingly) appear much more clearly, but in reality it *flattens* them. Electric light imparts much too much brightness and thus things lose body, outline, substance—in short, their essence. In candlelight objects cast much more significant shadows that have the power actually to create forms. Candles give as much light as things need in order to be what they are—optimally, so to speak—and allow them to retain their poetic element."[35]

Lighting with candles, as Hausenstein describes it here, appeared to the sociologist Thorstein Veblen, a contemporary of the first electrification wave of 1880–1890, as snobbism and empty convention, unsatisfactory in brightness.[36] The (depth) perception with which Hausenstein views things discloses the historicity of perception: it was only because of the catastrophe of war that the experience of things in a natural organic light became possible again, in which they did not, as in electric light, all seem equally flattened. In the department store (Zola), on the other hand, and contrary to perception in private, it was not a matter of presenting things (in a good Heideggerian sense) in their thingliness; rather

But the light is quite genuine. It is there, standing firm, not frozen—that would be false: stopped? could be! In any case, that is his depiction. Wait, the air is there too! The breath has stopped the light. . . . In the circus, leaps in zinc. Vaults in tin, executed by people. All by electric light. Expressionism rolling up, futurist spirals reeling out, by yellow-sprinkled, spiritedly powdered electric light.

Theodor Däubler on Seurat's paintings and drawings, in
Neuer Standpunkt (1916)

what appears is the commodity as an immaterial light form. Hausenstein, in his apologia for natural light, retrieves in bewildering form the argument Odilon Redon adduced against the impressionists, who "without opposing surfaces, without organizing planes" reproduce "a vibration of tone." In his opinion, "the expression of life can appear differently only in light and shade."[37] Electric light is as immaterial as impressionist light—both emphasize the beautiful appearance of things, without inquiring into their "substance."

If electricity is also an immaterial, invisible energy, far removed from the obviousness of a steam engine in its mode of operation, then it was still, or perhaps precisely for that reason, regarded as a life force: "For the century of Hermann von Helmholtz, electricity, energy, and life were synonomous."[38] The fantasies of creating an artificial human being gained new impetus from electricity. Villiers de L'Isle-Adam, in his novel, *Tomorrow's Eve* (1886), combined the myth surrounding Edison with a creation myth. Induction keyboards, fluctuating visions, electricity, nerve *fluida*, metallic wires, and animating currents bring the android into being, as the first product of a future "manufactory of ideals."[39] Alfred Jarry devised for his farce, *The Supermale*, an electromagnetic apparatus: "the machine-to-inspire-love."[40] There was an echo from Maeterlinck, who wrote about the automobile, that "monster": "Its soul, that is the electrical spark, which causes his breath to glow seven to eight hundred times a minute."[41]

Just as electricity produces life and even love here, so do people learn how to use it to put other people to death. The invention of the electric chair is the negative empirical complement to the fantastic inventions: the city of New York, according to a report, "can consider itself fortunate that the barbaric form of execution by hanging will soon be replaced by a more humane and scientific means of execution: beginning January 1, 1889, criminals will be executed on the electric chair."[42] Jarry, who likewise describes the electric chair, regards the "spasmodic convulsions" that beset the condemned in the moment the current flows as an ambivalent phenomenon—even death is perceived from the angle of electricity as a life force: the convulsions of the already dead inspire the impression that "the device that has killed it is falling upon the corpse in an effort to revive it."[43]

Electricity is not only effective for the animation and killing of the human body but was also used in agriculture like fertilizer and in medicine for electrotherapies, electric baths, etc.[44] In Huysmans's novel, *Là-bas*, reference is made to a doctor who allegedly made "green electricity" in liquid form and claimed that he was able "to fix in his globules and liquors the electrical properties of certain plants."[45] What is remarkable is that electric current, unlike mechanical forces whose effect remains external, is connected to the body for every conceivable reason, as if it were possible to use it to expand human forces into infinity. Here is a remedy for tiredness, which as "décadence," among other appellations, is one of the obsessions of the closing years of the nineteenth century that are spawned by the feeling of impotence in the face of the abstract and autonomous social apparatus: "If fatigue was the disorder of energy, electricity held out the promise of restitution."[46]

It is perhaps fruitful to look for the effects of the image of electricity as the flowing current of life in the aesthetics of the years after 1880, especially in symbolism and *Jugendstil*. Streams of flowing hair determine the image of the woman. Baudelaire is already describing the canonical symbol of seduction by female hair in his poem, "Her Hair":

> O toison, moutonnant jusque sur l'encolure!
> . . .
> J'irai là-bas où l'arbre et l'homme, pleins de seve,
> se pament longuement sous l'ardeur des climats;
> Fortes tresses, soyez la houle qui m'enlève![47]
>
> [O fleece, that down the neck waves to the nape!
> . . .
> I shall go there where, full of sap, both tree
> And man swoon in the heat of southern climes;
> Strong tresses, be the swell that carries me!]

But this image of sensual effusiveness transforms itself into the danger of entanglement, which appears with exemplary clarity in Stuck's "Medusa," whose hair is made up of ominously darting vipers. This anxious desire, this game of enticement and threat,

The Electricity Palace at the
World Exposition in Paris, 1900.

Gustav Klimt, *Fish Blood*, 1898.

is typical for the image of women of the time. The allegorical representation of electricity around 1900 takes up this symbolic complex of woman, hair, water, and flowing, now stripped of the component of fear, once again: just as the electricity palace at the World Exposition of 1900 appears as a fairy-tale water castle crowned with a naked goddess of electricity, so too does a contemporary representation of electric light present it as Venus with long hair suspended over the water. The fantastic constructions concerning the puzzle of flowing electricity are legible precisely in these aesthetic trivialities. They not only symbolize the network of energy supplying power plants as a fountain of youth but also lend electricity the appearance of flowing erotic power.

In art, hair supplies the streamlines of the soul. In his *Beethoven Frieze* Klimt translates Schiller's verse, "let the millions intertwine," in ornamental lines of force winding about the embracing pair. Erotic communication appears in the image of pairs woven or entangled together—as in Munch's woodcut, *Man's Head with Woman's Hair* (1896), as in the famous lithograph *The Kiss* by Peter Behrens (at the Allgemeine Elektrizitäts-Gesellschaft since 1907). Hair translates the flow of the soul into ornamental lines, comparable to the lines of force in a magnetic field, which are caused either by electrical currents or variable electrical fields: an image of immaterial communication, in which the currents conduct the bodies, that is, make the bodies conductors. In Jugendstil the person "becomes an organic, vegetable soul. The immediate body of bones, flesh, muscles, skin, nails, and hair disappeared,

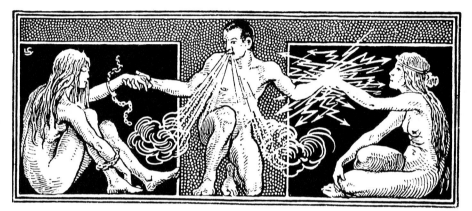

Symbolic representations of electricity from the turn of the century.

was dissolved into this driving yearning"[48]—and electricity, its constant invisible flowing, is possibly one of the empirical inspirations for the new, ethereal paradigm of the body.

6. "TELEGRAM STYLE OF THE SOUL"

AND COSMIC ENERGIES

The notion of invisible but still very effective energies that in some way have an effect on individuals is probably *the* phantasm of the last twenty years of the nineteenth century. The language is often ambiguous—is electricity an image of these energies or do the energies appear in the image of electricity? The application of this conceptual model reaches from psychotechnology and psychodynamics all the way to neoromantic theories of psychic energy. Psychology, like the science of work, searches for the laws of nerve excitations to be able then to get a better grip on the energies of a human being. In Eduard von Hartmann's *Philosophie des Unbewußten* (1869), a much-discussed work of the time, the transmission to a person's limbs of a decision to move is presented entirely in the image of the telegraph: the book speaks of "nerve circuits," of "will impulses" that are "received," of "outgoing currents," and "broken circuits."[49] The will thus makes use of something Sternberger compares to a telegraph keyboard. Hartmann, taking "electric current, which is so closely akin to the nervous currents," as his point of departure, conceives the transmission of the motivational energy of the psyche in the image of an electrical apparatus.[50] Currents flow through the person, and the point is to conduct these currents properly.

Hartmann speaks of "a keyboard in the brain"[51] that organizes the nervous currents. This conception of psychical phenomena as an electrical-telegraphic process is still to be found (and this demonstrates its range) thirty years later in Peter Altenberg, who popularized the "telegram style of the soul."[52] Altenberg's abbreviated style works with suggestions and is defined by the extensive use of accumulated dashes, that is, by elements of Morse code. What Thomas Mann dismisses as "infantile punctuation"[53] is a procedure for representing unnamable communicative processes as electromagnetic impulses. To read Altenberg is thus to decode nonverbal communication currents, which are apparently always present between the people involved.

For Altenberg the "telegram style" is no abstraction—as it was for the old Stechlin, for example, who complained, "Telegraphing

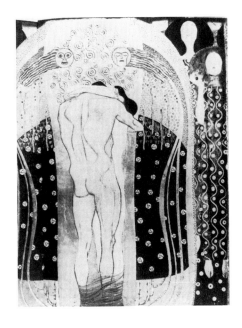

Gustav Klimt, *Beethoven Frieze*, 1902 (detail).

Edvard Munch, *In the Brain of a Man*, woodcut, 1897.

Edvard Munch, *Man's Head in Woman's Hair*, woodcut, 1896.

He understands the note of a piano as a personality, a note that does not linger in a surrendering feeling, but disappears in the moment of its existence, finds the entirety of its life in the stronger or weaker pressure of a finger, which commands it into existence, and which gains in mobility, nervousness, wingedness, freedom, in motorlike sensitivity what it cannot achieve in intensity.

Oscar Bie, *Das Klavier*, on Claude Debussy (1898)

Peter von Siemens has been reading Steiner's works for forty years. Thanks to the "meditative occupation" also connected with it, he says, he has in himself "established the clear impression" that the "master of solid matter, Ahriman," "has preserved" electricity, magnetism, and atomic energy. The utilization of nuclear power—this is the implication of Siemens's electro-mysticism—is thoroughly in Rudolf Steiner's spirit, so that "the earth will be conducted step by step into new forms of existence."

Der Spiegel, 38, no. 17 (April 23, 1984): 63

is one of those things . . . just the form, the composition. Brevity is supposed to be a virtue. But to cut it short usually means to make it crude as well. It does away with every trace of civility."[54] Rather, for Altenberg, it is a possibility of representing condensed psychic energy by means of abbreviated, impressionistic suggestions and the coded language of the telegraph. The psychic currents suggested by Morse code also provide a means of, as he says in another place, preserving the "vital energies," that is, "the force contained in our nervous systems," from fragmentation through crude linguistic tangibility and social dispersion.[55]

It is only a short step from the psychophysical telegraph, the potential of which is illumined from Hartmann to Altenberg, that is, from the proper organization of individual nervous currents, to the synchronization of the energy currents in a person with a total cosmic system, which appears to an American technologist of the will as a "hidden storehouse of energy,"[56] or to Maeterlinck as "an enormous receptacle of power."[57] Georg Simmel is also convinced "that the human individual does not, so to speak, come to an end where our senses of sight and touch define his boundaries; that it is much more the case that there is a sphere beyond this, whether one conceives it as substantial or as a kind of radiance, whose extension exceeds all hypothetical effort and which belongs to his person like the visible and palpable to his body." As an example he offers "the antipathies and sympathies between people not at all subject to rationalization, the frequent feeling of being captivated to a certain extent by the mere existence of a person, and much more."[58]

Neoromanticism and vitalism return here to notions of a "self-emanating world-soul," as Goethe and the romantics had already formulated it. In opposition to force-consuming modern life, to the "activity apparatus," the discussion of electricity, without a doubt inspired by its technological application, is reinvigorated. Siemens's prophecy, "of producing electrical currents of unlimited force," works like a signal to the thinkers in the last years of the nineteenth century that they should secure their share of the new. Currents from unnamed energy sources supply individuals, too, with unsuspected forces.

Electricity exercises its effect not only on the bodies of individuals but also on society, as appears especially clearly in Lenin's

statement: "Electrification + Soviet power = Communism."
Indirectly it also makes its way into the thinking of the electricity
magnate and writer Walther Rathenau, who conjures up the power
of the soul to counteract the dangers of mechanization. Rathenau
appears in Musil's novel *The Man without Qualities* as Dr. Paul
Arnheim, who pursues the "unification of the soul and economy":
"The sensitive minds of the time, endowed with the finest capacity for picking up the scent of things to come, spread the tidings
that he in himself united these two poles, usually separate in the
world."[59] Musil privatizes the social model of transubstantiation,
the unification of two poles, by describing a love scene in which,
according to Arnheim's notion, "souls would commune with each
other without the mediation of the senses": "The mysterious forces
in them collided with each other. What happened can only be
compared to the blowing of the trade winds, the Gulf Stream,
the volcanic tremors in the earth's crust: forces vastly superior to
man . . . were set in motion between the two of them . . . measure-
less, mighty currents."[60] Here the idea is put to the test privately;
the flowing, immaterial communication of souls quickly founders
on the mechanisms of convention. In Musil, put ironically, the
electricity magnate becomes the last representative of the belief
in psychic currents, the mysterious *fluida* of the romantics.

Nerves are the higher roots of the senses.

Novalis[61]

7.   NERVES: MACH, BAHR,

AND FREUD

For it is the enervating that benerves us—if

certain vital prerequisites are met—and

makes us capable of performances and

enjoyments in the world that are beyond the

compass of the unbenerved.

Thomas Mann[62]

The "Introductory Remarks: Antimetaphysical," with which
Ernst Mach preceded his *Analysis of Sensations*, contain the central
catchwords of self-reflection for the era between 1885 and 1910.
"Thing, body, matter are nothing apart from the combination of
the elements,—the colors, sounds, and so forth—nothing apart
from the so-called attributes."[63] That which appears as body is of
merely relative solidity; it indeed impresses the memory as having
fixed contours, but has none. "Further, that complex of memories, moods, and feelings, joined to a particular body (the human
body), which is called the 'I' or 'ego,' manifests itself as relatively
permanent."[64] Mach separates the body from the ego, and, in the
face of the merely relative stability of both element complexes,
sees here as well a merely contingent combination. Only in the
economy of thoughts—memory, perception, etc.—is the fiction
of a unity created; thus the momentous statement: "The ego must

Oskar Kokoschka, *Portrait of Hans Tietze and Erika Tietze-Conrat*, 1909.

be given up."[65] Freely moving elements, or element complexes (sensations, etc.), have taken over from the image of the consistency of the thing or the subject. Conceptions of substance or identity no longer have any object.

Mach generalizes the thought Nietzsche expressed thirteen years previously in "Über Wahrheit und Lüge im außermoralischen Sinn": "What is a word? The figure of a nerve stimulus in sound."[66] Nietzsche's reflections on language lead him to an insight into the merely relational character of truth, while, in Mach, the person appears to have dissolved into alternating currents of stimulation, each of which produces variable relationships: "The fact that the different organs and parts of the nervous system are physically connected with, and can be readily excited by, one another, is probably at the bottom of the notion of 'psychical unity.' "[67] The division between physical and psychological forces thereby becomes untenable. Mach's remark: "When I speak of my own sensations, these sensations do not exist spatially in my head, but rather my 'head' shares with them the same spatial field"[68] returns in the aesthetic of Viennese modernism in the figure of the sensitive soul who passively allows stimuli to flow through him, who is ruled by changeable moods.

This aesthetic was formulated by Hermann Bahr with much indebtedness to Mach. It was Bahr who coined the catchwords for young Vienna, who was always creating new fashions, ever new designations to describe the same symptoms. He departs

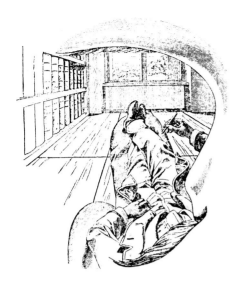

Illustration from Ernst Mach's *Die Analyse der Empfindungen* (Analysis of sensations), 3d ed. (Jena, 1902).

from a critique of naturalism, which, in its confinement to the surface of phenomena and apparent subjectivity, he thought stood in the way of a freely artistic mode of perception. The "new people," as Bahr wrote in *Die Überwindung des Naturalismus* (1891), have discovered a new medium of perception: "They are nerves; the rest is extinct, withered and barren. They live now only through the experience of nerves; they only react on the basis of nerves. The events they experience happen from the nerves and their effects come from the nerves. . . . The contents of the new idealism is nerves, nerves, nerves."[69] Idealism is set into opposition against naturalism, the ephemeral experience of the moment against barren objectivity. Events no longer exist, nor does reality; rather reality is only that to which the nerves react. Nerves become the central category of aesthetics.

Bahr replaces the catchword "idealism" three years later (in *Studien zur Kritik der Moderne*, 1894) with "décadence." The décadents want to shape "notre univers intérieur," "they are a romanticism of the nerves. . . . Not feelings, only moods do they pursue. They do not merely disdain the external world, but in the very interior self disdain all the rest that is not mood. They pay little attention to thinking, feeling, wanting and want to express and communicate only the stock they each find in their nerves. . . . These new nerves are sensitive, broad-ranged, and manifold and communicate all the oscillations among themselves."[70]

The new decadent idealism is joined to the old romanticism, which is thereby modified considerably. Feeling is played off against mood; where romanticism knew both perceptual categories, here only mood remains. And not without reason: feeling is bound to the subject, mood ultimately independent of it; feelings refer to concrete experiences, while moods are diffusely composed of imponderable factors. Moods tune a person, as an instrument is tuned by an alien hand. The return to romanticism is conflicted to the extent that the "univers intérieur" presupposes an interiority, an interior space, that is, a traditionally bounded subject. Bahr, in contrast, gives up the subject in favor of nerves, the oscillations of which produce nothing more than moods. The subject is, according to the unspoken consequence, nothing more than the rather accidental conjunction of stimuli, whereby the distinction between inner and outer is no longer tenable. Nerve stimuli are just as immaterial as electricity; they stand for a new, immaterial paradigm of the body, the product of postmechanical thinking.

In the *Dialog vom Tragischen* (1904) Bahr finds a less problematic concept for his concern than nerve idealism and nerve décadence turned out to be. Impressionism is the new formula. As Huysmans's Des Esseintes stood godfather to the concept of décadence, now it is another product of French modernism, namely, impressionist painting, that Bahr transports to Vienna. The impressionist, he says, "dissolves the appearance he wants to depict into many colorful flecks or points, which come strangely together only at a certain distance, and, having just been flickering wildly, shapelessly, suddenly take on the most beautiful form. . . . [The picture] disappears, it appears, as I want, under my eyes."[71] As nerve stimuli have no central impulse but vibrate diffusely, so it is with the objects of impressionist painting—dissolved into flecks and points, the figure has no fixed contours but appears and disappears according to the viewer's standpoint. The figure has only a relative stability. Bahr transfers the perceptual form of impressionist painting onto the image of the world, which is just as little "real" as the former. In doing so, Bahr makes an unacknowledged return to naturalism, the theory of which, at least originally, coincided with that of impressionism: the goal was (in particular with Seurat) to achieve the physically correct reproduction of light reflexes. But impressionism understood in this way was a naturalism without an object, and that allowed Bahr to forge his connection.

Only now, in 1904 with the catchword "impressionism," does Bahr refer to Mach's *Analysis of Sensations*, which he proclaims "the philosophy of impressionism." That Mach refers repeatedly to optical phenomena in the course of his analysis makes it easier for the aestheticist Bahr, departing from considerations on painting, to combine artistic with philosophical reflections. Mach's book became the justification of Viennese modernism and the cult of the immaterial scintillation of nervous moods.

Nerves are not only an aesthetically fascinating phenomenon— in the 1890s pyschologists also intensify their interest in the phenomenal forms of nervous life. In their hands the aesthetic sensitivity to nerve stimuli is transformed into a symptom of illness. Beard, Erb, Krafft-Ebing, Binswanger, Moll, Freud, and Adler are examples of those who published studies on the topic that inquire into the cultural causes of modern nervousness. Erb emphasizes the significance of mobility: "The illimitable expansion of communication brought about by means of the network of telegraphs and telephones encircling the world has completely altered the conditions of business and travel. All is hurry and agitation: night is used for travel, day for business; even 'holiday trips' keep the nervous system on the rack. . . . life in large cities is constantly becoming more elaborate and more restless."[72]

The rhythm of money and commodity circulation determines that of human life—the constant exchange of things and information suggests an image of social mobility as diffuse as the nervous oscillations of the lonely aesthete. Just as the contours of things disappear in impressionist art, so do the boundaries between day and night disappear in social life; the permanent flow of currents of goods and traffic in the large city, lit first by gas and later by electric lights, give notice of the dissolution of the social body into an oscillatory field, in which everything individual and bounded evaporates. Marx's remark concerning "this lack in the commodity of a sense of the concrete" ("A born leveler and cynic, it is always ready to exchange not only soul, but body, with any and every other commodity"[73]) is recalled here, though it represents an analogy in economic terms to the constant metamorphosis of moods and nerve stimuli propagated, or, as the case may be, constituted, by the aesthetics and psychology of the 1890s. Georg Simmel also emphasizes the relationship between the "intensification of nervous life" and the money economy in his 1903 essay "The Metropolis and Mental Life."

What interests the psychologists is something else, namely, the diagnosis of specifically modern neurasthenia, the first full-blown description of which as an illness was written by George Beard, an American doctor, in the early 1880s. In the general formulation of the thesis advanced by Beard and his successors, the intensified demands placed by modern life on the nerves ultimately lead to fatigue in the psychological system as a whole.[74]

In his essay " 'Civilized' Sexual Morality and Modern Nervousness" (1908), Freud acknowledges the social-historical influ-

Enamel sign, *ca.* 1907,
Werkbund-Archiv.

ences the other psychologists hold responsible for the malady, but he fails to see a precise correspondence between these factors and the concrete symptoms of illness. Freud attempts to remedy this deficiency by referring to the repression of sexual life, which he took to be the basis of culture. At the same time he travels backward along the path of his predecessors, conducts research strictly in the sense of his theory of sexual repression, and develops the precise diagnosis that had previously been lacking. But in filling this gap he dehistoricizes nervousness by refusing to connect his description of the illness, the validity of which is general, with novel social-historical phenomena. For culturally based sexual repression is in no way identical with or to be derived from modern mobility but is rather a general cultural-historical phenomenon. Freud's psychoanalytical initiative remains unconnected to the social-historical initiatives of his predecessors. Bahr, Erb, and Simmel, and ultimately Freud, offer various interpretations of nervousness, which agree on only one point: the dominance of nervous stimuli in comparison with less diffuse, bounded forms of perception directed toward goals and objects.

8. STRINDBERG AND ELECTRO–HYSTERIA

In 1884 de Maupassant brings together the traditional diatribe on magnetism and electricity into a small fantastic story, "Mad?" The hero's ego boundaries, particularly on "electric" evenings, are permanently compromised by an onslaught of objects set in motion by an extraordinary "magnetic" force. This power of attraction is simultaneously experienced as draining, as a force that "gnaws . . . and wears out."[75] The subject feels himself to be located at the center of forces that destroy it. De Maupassant's literary fiction manifests the fear of invisible forces in romantic terminology, which allows no direct connection to actual historical experience.

Strindberg's journals from 1894 to 1897, published under the title *Legende*, in contrast, sometimes connect his own crisis of consciousness very precisely with the phenomena of nervous-making modern life, which produces uncanny states of electrical tension. Thus in the example of the modern traffic system: "Step into a fully loaded train car on your own. No one knows each other, all of them sit quietly. All of them, depending on how sensitive they are, feel quite discontented. There spreads a com-

Emile Zola, *Self-Portrait*.

plicated network of various rays that generally stifles the air. It is not warm, but it feels like you're suffocating: the spirits that are excessively charged with magnetic *fluida* feel a need to explode; the intensity of the currents, fortified by influence and condensation, perhaps even by induction, have reached its peak. Then someone speaks: the discharge has taken place and neutralization sets in."[76]

The experience of anonymity in the means of mass transportation, the unification of foreign individualities who only see each other without speaking, signifies an alienation from accustomed communication: the form of familiar intimacy mediated over language is replaced by a situation in which the subjects feel themselves to be close, and simultaneously alien. There arises a communicative situation in which mutual perceptions are not produced linguistically, that is, palpably, with clear acoustic contours like those of things, but flow diffusely. The experience that irritates Strindberg, which he fixes in the image of nervous-electrical states of tension, is the same as that which Simmel had described as the "preponderance of occasions to *see* rather than to *hear* people" in the public means of conveyance.[77]

Strindberg is irritated by the feeling of being pursued by invisible, anonymous forces. The anonymity of social relations in a big-city (Paris) hotel becomes threatening, since it makes autonomous behavior, like that in comprehensible situations of concrete contacts, impossible. The invisible proximity of people who move without being capable of insight into their motives induces anxiety. Thus his report of a neighbor in the next room: "What is strange is that he pushes his chair back when I move mine; that he repeats my movements, as if he wanted to provoke me with his imitations. . . . When I go to sleep, the other one lies down. . . . I hear how he stretches out parallel to me."[78] Anonymity promotes this delusion of relationship; an actual interchange of reactions is impossible under these conditions. It is comparable to another perception: "As soon as I've moved into a hotel, noise erupts. . . . Feet dragging and furniture being shoved. I change rooms, I change hotels: the noise is there, above my head. I go in the restaurants: as soon as I sit down in the dining room, the rumble begins."[79] The environment is constantly present; the sub-

Now I would like to speak of two **social projects**. The first was the great alliance against unnecessary noise, which I founded in 1908 once I was finally settled permanently in Hanover. It expanded so quickly that I had to keep an office with two secretaries. The various types of noise, like the piano nuisance, the automobile nuisance, the church-bell nuisance, the carpet-beating nuisance, the wrong kind of paving stones, and so on, had to be fought one by one. The association's magazine, *Der Antirüpel*, which I wrote completely by myself, has become very rare today. In London I met with the founder of the American alliance, a millionaire New York woman, and with the head of the English "anti-noise" campaign.

Theodor Lessing, *Einmal und nie wieder* (1935)

ject cannot shut itself off, is permanently penetrated by noises that absorb all the forces. The subject is degraded into a surface on which the movements of others are written. The nerve stimuli of Bahr have become a permanent condition of torment.

Social life appears as a force field into which subjects are drawn without regard to will and in which they dissolve: "[Alone] he felt how his nerves settled and calmed down. He became aware again of his identity, that special something which exists independently. Instead of dissipating, his personality concentrated inwardly."[80] The nervous currents become materialized and appear as entanglement: "When I am alone, I immediately experience indescribable relief; lethargy ceases, the headache disappears, and it seems as if the convolutions of the brain and the wickerwork of nerves had been tangled up with someone else's but now are beginning to straighten themselves out."[81] Yet there also exists for the ego, which is without boundaries, is always trapped in the currents and entanglements, the reversal of the ties responsible for dissolving the self: now separation destroys the connection, experienced by the ego as unity, with another person. The path away from the beloved woman is an emptying of the self: the ego is like "a stretched rubber cable. . . . I feel like the pupa of the silkworm which is being unwound by the engine of the steamer. . . . Now it is the train engine which unreels my intestines, the convolutions of my brain, my nerves, my veins, my guts, so that I am a mere skeleton when I arrive in Basel."[82] The subject conceives itself in the form of the technologically new, like rubber and electricity. What is new is manipulable; it becomes the image of that which destroys.

The nervous body is noncorporeal, immaterial, arbitrarily subject to being charged with tensions. Nervous conditions assume in Strindberg the form of an electro-hysteria: objects transform themselves into electrification machines that render the subject a victim of currents. "A blanket has been hung over a cord, obviously to hide something. On the mantle above the chimney there are metal plates hung up in rows, separated from each other by wooden posts. On every row there is a photograph album or some book or other, clearly to give these hellish machines, which I am inclined to consider accumulators, an innocent appearance."[83] Or

It will be possible to send anywhere or to re-create anywhere a system of sensations, or more precisely a system of stimuli, provoked by some object or event in any given place. Works of art will acquire a kind of ubiquity. . . . Just as water, gas, and electricity are brought into our homes from far off to satisfy our needs in response to a minimal effort, so we shall be supplied with visual or auditory images, which will appear and disappear at a simple movement of the hand, hardly more than a sign. Just as we are accustomed, if not enslaved, to the various forms of energy that pour into our homes, we shall find it perfectly natural to receive the ultrarapid variations or oscillations that our sense organs gather in and integrate to form all we know. I do not know whether a philosopher has ever dreamed of a company engaged in the home delivery of Sensory Reality.

Paul Valéry, "The Conquest of Ubiquity," in *The Collected Works of Paul Valéry*, ed. Jackson Mathews, vol. 13, *Aesthetics*, trans. Ralph Manheim, Bollingen Series, vol. 45/13 (New York: Pantheon Books, 1964), pp. 225–226

On some evenings in April, the statue of Friedrich looks quite pretty from a distance: the slightly tilted three-cornered hat against the background of the sunset and the triumphal arch, and not far above him, a headdress of forty telephone wires.

Jules Laforgue, *La cour et la ville* (1887)

he notices "the American iron bed, whose four posts, topped by brass spheres, look just like the conductors of an electrification machine."[84] Pursued by electricians, he takes "electric showers," wears an "electric belt," etc.[85]

The wickerwork of the nerves finds its counterpart in the transmission cables threatening to connect to the subject from all sides and annihilate him. The invisible electrical currents are the metaphor of the life of the nerves: the body becomes a force field, a contingent intersection of effects determined elsewhere. Strindberg's electro-hysteria unfolds before the background of the quickly changing anonymous social relationships in the big city, in which objects, things as well as people, are experienced as nothing more than nerve stimuli.

12

THE CONSTITUTION OF PERCEPTION

FROM 1900 TO 1914

1. Mach, Simmel, and Hofmannsthal

But the separation between a thing and its

environment cannot be absolutely definite

and clear cut; there is a passage by insensible

gradations from the one to the other.

Henri Bergson, *Matter and*

Memory (1896)[1]

And three are One: one person, one thing,

one dream.

Hugo von Hofmannsthal, *Terzinen*

über Vergänglichkeit

Viennese modernism is inspired by Mach's theories on the deterioration of the ego, the dissolution of personal unity into variable aggregates of sensation. Georg Simmel, a contemporary in Berlin, undertook to combine Mach's thoughts with a *Philosophy of Money* (1900), which then worked its retroactive effects on Viennese modernism. Simmel speaks, as does Mach, of the "aggregates of qualities that we call objects," and of the impossible separation between subject and object.[2] Moving beyond Mach's purely epistemological posing of the problem, he defines money as the instance that brings subjects and objects into an exchange relation: for him, money is "a means, a material or an example for the presentation of relations that exist between the most superficial, 'realistic' and fortuitous phenomena and the most idealized powers of existence, the most profound currents of individual life and history."[3]

The beginnings made by Mach and Simmel intersect in Hugo von Hofmannsthal: he describes the flowing over of the subject into inanimate matter,[4] that is, the deterioration of personal unity, and, in the essay on Balzac of 1906, sketches the social background to the continual metamorphosis of subjects: "Everything is flowing, everything on the way. Money is merely the brilliantly conceived symbol of this constant motion, and at the same time its vehicle. Through money everyone gets everywhere. . . . We find transitions everywhere, nothing but transitions in the moral as well as in the social world."[5] Hofmannsthal was, like Musil, a reader, or, as the case may be, listener, of Simmel's, and in 1906, under the influence of his reading of the *Philosophy of Money,* conceived a plan for a drama in which the "value-destroying magic" of money was supposed to have been given expression.[6]

The crisis of perception and the disappearance of subjects, the central aesthetic theme of Viennese modernism, finds a correspondence in the exchange abstractions of the circulation of goods, in which—and here he follows Marx, expanding his theory into a general cultural analysis—the ego "becomes so far removed from the objects that they can measure their significance by each other without referring in each case to the Ego."[7] In exchange circulation the relationships of the person to the objects is dissolved, with retroactive effects on the relationships of persons among themselves, whose circulation is likewise threatened with being made subject to an abstraction: following the differentiation of the world of things in industrialized society, people operate (and communicate) with "a growing number of ideas, concepts, and statements, the exact meaning and content of which they are not fully aware. . . . Just as our everyday life is surrounded more and more by objects of which we cannot conceive how much intellectual effort is expended in their production, so our mental and social communication is filled with symbolic terms."[8] The predominance of objective culture has effects extending all the way into the interiority of subjects. The aesthetic consequence is the search for new forms of perception and communication that attempt to escape the abstraction of both the world of things and of language.

2.   SILENCE

Physics is bound to words only in its doctrines, not in its phenomena. We experience the power of nature wordlessly; we comprehend wordlessly and measure without resort to numbers the mechanical and acoustic, visual

Silence is a form of communication in which no purely verbal "exchange" takes place. The modern metropolis sets the space for an experience in which communication is reduced to fleeting visual contacts. The emphasis on the sense of sight manifests the distance that exists between the individual subjects: the purely visual reception of contacts does without tactile or verbal communication, which presuppose a concrete other or a concrete desire. In the circulation in large cities there arise only a few situations, as they might typically be for a small town, in which everyone knows everyone else: the overwhelming majority of contacts take place with anonymous persons. Passengers on the train or streetcar react, like "The Man of the Crowd," silently to the

and electrical movements.

Fritz Mauthner, *Beiträge zu einer*

Kritik der Sprache[9]

ephemeral meetings, to the constant changes of constellations in which they move. This silence is the expression of the reduction, or abstraction, of social communication in the conditions of the modern metropolis. The relinquishing of speech, that is, the transferral of communication onto the sense of sight, brings people into conformity with the new conditions of social intercourse. Where people circulate like commodities, language as a medium of intercourse has become obsolete.

Against this silence, which, given the anonymity and abstraction of movements in a permanently altered environment, is sooner dumbness, the *fin de siècle* aesthetes and Viennese modernism play out the signifying silence as ideal communication completed beyond the senses and language. Speechlessness, euphemistically reinterpreted, becomes the guarantor of inner experience. Maurice Maeterlinck won the position of the apologist of silence: "If you want truly to give yourselves to someone, stay silent; and when you fear to stay silent with him, then flee." "We speak only in the hours in which we do not live. . . . As soon as we speak, something inside of us says that divine doors somewhere are closing." "As soon as the lips sleep, the souls awake and set themselves to work." These are typical statements from the essay "Das Schweigen,"[10] which make it clear where Maeterlinck referred for his theories, namely, the mysticism of Cusanus or Meister Eckhart, in which silence is the precondition of religious experience. Maeterlinck excises this dimension in that he makes silence into the ideal form of interpersonal communication, which is not to be allowed to be robbed of its purity by words.

The medium of this communication is the soul. The sign of the intercourse of souls is speechlessness, the complement of which is bodilessness. Maeterlinck is thus reacting indirectly to Mach's theory, in which the bodilessness and egolessness had been formulated soberly: Maeterlinck's ego exists only inside the soul; an inner without an outer, which is denounced as externalization. This ego is paradoxically defined by speechlessness and bodilessness, that is, by sensual absence. The data of sensation, the registration of which Mach had still left to the putative ego, are replaced in Maeterlinck by the unnamable qualities of the soul, in which the ego has utterly disappeared and—this is the consequence—is precisely for that reason utterly present.

Hofmannsthal, unlike Maeterlinck, is conscious of the social-historical implications of silence: as protest against the permanence of (ex-)change. This protest shows its true colors in the late Hofmannsthal—it is the conservative revolution, which opposes aristocratic substantiality to the leveling of all values. Exchanging *values* is, indeed, according to Simmel's insight, also the *exchange* of values.[11] After the collapse of the monarchy, Hofmannsthal, in the comedy *Der Schwierige*, plays ironically with the possibilities—the difficult one of the title falls silent: "That you," a character addresses him, "have taken up residence in the manor for a year and a half now, but have never spoken a word. Exactly as it should be for a gentleman like yourself! Such a gentleman speaks through his mere presence!"[12]

Expression (externalization of the self through speech) or alienation (externalization of a possession) is not appropriate for the feudal gentleman, whose property was not mobile like money, but had the substantive existence of land and soil. The money economy is in contrast the sign of the developing bourgeois society, from the talking of which the difficult gentleman withdraws: "He did not wish to become accustomed to the paper money of daily dealings. With speech he can only give away his intimacy, and that is invaluable."[13] Through silence, words, and thereby the person, are withdrawn from the abstracting intercourse of exchange; verbal intercourse is made the equivalent of the intercourse of money, the stripping of things of their qualities is proscribed through silence. But that—and this is the point of the play—offers no escape: silence, like speech, produces confusion.

The critique of language in the early Hofmannsthal aims at the surfeit of momentary experiences comprehended in words: "We experience so much, we touch many too many things; we also speak too loudly, too fast, and of too much; we are not healthy enough for grace and are all too poor in inner music."[14] A review of 1895 expresses the problem of language more precisely: "Words have put themselves in front of things. Hearsay has swallowed up the world." Through the abstraction of the language of the bureaucracy and science, etc., the claim continues, thinking has been caught in the Augean stables of concepts, the result of which is a conflict between (objective) language and (subjective) sensation. Independent of people, words develop a "ghostly connectedness."[15] The autonomous life of words recalls that of commodities, whose values are established in mutual reference and independently of people. The person has become absent within his own language.

Hofmannsthal names very precisely the social-historical causes of the loss of language; he reacts, however, with a typical *fin de siècle* strategy: the cultivation of sensibility as the escape from alienation in the form of a "desperate love for all of the arts . . . that are executed wordlessly: music, the dance, and all the arts of the acrobats and jugglers."[16] To the deterioration of experience (*Erfahrung*) (compare Benjamin's analysis), the young Hofmannsthal (unlike his imaginary contemporary Monsieur Teste) replies with the construction of a perception that restores in speechless interiority that which has been lost through externalization. Dance and pantomime are ideal art forms for the *fin de siècle* aesthete—for are they not, "emanations of absolute sensuous beauty,"[17] practiced wordlessly? These beauties work to counter the petrifying conventionalization of language and the world of things, in that everything that has been scattered in the flow of movement is taken up and maintained. The body moving in pantomime or dance is for Hofmannsthal a whole, the expression of an "inner plenitude . . . of the soul,"[18] beyond any possible utilitarian distribution: gestures, tones, bodies, and things flow together into one. The silent arts appear as the restoration of cultural experience (*Erfahrung*)[19] at which the aesthete is passively present as a spectator.

Only in silence are the disparate elements of reality unified. In silence things are brought into congruent moods with each other; mood is conceivable only in silence. Hofmannsthal frequently uses the concept of mood in theater reviews: mood is theater as, vice versa, theater produces moods. Mood is the contrary of concrete reality, of conflict and work, or, in Hofmansthal's words, of "deeds and things";[20] mood is not consciousness but consists rather in a "dark mass of images";[21] mood is changeable; those in the mood are present at a theater presentation determined by another just as completely as in reality.

Artists and spectators are one: the writer "is there and silently changes his position and is nothing but eye and ear and takes his color from the things on which he rests. He is the spectator, no, the secret comrade, the soundless brother of all things."[22] The writer is pure permeability. Withdrawn into soundlessness and inconspicuousness, he is wholly passive sensibility: "He lives, and lives ceaselessly, in the pressure of immeasurable atmospheres. . . . He is the place in which the forces of the time strive for equilibrium. He is like the seismograph that translates every jolt . . . into vibrations. . . . His pains are inner constellations, configurations of things in him, that he lacks the power to decipher. His ceaseless activity is a searching for harmonies within himself, a harmonization of the world that he carries inside."[23]

"Atmosphere" is here only an alternative expression for mood that implies the physical: the writer as seismograph of the moods of the time. Baudelaire's artist, the kaleidoscope endowed with consciousness, seeks to process the shocks of reality—in Hofmannsthal a strategy of harmonization has been made of the enterprise. Just as the wordless arts reveal the soul, so does the writer reveal the harmony of the world, in that he decides against consciousness and for mood, the effects of which he allows to work on him and from out of him. Only in this way can he "bind the elements of the time" and produce "transitions"[24] among things that have long since deteriorated. Only in silence and mood do subjects communicate with each other and with things.

Musil, in the novel *The Man without Qualities* set in 1913–1914, indicates the limits of this mode of perception. His reference figure is Maeterlinck, whose theories of silence he analyzes as "batik-adorned metaphysics," as a powerless "expression of spiritual and artistic protest against the machine age."[25] Concealed Maeterlinck quotations enter into the depiction.[26] Diotima speaks to Arnheim: "Let us be silent! The word can accomplish great things, but there are things still greater! The true truth between two people cannot be uttered." And Arnheim answers: "A time will perhaps come . . . when souls will behold each other without the mediation of the senses."[27]

Silence and souls are the figures of integration for the uncombinable. With them anxieties of contact in personal life are idealized and thereby defused: both are silent concerning that about which they could also speak. Silence is the formula of false harmonization in the social space as well: Arnheim works, analogously to his behavior toward Diotima, on "the fusion of interests

Edvard Munch, *Rathenau*.

between Business and the Soul," and the parallel action can unify the diverging social interests only under the catchword of the liberation of the soul.[28] The "consolidation of appearance,"[29] on which Arnheim places value personally and in his thinking, is nothing other than the appearance of unity: the political and erotic reality is taken up and maintained in a higher third reality, which is the only guarantor of the soul and of silence.

3.   ORNAMENT

The ornament determines the aesthetic of Jugendstil and, beyond that, that of the turn of the century. Ornamental forms are to be found in painting and architecture as well as in the forms lent to the world of things. The interlaced ornamental forms of Jugendstil are the beginning of industrial design. The form of things was not derived from their function; rather, the bodies and lines appear as if in a flowing movement. Unlike historicism, Jugendstil is a style, that is, is possessed of a common formal constant. The adaptations of traditional styles are overcome by way of a resort to a formal language, which opposes to the stale traditional motifs an apparently timeless one: it is nature in whose image abstract technical things are also made. The design sponsors universal correspondences among electric lamps, flower vases, and nature; the ornament transforms the isolated things into a unity.

One of the traditional forms of application of the ornament is the carpet: the abstract or objective decorative forms are arranged on a surface, formally as well as materially woven together. In weaving, things are both isolated and bound together; it is not organized according to perspective, or to the coordinates of space and time, but admits of overlappings and ambiguous references back and forth of the individual forms. For Hofmannsthal, this is the fascination of the tapestry: "What a unified, special world! What an opportunity to treat the angel like the flowers, to bring the gesture of a virgin into a secret harmony with the bow of a lily's stem, the coat-of-arms on a shield in enigmatic correspondence with the smile on a face!"[30] The things are bound together in a decorative concept, but it is precisely this abstraction which allows them to share correspondences as if in a dream; they are just as exchangeable as they are combined.

The ornamental carpet-weave not only displays a relatedness between things on the level of the forms but also embodies, like

Gustav Klimt, *Portrait of Margaret Stonborough-Wittgenstein*, 1905.

the commodity fetish, social labor. To the inspired observer it is a revelation: "that there is connectedness, connectedness wrought by human fingers in endless hours and thousands of knots, and in one instant this thousandfold knottedness lights up and yields to sight the stiff vitality, the arbitrariness of the conjoined colors and shadings become form."[31] Weaving is the unification of things with the labor that created them; reality is legible in the ornament, in which everything has come together in a timelessly ambiguous pattern. The weaving depicts the pattern of the world, as, vice versa, the writer weaves the world together: just as he deciphers the weaving on a carpet, so too does the world appear to him as a "weaving of things." The writer's labor of unifying them allows the most disparate things to come together, the forms in a tapestry as well as "the contents of certain industries or the equivalent," for they consist of "integrating every new thing in the whole which they bear within."[32] The ornament is the aesthetic guarantee of unity in a particularized world.

The poetic topos of the weaving, related to the sign structure of the ornament, is widespread in *fin de siècle* literature. Musil writes about the poems of Rilke: "In his poetry, things are woven as in a tapestry. If one observes them, they are separate, but if one regards the background, it connects the things with each other."[33] But Musil, unlike Hofmannsthal, distinguishes very sharply the legitimate procedure in poetry of interweaving things from a concept of weaving as a description of social reality. Thus he writes in an essay: "The social life of human beings has become so broad and so dense, and relations so inextricably entangled, that no eye or will is any longer able to penetrate great stretches of it, and outside the tightly restricted circle in which he functions every person remains a child."[34]

This image of social reality becomes the point of departure for the novel: " 'It doesn't matter what one does,' the Man Without Qualities said to himself, shrugging his shoulders. 'In a tangle of forces like this it doesn't make a scrap of difference.' "[35] The ambiguously ordered weaving of the poets has metamorphosed into multiple interwoven social interdependencies; the ambiguity has become arbitrariness and unfreedom. The tangle is not legible like the ornamental weaving; here it is not things that are tied together, but individual threads pressed formlessly together. Musil takes up

Gustav Klimt, *Portrait of Fritza Riedler*, 1906.

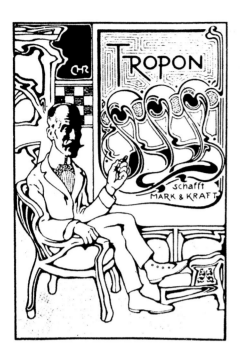

Franz Christophe, *Henry van de Velde.*

the set of *fin de siècle* textile metaphors in that he turns their sense, namely, to depict the poetic connectedness of things, into its opposite and thus reveals the ambivalence of the interweaving.

The aesthetic debates between the architects van de Velde and Loos are equally reflective of the problems of ornamentation. Van de Velde searches for a "purely abstract system of ornamentation"[36] that lends expression to the functional "harmony of the designs." In this new ornament, engineering and decorative forms no longer pose any opposition; they are transcended in a mutual third term. The concept of harmony, however, refers back to Hofmannsthal, and has the same phantasmal quality as mood, soul, or silence. The new ornament has a single aim, that the objects "make manifest the common will, out of the unity of which we unconsciously create nervous forces."[37] In the factory van de Velde is fascinated by "the unitary direction . . . which commands all of these machines, [the] unitary thought that has regulated these movements."[38]

The new ornament consists in the equivalence struck between the harmony of the soul and the strictest functionality of factory organization responsible for the reification of people. It is a model of unification which, precisely in its phantasmal quality, is thoroughly concrete. The etymology of the word "ornament" provides some clarification here: in the word stem is "ordo," "ornament" is derived from "adornare" and "ordinare." Decoration is thereby referred to the creation of order. It is always directed against the autonomy of the singular. In this sense, ornament is destructive; it dissolves individuality and combines the elements of the decor into a unity. This refers to the poetic quality of the "unity" of the psychic effect of which van de Velde speaks. The ornamentation of the masses in the revues of the 1920s,[39] and later in fascist ritual, manifests this aspect of self-surrender, which becomes adjustment to the given line.

But Loos's thesis of "ornament as crime" (1908)[40] is, in another way, no less dubious as the apologia for harmonious design than is psychic harmony in van de Velde. By referring the ornament back to erotic symbolism and, at the same time, denouncing it as a squandering of labor, he propagates a rationality that forbids all manner of pleasurable waste.[41]

The relation between the person and the ornament is more precisely defined in the paintings of Gustav Klimt. The portraits of women from the years 1905–1907 display an increasing preponderance of the ornamental surroundings over their subjects. If in the portrait of Magret Stonborough-Wittgenstein her person is to be seen in front of a wall, then the wall and the clothing are interpenetrated in the portrait of Fritza Riedler, while in the likeness of Adele Bloch-Bauer I, the face, décolleté, and hands just barely emerge from the flowing forms.[42] The ornamentation has enclosed the persons; the body has disappeared into a hieratic decor, which cites the gold backgrounds of Byzantine painting. Klimt's pictures manifest the ambivalence of the ornament: the liquefaction of things and the enclosure of people.

Also characteristic of the Jugendstil *interieur* is that the formal language unifies the heterogenous forms of the world of things and turns them into nature, which, however, encloses the people: "In this way, all that remains of the home's content becomes exchange circulation, while the inhabitant himself is dispossessed of his freedom of movement."[43] The fiction of an all-pervading nature created through the art of the ornament is counterposed to abstracting circulation. The ornament's organic forms guarantee the continuity of a natural context. The conflicts between the interior and exterior world, between society and the individual, are confined in the mutual expression of all things.

In the *fin de siècle* period, the ornament is an aesthetic strategy suggesting unification on the surface of things. The ornament is transferred onto reality, while, according to Benjamin, it can be experienced only as intoxication. He makes reference to the fact that the "multiplicitous interpretability, of which the originary phenomenon is the ornament, merely represents the other side of the peculiar experience of identity opened up by the crock. . . . Ornaments are ghost settlements."[44]

Gustav Klimt, *Portrait of Adele Bloch-Bauer I*, 1907 (detail).

4.   THE LIFE OF THINGS:

RILKE'S THING-POEMS,

ANIMISM, AND SILENT FILM

a) Rilke—"Only Things Speak to Me"[45]   To perceive animistically is the final prerogative of the lyric poet. Rilke's conception of the thing-poem in *Das Buch der Bilder* (1902–1906) and in the *Neue Gedichten* of 1907, however, establishes new standards to the extent that here things from the world of daily life are nearly systematically poeticized as living things, that is, verbally "made" anew.

> Welche Gebärde des Einsamen fände
> sich nicht von vielen Dinge belauscht?
>
> [What gesture of the lonely would not
> be overheard by many things?]

In the poem "Die Stille"[46] loneliness is named as the cause of the animistic investment of the world of things, which is always an expansion of the isolated subject. The absence of the beloved is the precondition of the subject's search for completion within itself, to melt, from the desire for communication, together with things:

> Auf meinem Atemzügen heben und senken
> die Sterne sich.
>
> [With my breaths, the risings and settings
> of the stars.]

Without this connection, which it produces for itself, the subject threatens to disappear; it becomes "indestructible" only once it sees the "impression" of its "tiniest motion" becoming "visible in the silken silence." The extremely intensified sensitivity to the self is the substitute for the absent one. "Progress," as one poem is named, can only be this:

> Immer verwandter werden mir die Dinge
> und alle Bilder immer angeschauter.[47]
>
> [Things become ever more closely related to me
> and all images ever more intuited.]

To become related, "to entwine" the self, is also the intention of the "reading subject," for whom, as he raises his eyes from the book, interior and exterior become one:

> Dort draussen ist, was ich hier drinnen lebe,
> und hier und dort ist alles grenzenlos;
> nur daβ ich mich noch mehr damit verwebe,
> wenn meine Blicke an die Dinge passen.[48]
>
> [Outside is that which I live here within,
> and everything, here and there, is boundless;
> it is just that I entwine myself the more,
> when my glances fall upon the things.]

The interlaced ornamentations of Jugendstil, in which things and people melt decoratively together, are made into a poetic principle here. Everything individual appears, as if a current is flowing through it, to be united with everything else—in the paradox of a universalistic solitude.

The experience of the world transpires only reactively; the subject feels itself as:

> . . . eine Saite,
> über rauschende breite
> Resonanzen gespannt.[49]
>
> [a string,
> across turbulent broad
> resonances spanned.]

As string it is itself a thing, while things conceal life:

> Die Dinge sind Geigenleiber,
> von murrendem Dunkel voll;
> drin träumt das Weinen der Weiber.
>
> [Things are violin bodies,
> with muttering darkness full;
> therein dreams the weeping of women.]

Here the subject is part of an instrument on which an unknown person is playing; Rilke personifies this anonymous power in another place as "wind": the ego stands as "a thing of the world in your hands."[50] Or:

> . . .
> liessen wir, ähnlicher den Dingen,
> uns *so* vom grossen Sturm bezwingen,
> wir würden weit und namenlos.[51]
>
> [If only we let ourselves be dominated
> as things do by some immense storm
> we would become strong too, and not need names.]

If the isolated ego, the melting together with things, aims, in exceeding its boundaries, at a bodily expansion, so is there present in the image of the wind a cosmic reference—the solitary ego wants to swell into the boundless expanse.

In what conditions is this metamorphosis completed? Not in the bright, clearly distinguishing light, but in the night, which causes the contours of things to disappear. The night—by elevating things into "A darkness A silence"—creates that unification of opposites for the sake of which they can be offered prayers like a divinity. In them, subject and object are ornamentally "entwined"[52] with each other. The ego no longer wants to "lift" itself from the "objects." The motif of turning away from the light is concretized in the dialogic poem "Die Blinde."[53] Upon the loss of the eyesight there ensues first of all the feeling of being an island, abandoned and devoid of ties to others—isolated in the original sense of the word. Being cut off is experienced as the collapse of the accustomed perspective: "Space has collapsed. . . . I cannot live this way, with the sky upon me." But then, the sudden change. The things that have collapsed from an external perspective begin to live internally: "My foot speaks with the stones, it steps upon." The exterior world is now existent only as the interior world: "Now everything goes around in me, . . . feelings move like newborns . . . through my body's darkened house."

More precisely can interiority scarcely be defined: the world is now present only in a dark space of feeling, where it undergoes passive tactile investigation. Reflections on enlightenment, expressed in images, would require light. The looking propagated by Rilke does not contradict this blindness as an interior seeing. In lines such as these,

> ich schaute an;
> blieb das Angeschaute sich entziehend,
> schaut ich unbedingter, schaut ich knieend,
> bis ich es in mich gewann[54]

> [I looked;
> What I saw remained removed,
> I looked more absolutely, looked on my knees,
> till I gained it in myself,]

the looking is not directed at recognition, but at a process of becoming related, at incorporation.

Buildings, artificial shells around people, are likewise filled by the subject with life: "a feeling was in every house façade,"[55] the "houses young and laughing."[56] But this fraternization with the building has another, potentially threatening side: if the poet invests a thing with life, so must he too—this is the old drama of the golem, or of the sorcerer's apprentice—count on the thing's independence. Living things can turn against their creators. Rilke's building that consumes its inhabitants like a cannibal is the logical expression of this ambivalence: the opera house, which unites people with each other under its roof and with the help of music, begins like a "monster" to "chew the thousands pressed within its walls."[57] The ties of unity become chains from which no escape is possible. That is the dilemma of this remythologization strategy: the desire to overcome independence, juxtaposed since the Renaissance to mythical dependent minority and now experienced as isolation, while at the same time preserving it—in the intention of dissolving all manner of petrifaction and yet remain, as the individual responsible for arranging this poiesis, separate.

Rilke sees this conflict and nevertheless attempts an apology for the "art-thing," historically coincident with Jugendstil, that seeks to melt the world of commodities together with the dream energies. A key letter to Clara Rilke of June 24, 1907, extols the creation of the art-thing as self-preservation: it is "for the life of the person who must make it" a summarization, the "ever-recurring proof of his unity and trueness" that, however, is "directed only toward himself and to the outer world [works] anonymously." When a thing is perceived "in its essence . . . to the verge of personification" (letter to Clara Rilke of January 20, 1907), Rilke is thoroughly aware of the danger of "personal madness" (letter to Clara Rilke of June 24, 1907); in one place he says about the "Mad":

> sie schweigen, weil die Scheidewände
> weggenommen sind aus ihrem
> Sinn.[58]

> [they are silent, because the partitions
> in their minds have been removed.]

And nevertheless, he defends his cult of things, if ironically, in his letter of March 20, 1919, to Ilse Erdmann, where he is also cognizant of the danger of the "pathological fixation" of this "mythologization confined to the bourgeois and to interior space": "Savings tins, yes, that was it, what I meant from the beginning; that is how all these talismans appeared to me, collectors, little batteries of the life force, charged by us with what we otherwise give off into the caprice of the blowing breeze." This mythologization in interior space reflects on the isolation of the poet, which is supposed to be overcome inside the bounds.

The work of the collector to which Rilke alludes belongs here to the activity of the poet: in Benjamin's words, through the agency of the collector, "things were free from the bondage of being useful. . . . He made the [transfiguration] of things his concern."[59] The Rilkian cult of things aims at the restitution of a presumedly magical-animistic state of unification with things. In this Rilke is thoroughly conscious of the artificiality of his procedure: the comparison with the batteries refers ironically to the parallelism of the technical and imaginative processes of transformation.

The Rilkian perception of things aims at a brotherly relation to things, at that "delicate empiricism" (Goethe[60]) which, in the face of the total domination of nature, seemed to open a utopian way out. It is a gaze at things "that is no longer directed ahead."[61] To the gaze of linear perspective, which isolates and instrumentalizes things in space, Rilke opposes a comprehensive perception. The simultaneous gaze, the simultaneous perception of various views of things, with which the cubist avant-garde destroyed linear perspective, is replaced in Rilke by the simultaneous experiencing of things.

b) Animism   The search for new forms of perception and communication is a reflexive reaction to the abstraction of the world of things and social relations in commodity circulation. The search aims at restoring lost relationships. Silence and ornamentation, for example, are models of unification that attempt to construct aesthetic ways out of social particularization. Rilke's attempt to communicate with things rather than people draws the poetic conclusion from this predicament. Ethnologists, in a parallel undertaking, research the thinking of "primitive" cultures under the rubrics of myth, magic, and animism. Between 1900 and 1910 fundamental works by Spencer, Tylor, Frazer, Wundt, Mauss, Levy-Bruhl, etc., appear and ethnological collections in museums attract the attention of the artistic avant-garde, for example, of cubists or the painters of "Der Brücke." The shared point of departure for the ethnologists,[62] writers, and artists is their attempt to present models that seem unaware of the distance to objects created by the money economy. The projection of this desire onto foreign cultures amounts to an indirect critique of the abstraction of modern civilization.

In the study *Totem and Taboo* (1912–1913), subtitled *Some Points of Agreement between the Mental Lives of Savages and Neurotics*, Freud brings the two aspects together by defining animistic thinking as a form of neurosis. From this point of view, aesthetic strategies move into the vicinity of psychopathology. Animism makes it possible to treat mental images like things, and things like mental images. The ego and the object world are not separated but compose a mutually coherent relationship. Utilitarian action undertaken in reference to a series of goals and according to abstract regularities, as is typical of the money economy, is impossible under these conditions: "Relations which hold between the ideas of things are assumed to hold equally between the things themselves. Since distance is of no importance in thinking—since what lies furthest apart both in space and time can without difficulty be comprehended in a single act of consciousness—so, too, the world of magic has a telepathic disregard for spatial distance and treats past situations as though they were present. In the animistic epoch the reflection of the internal world is bound to blot out the other picture of the world—the one which *we* seem to perceive."[63]

It is not difficult to recognize here Rilke's strategy of poeticization, the one Freud terms "the omnipotence of thoughts," which allows one to enter into contact with things as if with living beings. Money currency, which creates abstract relationships between things, is replaced, in Freud's apt expression, by "neurotic currency,"[64] which makes possible a relationship to things. The abstraction of money is disguised by way of a unification with things, which can develop to the point of neurosis in the form of an obsessive relational mania.

We will be, we are: old animistic rudiments and the new technological reality. Everyone is included—but no one is capable of surpassing a somewhat general validity stamped by the situational. Therefore Ellen Lohmeyer writ large—led to the table by genetics and paleontology, the overture takes up, composed in the supersonic, performed on seashells!

Gottfried Benn, *Der Radardenker* (1949), in *Gesammelte Schriften*, ed. Dieter Wellershoff (Wiesbaden, 1968), 6:1451

Freud links this unification with things, which can also take on the character of the "uncanny," not only to the thinking of the "primitives" and neurotics but also to narcissism: it is not that which really happens that is perceived, but only one's own mental reaction. That means that animistic perceptions are sealed off from the experience of reality.[65]

Modernism, in contrast, is cognizant (not only in aesthetics, where everything becomes *Erlebnis* and *Erlebnis* becomes the expression of everything) of animistic perceptions that do not bear the stigma of a loss of reality but constitute an alternative approach to reality. Thorstein Veblen, in his *Theory of the Leisure Class* of 1899, locates the gambler and the athlete in the context of animistic thinking.[66] To be sure, he judges the trust in a coup—a single act by which all wishes are fulfilled and an ideal constellation of all things is established suddenly and without the assistance of consciousness—to be the issue of industrial rationality. Sport and gambling are, like art, possibilities of an experience (*Erfahrung*) that surpass the bounds of bourgeois and industrial instrumental thinking. According to Musil in *The Man without Qualities*, the athlete comes close to the mystic in seeing a "transcending" of consciousness "in the moment of the act" as a feat of liberation for the "whole and chief person as identified and defined by civil law."[67]

Sports, as they are practiced in the modern world, are a reaction to the end of bodily experience (*Erfahrung*) in the industrial labor process. If Veblen and Musil see in them the reactivization of animistic, or mystical, modes of perception, then the *Erlebnisse* of the athlete are being identified with as structurally related to artistic-animistic operating procedures. The same applies to gambling, an important topos in Baudelaire's work, as a remedy against boredom in a world of progressive utilitarianism: for "Gambling invalidates the standards of experience (*Erfahrung*)."[68]

The critique of animism as a loss of reality, as Freud undertakes it, falls short to the extent that it is precisely not animism that causes the deterioration of *Erfahrung* in reality; rather, animism reflects it and establishes in opposition a subjective order of things that appears to have become impossible in reality. Freud judges modern forms of animism to be symptoms of illness, while the modernist aesthetic takes note of animistic *Erfahrungen* in the intoxication of the moment. That is a reaction to illness, not the illness itself.

c) Silent Film   Jean-Paul Sartre is born in the same year as Little Nemo. The seven-year-old Poulou has the same *Erfahrungen* in the cinema as the hero of Winsor McCay's comic strip in his dreams: "I was utterly content, I had found the world in which I wanted to live."[69] As does Little Nemo's awakening from sleep, so does the end of the film return the little Sartre to reality: "What an uneasy feeling when the lights went on: I had been wracked with love for the characters and they had disappeared, carrying their world with them. I had felt their victory in my bones; yet it was theirs and not mine. In the street I found myself superfluous."[70]

McCay's drawings are stylistically related to the poster art of Jugendstil. They draw the conclusion from the liquefaction of the individual things in Jugendstil, in that they carry them over into a fantastic, dreamlike plot. That brings the comic strip into proximity with film: the vivification, the making fluid of rigid things, suggested by Jugendstil through the use of organic ornaments, becomes a mechanically accomplished matter of fact in the succession of film images.

In Little Nemo's dreams things come to life; a bed begins to fly, trees become people, dimensional relations are subjected to continual change. Little Nemo dreams with the stage sets of his daily experiences and desires, which, fantastically amalgamated, set all things in motion beyond the laws of causality. Comics visualize the movement of things in static pictures, while film presents "moving" pictures. The former are a handicraft form of film, drawn by hand and equally traditional on the level of reception: unlike in the cinema, where the apparatus (like the conveyor belt, which was developed at the same time) determines the tempo of perception, a comic, both the pictures and the language, is read at a pace determined by the individual and not from without.

Where the comic is a succession of individual isolated pictures, film renders visible the continual mobility of things beyond the temporal and spatial order, as had previously been possible—in the medium of language—only in fantastic literature. Early film presents reality in the mute picture-language of the dream. In 1913, Georg Lukács sees a parallel to romanticism, and in doing

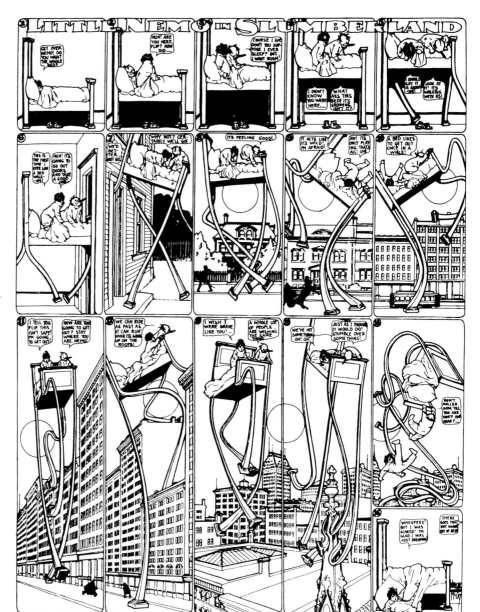

Winsor McCay, *Little Nemo in Slumberland.*

so he is by no means alone in the reception of cinema at the time: "In the 'cinema' everything can be achieved that the Romantics hoped (in vain) to achieve from the theatre: the total unhindered movement of the characters, the background, nature, interiors. . . . and the 'cinema' can create fantasy purely mechanically— when films are projected in reverse and people stand up from underneath hurtling cars, when a cigar butt grows longer as it is smoked."[71]

Two factors, which have nothing to do with the images but which influence the perception of them, are important in the reception of silent films. One is the music, which helps make the actions of the heroes comprehensible, and the other is the silence. Sartre recalls his impressions in the cinema as a child in 1912: "the young widow who wept on the screen *was not* I, and yet she and I had only one soul: Chopin's funeral march. . . . We communicated by means of music; it was the sound of their inner life."[72] What Sartre describes as his own childhood reaction corresponds exactly to the *fin de siècle* musical aesthetic: while the music is allowing him to meld his soul with that of the young widow, Hofmannsthal writes, with no reference to the cinema: "But the mute things live most intensively within the fascination of the music. It makes the dimensions palpable: the height, the depth. . . . It lets the statues in their niches eavesdrop on life. It lends existence to the shadows."[73] This power of animation and mood is purposefully employed in the cinema—is no longer an independent quality as it is in Hofmannsthal, but the emotional determinant of plot. Pieces from the classical repertoire, the reception of which has long since become solidly habitual, establish in turn the mood of the film treatment; this music is what makes the things and people appear to be alive.

Silence, as has been mentioned above, is one of Jugendstil's typical communicational forms. In the same text in which things under the influence of music appear animate to Hofmannsthal, he describes the life of things in silence.[74] What can be achieved here in an inspired moment, the silent film transforms into a matter of fact. But it is not the apparatus-like character of the life of things in film that interests the early observers, but, beyond technology, the life of things itself. The demonization of the machine world around the middle of the nineteenth century is repeated in theoretical confrontations with the new visual medium by way of an emphasis on the latter's magic.

The film critic Béla Balász writes in "Der sichtbare Mensch oder die Kultur des Films" (1924): "In the world of the speaking person, mute things are much more lifeless and insignificant than the person. They acquire a life of merely the second or third degree, and that only in rare moments of particularly clear-sighted sensitivity on the part of the people who observe them. . . . In the

Grete Wiesenthal in the mime drama *Das fremde Mädchen*, from a text by Hofmannsthal.

universal muteness [of film] they become nearly homogeneous with a person and gain thereby in liveliness and significance. . . . That is the puzzle of that special film atmosphere."[75] In Balász (who, incidentally, supplied Bartók with the libretto for "Herzog Blaubarts Burg"[76]) the life of things in silence, as Hofmannsthal described it, is only gradually distinguished from the silent film. The boundaries between subject and object fall; the two become "nearly homogeneous." In his essay on Balász, Musil compares this perception of things with the "participation" (in Levy-Bruhl's terminology) typical of "primitive" peoples, and places it in the context of the immediate experience of art and psychopathological phenomena.[77] The vanishing point of Musil's considerations is a proof of the "other condition," which is of central importance in *The Man without Qualities*. He adopts Balász's theory of the life of things in a silent film and neglects consideration, like the former, of the apparatus-like character of this type of animism.

The silent film is much more completely reliant on the language of gesture than the sound film. In this there arises a proximity to pantomime. Hofmannsthal saw pantomime as a ceremonial form of expression, in which the soul discharges its "inner plenitude."[78] Parallel to the rise of the silent film, the silent arts of dance and pantomime enjoyed a renaissance. Max Bruns writes in 1913: "The nearest relative of the kinodram is pantomime"; Bruns, like Hofmannsthal, emphasizes the proximity of the silent film to dreams.[79] The lightning-quick changing of elements, the silent cooperation of people and things in film are explained here in reference to pantomime and dreams and thereby de-concretized historically. For the language of gestures in the silent film is not only the new form of pantomime, "the new mime through the camera," as Bloch writes,[80] but simultaneously a mirror of the changed conditions of communication in the modern metropolis introduced by the preponderance of visual perception and the rapid succession of impressions. "The human look, the human gesture, the whole physical bearing of a person is occasionally capable today of saying more than human speech."[81]

The copy of reality in film corresponds to this kind of fragmentation of communication—less as the expression of a rediscovered ceremonial pantomime than in the latter's sense of rendering the apparatus-like character of society visible. This

The machine had done its job: It had taken the man apart and then reassembled him. His hands moved faster, his eyelids blinked less often. On the outside he looked like an ordinary person. He had eyebrows and a vest. He went to the movies. But you couldn't talk to him. He was no longer human. He was merely a part of the belt: a bolt, a wheel, or a screw. Unlike others, he didn't live simply to eat, sleep with women, laugh. No. His life was imbued with profound meaning. He lived in order to produce cars; ten horsepower, noiseless engine, steel body.

Ilya Ehrenburg, *The Life of the Automobile*, trans. Joachim Neugroschel (New York: Urizen Books, 1976), p. 25

distinguishes the expressive dance from slapstick—"The attitudes, gestures, and movements of the human body are laughable except in exact proportion as that body reminds us of a mere machine."[82]

The gesture is not performed directly but is mediated over the apparatus: "The camera that presents the performance of the film actor to the public need not respect the performance as an integral whole."[83] The alternation of close and full shots, employed for the first time by Griffith, indicates that in film there is no longer any unified standpoint. Camera instructions and settings determine the course of the action. A second form of displaying perceptions in a way that violates accustomed visual norms is the slow-motion shot. Musil compares it to a view through binoculars: the perception through a telescope of a streetcar traversing an S-shaped double curve yields a reality altered by the apparatus, an unaccustomed liveliness of things: "an inexplicable force suddenly pressed this contraption together like a cardboard box, its walls squeezed ever more obliquely together (any minute it would be completely flat); then the force let up, the car grew wide to the rear, a movement swept once again over all its surfaces, and while the flabbergasted eyewitness released the breath he had held in his breast, the trusty old red box was back to its normal shape again."[84]

By isolating things outside of reality, the apparatus (the binoculars or the slow-motion camera) destroys the perception of perspective and the usual course of events in space and time. Benjamin sees in slow-motion and full shots a "deepening of apperception," with which film, analogously to the discoveries in Freud's *The Psychopathology of Everyday Life*, makes visible that which until then had been invisible in the communication and relation of people to things.[85] But Musil is more skeptical in his emphasis on the ambivalence of this mode of perception. It could lead either to understanding or to the loss of it: the apparatus-gaze on things and people is, on the one hand, objectifying, but at the same time it causes them to appear "ununderstandable and terrible . . . more primitive and demonic" in their isolation, cut off from the environment responsible for defining them in the first place.

The apparatus transforms vitality into a technical form; it shows a different nature from the one the eye sees. Film makes it possible to humanize things, to allow them to seem alive, and at the same time to treat people as things. It redeems the fantastic-animistic dreams of the romantics, but the medium of this metamorphosis is the machinery. Film is equally the phantasmagoria of commodity circulation: an image of the unending communication of people and things. The living-mute pictures crash down on the spectators like the impressions in the metropolis—like shocks that are either absorbed by a "heightened presence of mind"[86] or, on the other hand, perceived like a dream mediated through the apparatus, which produces a liveliness of things and relations as it can no longer be experienced in reality. In film, as in no other art form, technology is constitutive of the product and, simultaneously, the product is an expression of the technology—things appear in functional relationships that had previously been invisible, or, on the other hand, visible only as magical fetishes.

5. ANIMATED THOUGHT

After the turn of the century, there developed strategies in art designed to vivify the world of things—attempts to escape the abstractions of the technical rationality of the money economy. Analagous endeavors are to be found in the derivatives of philosophical vitalism, in which the "soul" is played off against the "butcher standpoint of materialism," in the words of Karl Joël in *Seele und Welt* (1912). "Experience" (*Erleben*) and "living form" (*lebendige Form*)[87] are the formulae by which Joël confronts abstraction with nothing more than mood painting. The latter remains as empty as that against which it thinks it has protected itself.

It is similar with Rudolf Kaβner in "Moral der Musik" of 1905: "My thoughts are not thought in the atelier. My thoughts must give one the feeling of light and air. The French moralists are very clever, but when I read them I do not breathe freely enough. Their thoughts suffocate in themselves, in the airless space of reason. Thoughts have to affect me physically, like pictures, like people, like trees, like flowers, like a sunny day. . . . To think in the free light—that is art."[88] Thinking here is a question of the cult of *en plein air*—free breathing takes over its function. The thoughts that thereby arise—this is stated explicitly—stand in opposition to reason. They are thought pictures, pictures of thoughts, but not mental images.

Robert Musil was also a proponent of "animated thoughts." His writings are in many ways indebted to the *fin de siècle* aesthetic, even the latest works of the thirties and early forties. One example would be his lifelong interest in the theory of the "other state." But Musil's involvement is fundamentally distinct from that of, for instance, Maeterlinck, in that Musil understands mysticism as a critique of rationality rather than as a replacement for it. The difference can be clearly indicated in the formula for "animated thoughts" first appearing in *Torless*. The novel includes an epigraph from Maeterlinck's *Schatz der Armen* in which speaking is described as devaluation. But even here the epigraph is indirectly contradicted in the course of the story, a first step toward the devastating critique of Maeterlinck in *The Man without Qualities*. For Torless attempts a verbal approach to that which Maeterlinck regards as possible only in silence: he tries to express in words precisely that which is inaccessible to daily speech. The vehicle is the animated thought: "thoughts have dead and vital seasons. We sometimes have a flash of understanding that amounts to the insight of genius, and yet it slowly withers, even in our hands—like a flower."[89]

The images in which animated thought is embedded are the same as those Kaßner uses. The relative importance of these images, however, is a completely different one: where image and thought become one in Kaßner and the thought disappears into the image, losing all independent content, in Musil the animation does not change the thoughts but only the significance they have: "we still remember it all, word for word, and the logical value of the proposition, the discovery, remains entirely unimpaired, and nevertheless it merely drifts aimlessly about on the surface of our mind. . . . And then, perhaps years later—all at once there is again a moment when we see that in the meantime we have known nothing of it, although in terms of logic we have known it all."[90]

This animation of the thought is not very distant from the *mémoire involontaire,* as Proust describes it. Proust distinguishes the *mémoire involontaire* from the *mémoire volontaire,* and Musil draws a distinction between the logical structure of a thought and its actualization for the subject. It is not a matter of replacing the thought but of combining it with that for which Maeterlinck substitutes a hypostatized silence: the thought becomes animated only once something "that is no longer thought, something that is not merely logical, combines with it. . . . Any great flash of understanding is only half completed in the illumined circle of the conscious mind; the other half takes place in the dark loam of our innermost being."[91] Unlike the apologists of a silently blossoming feeling of thought, Musil separates the components, rationality and interiority, and at the same time amalgamates them in the figure of the darkness of our "innermost being"—as an expression of the confusions of Torless in his school days.

Only in a later text does Musil deliver a theory of animated thought—as a theory of the essay. The essay, a much-used literary form during the *fin de siècle* crisis of speech and consciousness, frequently with an irrationalist ring (compare the examples of Maeterlinck and Kaβner), was rarely examined as to its theory. About the same time as Lukács's famous text in *Soul and Form*, and coming, in part, to the same conclusions, Musil endeavored to locate the significance of the essay in a posthumously published text dated 1914 by the editor.

The cognitive goal of the essay is "the strictest form attainable in an area where one cannot work precisely."[92] The area is that between science, on the one hand, and life and art, on the other. This dichotomy, characterized by the opposition between systematic order and the equally complete impossibility of any such thing, is not resolved in the essay; rather it "takes its form and method from science, its matter from art. . . . It presents not characters but a connection of thoughts, that is, a logical connection, and it proceeds from facts, like the natural sciences, to which the essay imparts an order. Except that these facts are not generally observable, and also their connections are in many cases only a singularity. There is no total solution, but only a series of particular ones."[93]

Just as there exists for combinations of thoughts a distinction between total (that is, universally valid) and particular solutions, so are thoughts themselves subject to a distinction between the rational and the sentimental. The true-false criterion applies to both, but the material of the sentimental chain of thought is not universally comprehensible. It presupposes a "resonance," which can arise only under specific subjective conditions. Here, too, the reference to Proust's *mémoire involontaire* might be helpful in rendering what happens in the area of subjective thinking comprehensible: "This sudden coming alive of an idea, this lightninglike reforging of a great complex of feeling . . . by means of the idea, so that one suddenly understands the world and oneself differently. . . . On a smaller scale it is the constant movement of essayistic thought."[94] The experiences (*Erfahrungen*) of the mystic are transformed in the animated thought of the essay into a profane (and verbal) epiphany. To treat thoughts like these experiences is Musil's utopian program.

6.   ABSTRACTION AND EMPATHY

Not without influence on the artistic theory of the "Blauer Reiter" was Wilhelm Worringer's text, *Abstraction and Empathy*, first published in 1907. Worringer juxtaposes two aesthetic procedures—first, Theodor Lipps's doctrine of empathy, according to which aesthetic enjoyment is objectified enjoyment of the self. There is no difference between subject and object (Mach had already denied this difference), for, as Lipps writes, "The form of an object is always the state of having been formed by me, by my inner activity." Things become a mirror of the self; subject and object are transcended in their mutual context of nature, bound together by a "vital feeling," which causes a form, as self-expression, to appear. This theory is formulated in extraordinarily general terms and does not take into account the modern *fin de siècle* strategies of empathy (Rilke's, for example), in which they are precisely not the expression of a mutuality between the subject and the external world, but the consequence of their separation, a highly artificial attempt to reconnect with things in the aftermath of general alienation.

To the "need for empathy" Worringer contrasts the "urge to abstraction." While the urge to empathy is conditioned by an unbroken relation between the person and nature, "the urge to abstraction is the outcome of a great inner unrest inspired in man by the phenomena of the outside world." Things can be perceived not through an empathic submersion but through abstraction, which lifts them out of an incomprehensible natural context and thus places them in an understandable order.[95]

While Worringer separates abstraction and empathy as poles of aesthetic experience, Kandinsky attempts to combine the two.

In his *Concerning the Spiritual in Art*, written in 1910, he defines the means by which painting will become "an art in the abstract sense": color and form. He attributes to color just as much as to form the power of causing "the human soul" to vibrate, according to the "principle of inner necessity." That means that the elements of which a picture is composed touch the soul, the internal, etc., independently of the object, that they themselves form a context that can replace empathy in the context of nature. Thus, for example, does "form itself, even if it is quite abstract and essentially geometric," have "its inner harmony"; it "is a living being with characteristics that are identical with that form." Kandinsky does not conceive abstraction as alienating but as a complete purging of materialist utilitarianism. The inexhaustibility of the combinations of colors and forms, whereby forms are changed by color and vice versa, causes the opposition between harmonious and unharmonious to disappear, in that—always according to the proportions of the principle of inner necessity—every combination is harmonious. (This is analogous to Schönberg's conception in his "doctrine of harmony," that dissonances are only widely separated consonances.[96]) The object, the representation of which is not ruled out, is only "one of the elements in the harmony of form."[97]

Kandinsky construes the inner harmony, the inner necessity, etc., precisely on the basis of the deterioration of perspective and the disintegration of line, drawing, and color, which no longer allows any arrangement of individual elements in reference to objects. The meaninglessness of the compositional elements creates internal meaning. Kandinsky draws the consequence from the experiences of impressionism (the lack of an object became conscious in 1895 with Monet's "Haystacks"), Cezanne, and cubism: he works not with atmospheric effects, geometricizing abstractions, or polyperspectival processes, but reduces the pictorial composition to the simplest elements, color, line, and shape.

This marks a turn away from the most advanced possibilities of pictorial composition as well—but precisely this most extreme point of the nonreferential character of the elements, the arrangement of which is released from all rules, all prior processes, and all sense, can be rationalized only as harmony by Kandinsky. The critical de-organization of the pictorial language transforms unexpectedly into an "inner" unity. Where no form is any longer valid, "The artist may use any form . . . to express whatever is mystical."[98] Abstraction appears here as the expression of the internal, which, in a paradoxical unification of opposites, becomes objective precisely in the abstraction. The loss of a structure of external references guarantees its internal restitution. There remains the question of whether such a model of harmonization, inspired by theosophy, does not cause Kandinsky as theorist to fall behind his achievements as a painter.

The "inner value of a picture" can only be perceived with the "spiritual eye": thus, as color must not only be "perceived" by the eye as an external impression but also be pondered by the "soul," so must a painting not be judged according to its imitation of nature or anatomy and perspective and mood; rather, what must be seen, beyond external effects, is what "lives by virtue of these effects."[99] The meaning of a picture is always something else, something that is not visible. Every visible meaning is obliterated in order to produce the invisible one. For that is the matter at hand: the production of what is supposed to appear in the painting as an internal necessity. Internally necessary is what remains after reality has been excluded and what appears through the conscious reduction of technical painterly means: to achieve "corresponding vibrations of the soul," "the forms, movements, and colours which we borrow from nature must produce no outward effect nor be associated with external objects. The more obvious is the separation from nature, the more likely is the inner meaning to be pure and unhampered. The tendency of a work of art may be very simple, but provided it is not dictated by any external motive and provided it is not working to any material end, the harmony will be pure."[100]

This construction of vibrations of the soul is reminiscent of the effects achieved by the cinema: movements whose succession and relations do not proceed according to the laws of logical and mechanical causality take on a fantastic quality, which is produced by the technique of editing, by running the film backward, etc. Kandinsky proposes a similar procedure for painting: the stripping of the composition of the preconditions of customary perception, narrative order, and so on. Where the cinema plays with fragments of reality, combines them anew analytically or in fantastic-comic form, Kandinsky proposes that painters work with compositional elements, which affect inner reality, without any reference to external reality, through the pure kinesis of colors and forms. The purity of the vibrations of the soul is defined by the absence of the external. What he says about the hidden construction of the forms on the canvas applies as well to reality (and characterizes his thought process): "Their external lack of cohesion is their internal harmony."[101]

Kandinsky quite clearly reflects the deterioration of things and their perception in modernism—thus he writes concerning the experiments of physics: "The deterioration of the atom was equivalent in my soul to the deterioration of the whole world. Everything became insecure, wobbly, and weak."[102] In his theory he dismantles pictorial language and gives up the project of copying external reality, but only to save both phantasmally in the inner reality. He repeatedly refers to Maeterlinck as the literary parallel to his own intentions. Precisely as in his theory of color, Kandinsky claims, the word in Maeterlinck has that "inner harmony," independent of the object it denotes. Only the "inner harmony" contains the spiritual elements of the word: the soul vibrates without objective reference.[103] The ambiguity of the formulation may not be intended but points nevertheless to the basis of the principle asserted as regards inner necessity: the inner is nothing but the absence of the external. Musil comments sarcastically that Kandinsky has not gotten beyond "the batik-adorned metaphysics of his teacher Maeterlinck."[104]

7. *THE LORD CHANDOS LETTER*

Hofmannsthal's text of 1902 displays in microcosm the aesthetic procedures and problems of the time. From the theory of empathy to the crisis of language and the idea of a new language, all the way to the ecstasies, thrills, and vibrations of a moment, the themes are gathered and played off one another. The presentational succession chosen by Hofmannsthal issues, almost incidentally, in an organization of the phenomena subject to analysis. This takes place in the context of a fictional letter to Francis Bacon, the founder of English empiricism.

Chandos recalls the time before his transformation when "the whole of existence struck me as one vast unity," with no opposition between subject and object—"I perceived nature in all things."[105] That conjures up a prehistoric-animistic mode of perception, which is possible only for the artist or for one contemplating art. That, at a minimum, is the fundamental idea of the doctrine of empathy according to Theodor Lipps, which Hofmannsthal transfers to Chandos before the crisis. Personal experience (*Erleben*) is projected onto objects; the latter appear, analogously to the experiences (*Erfahrungen*) of early childhood, as a non-externalized part of the ego. Thus, as objects bind themselves to the subject, so does the subject bind itself to objects: aesthetic enjoyment, following Lipps, is objectified enjoyment of the self.

In the formulation of the theory of empathy around the turn of the century, the empathy (or compassion) theory of the eighteenth-century Enlightenment was no longer resonant. According to the latter, the theater audience in particular, by putting itself in the position of the sufferer, was supposed to have been prompted to reflection. This foundation of what happens in the theater by virtue of the effects of the drama was replaced by the romantic notion of empathy as a poeticization of the world. If the element of metamorphosis in the form of a recasting of the world through imagination and the universal science of romanticism is yet resonant here, then this point of departure changed in Lipps and his predecessors (Friedrich Theodor Vischer) into a posing of the question on the epistemological plane, which is only interested in the perception of that which already exists.[106]

By describing empathy, in which the opposition between subject and object falls away, as a bygone state succeeded by a crisis of perception, Hofmannsthal renounces this basis of aesthetic perception. He turns back to the preromantic empiricist Francis Bacon to describe the deterioration of this nonempirical form of perception. Chandos—who was acquainted with empathy without distinguishing between the "intellectual and physical spheres,"[107] that is, who had an equally empathic understanding in the world of speech and the world of things—describes the primary expression of his crisis as the loss of speech, the loss of a few particles in the previously flowing continuum of words, a process of verbal reification. Words, which before had combined with one another in ever new constellations, suddenly become abstract and meaningless, lose their communicative quality.

Lipps touches on this problem ("Tatsachen des Seelenlebens") without discussing the consequences: "My here and now is the final pivot for all reality, and therefore for all knowledge. Assuming that the connection with this point was broken, the continuity of personality canceled, then the whole world of our experience would be a fiction in which we find enjoyment, whose content we really could believe for moments, which, however, would always dissolve into nothingness, like a nice and internally coherent dream in the moment of waking."[108] Here the dilemma of the doctrine of empathy is evident, namely, to be able to comprehend the world of experience ultimately only as a fleeting dream. Lipps discusses the confrontation between continuity and discontinuity, which would point to the problems of this mode of perception, only as a possibility.

The possibility of the deterioration of empathy, however, which Lipps sketches rather incidentally, has become reality for Chandos. Words and concepts acquire their own independence, become elements devoid of content. Language becomes amorphous nature—"the abstract words . . . fell to dust in my mouth like decaying mushrooms."[109] Nature, objects, and speech, associated with one another in the act of empathy, suddenly lose all relationship. Just as absolute as empathy is its deterioration—the omnipotence of the aesthetic individual corresponds directly to impotence.

Empathy is no less sealed off from the objective reality of time and space than Perle, the capital city in Kubin's dream realm, is secured by the high wall that surrounds it "against everything progressive, to be precise, against that from the area of science."[110] Empathy is the confinement of perception within subjective reality. For Chandos, language deteriorates as soon as he, moving out of himself, communicates with others. In the isolated dream realm, matter deteriorates: "The crumbling. It lays hold of everything. . . . The buildings of such various materials, the objects gathered over the years, all of that . . . was consecrated to annihilation. At the same time cracks appeared in all of the walls, wood rotted, all the iron rusted, the glass became clouded, fabrics decayed. . . . A disease of lifeless matter."[111]

The individual loses his relation to words, which are no longer associated with experience. Hofmannsthal employs a comparison that relates his verbal incapacity to the abstraction of the scientific gaze: "My intellect forced me to examine at curiously close range all of the things that surface in such conversation. Just as I once saw a bit of the skin of my little finger in a magnifying glass, and found it to resemble a huge field full of ridges and hollows, so it was for me now in my encounters with men and their conduct. I could no longer comprehend them with the simplifying glance of habit. Everything fell into fragments for me, the fragments into further fragments, until it seemed impossible to contain anything at all within a single concept."[112]

Goethe in *Wilhelm Meister* and Musil in "Binoculars" offer epistemological reflections on the de-concreticization of perception through optical instruments. While empathy suggests an ideal and transhistorical state of affairs, the world deteriorates under the instrumental gaze of the natural scientist—as it does for Chandos as soon as he enters into communication. Empathy is the phantasm of a nonalienated world with which abstraction is impotently repressed. What Goethe writes about the telescope, that it destroys proportionality between things—"the sharper images of the world do not harmonize with my internal ones"[113]—Hofmannsthal takes up by describing the loss of the relationship between language and reality in just this image.

Chandos's crisis of language is not only a subjective phenomenon but points to the increasing abstraction of language, which Georg Simmel had only recently analyzed in the *Philosophy of Money* as a phenomenon typical of the time: the proportionality between objective and subjective knowledge (the two were for Chandos phantasmally united before the crisis) was destroyed by the preponderance of the objective: "The tremendous expansion of objective, available material of knowledge allows or even enforces the use of expressions that pass from hand to hand like sealed containers without the condensed content of thought actually enfolded within them being unfolded for the individual user." The abstraction of concepts which Chandos experiences as soon as he begins to communicate is a barely encoded expression of the problem Simmel sees as a consequence of the division of mental labor,[114] in which subject and object take leave of each other.

Chandos's verbal deterioration is explicable only as a consequence of that which preceded it: empathy, which acknowledges no abstract instance of mediation between the ego and the world but unites the two in the here and now, necessarily deteriorates in a historical culture with divided labor; from the other direction, it is an expression of the various forms of alienation that produce the culture in that it insists on the immediacy of experience.

The deterioration of accustomed object perceptions follows the deterioration of speech—the objects, like the words, are detached from any context. What appears in empathy to be a static and harmonious matter of fact ("I perceived nature in all things"[115]) recurs as a sudden ecstasy prompted by arbitrary and banal things. No longer aesthetic enjoyment as objectified enjoyment of the self, that is, aesthetic understanding through empathy, but "rare occurrences," "trifles," that cause in the subject "a thrill at the presence of the infinite."[116] "A watering can, a harrow left standing in a field, a dog in the sun, a rundown churchyard, a cripple, a small farmhouse—any of these can become the vessel for my revelation. Each of them, or for that matter any of a thousand others like them that the eye glides over with understandable indifference, can all at once, at some altogether unpredictable instant, assume for me an aspect so sublime and so moving that it beggars all words."[117] There is no longer any act of empathy present here; it is rather the other way around: it is the things that empathize with the subject, bring the latter to life through their presence. The subject does not extend itself through the world of objects but is permeated by the latter: "All of it was there within."[118]

Rilke locates the modern urban experiences of Lord Chandos in Malte: "Electric street-cars rage ringing through my room. Automobiles run their way over me." Above a wall bearing the traces of old apartments appear the words: "I recognize everything here and that is why it goes right into me: it is at home in me."[119] There appears here the city as the empirical historical site in which the subject is constantly penetrated by objects, under the pressure of which it becomes permeable. The permanence of shocking impressions hinders any sort of empathic contemplation. Rilke's text is the more concrete in that he describes the process of the subject's domination not, like Hofmannsthal, as a profane epiphany but as the result of the bad infinity of circulation in the modern metropolis, in which the traffic of things overlies that of people. The transformation of the world of things becomes an indicator by which the course of one's own life becomes visible.

Chandos distances himself explicitly from empathy as a form of compassion; he characterizes his condition as a "flowing over,"[120] which is not guided, as compassion is, by consciousness. It is, as it were, a condition of physical sensation randomly stimulated, and not empathy as aesthetic understanding. That is what makes him so fragile, so removed from the guidance of thought, and, consequently, lost to the powers of verbalization as well.

Unlike Malte, who departs from the given as it has been formed by the conditions of living in the big city, Chandos wants nevertheless to ensure for himself "nameless, but unbounded delight," although it is accidental and not subject to control, because he has pushed it into the realm of thought. If it is a matter of thinking, then it does not proceed in words but, as it is transcribed, is an attempt "to think with the heart": "All of that is only a kind of feverish thought, but thought in a medium more direct, more fluid, more incandescent than words."[121] This recalls Musil's theory of animated thought, but, while in Musil the emphasis falls on thinking, here nothing more than a fiction of thought, of *ratio*, is maintained from which all preconditions have long since been withdrawn. Chandos is searching for a language "used by the dumbest of things in speaking with me."[122]

The crisis of language and perception is banished to a paradox as the last salvation of the aesthete in the face of the deterioration of the ego in modernism. Hofmannsthal describes quite precisely its phenomenal form—from a position that confronts abstraction with the no less brittle vision of immediacy, in the expectation of failure. With the Chandos letter, Hofmannsthal's lyrical production comes to an end.

EPILOGUE: THE EMANCIPATION OF

MATERIAL FROM THE SUBJECT

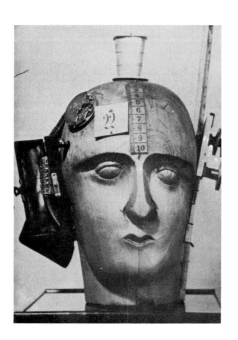

Raoul Hausmann, *Mechanical Head*, 1919.

Chandos suffers from the decay of language—the dadaists systematically promote its destruction. The difference points to a distinction in the reaction to a problem, not in the problem itself. When Hugo Ball sees a tin of shoe polish labeled with the words "the thing in itself" and simultaneously reflects on the lack of a relation between the worker and the product,[1] he is seeing the specific quality of the world of commodities and things, its independence and autonomy: "Everything is functioning; only man himself is not any longer."[2]

Language can no longer be there to connect subject and object; rather it separates itself from the subject, from the transmission of meanings, and becomes independent. Inspired by the futurist experiments of Marinetti, in 1916 the dadaists of the Club Voltaire renounce logically constructed sentences and contexts and remove the word from its grammatical frame. They renounce language as painters renounce the realistic reproduction of people and things. The "Poème simultan," in which the human voice and noises are mingled, is supposed to show that "man is swallowed up in the mechanistic process."[3]

Unlike in the Chandos letter, the destruction does not take place inside the subject; rather, subjects use language as arbitrarily manipulable material to portray the destruction of referential meaning. That is perhaps the essential distinction between the art of the turn of the century and its successor around 1910–1915: the emancipation of the artistic material from the subject.

Words no longer express subjective interiority, the sense and unity of subject and object; rather, the artist fragments long since reified particles. Or, to take an example from painting: van de Velde speaks of the line as "force . . . borrowed from the energy of the one who drew it" (*Kunstgewerbliche Laienpredigten,* 1902), comprehends, that is, the line as an expression of the personality; while Klee (who maintained ties to Hugo Ball and dadaism in Zurich) writes in the *Pädagogischen Skizzenbuch* (1905): "An active line that strolls freely, a walk for its own sake, without a goal."[4] There is mention here only of the line, that is, of the aesthetic material, and no more talk of the one who drew it. As Klee investigates the autonomous line as a pictorial element, so did the Zurich dadaists break language into elements.

Behind the project is an anarchist-mystical impulse; in his thoughts on Proudhon, Ball sketched an anarchist theory of language: "For once it is recognized that the word was the first discipline, this leads to a fluctuating style that avoids substantives and shuns concentration. The separate parts of the sentence, even the individual vocables and sounds, regain their autonomy. . . . The language-forming process would be left to its own resources. Intellectual criticism would have to be dropped, assertions would be bad, and so would every conscious distribution of accents. . . . No traditions or laws of any kind could apply."[5]

With this assertion, self-assertion disappears as well; the sedimentation of syntactical rules is dissolved. The "Poème simultan" and the "wordless verses" (sound poems), two of the typical expressive forms of Zurich dadaism, are pursuing a twofold goal: in view of the First World War, to destroy the murderous authority of offical language in order, second, to retreat to the individual element and expose, beyond conventional meaning, the "magically inspired vocables": "We have loaded the word with strengths and energies that helped us to rediscover the evangelical concept of the 'word' (logos) as a magical complex image."[6] The vanishing point of language destruction is for Ball a void into which new sense can flow. The de-objectification of linguistic material appears as liberation. The site of this liberation is not, as in Hofmannsthal, interiority, but language; its method is destruction.

In the visual arts, Malevich's *Black Square on a White Background* (1914–1915) marks the extreme of abstraction from any reference to the object. "The whole of previous and existing paint-

Contemporary caricature of Duchamp's *Nude Descending a Staircase.*

ing before suprematism, sculpture, literature, and music were slaves to natural forms; they are waiting to be liberated so that they can speak their own languages and escape their dependence on understanding, sense, logic, philosophy, psychology, and the various laws of primary objectivity, as well as the technological transformation of life."[7]

Where the dadaists in Zurich used the existing linguistic material in order to change it, Malevich in the medium of painting can forsake natural forms and, as a radical gesture, oppose to them the pure form of a black square. His theory of suprematism is directed against the futurists, more precisely, the cubofuturists, who had indeed overcome perspective and depicted the dynamic of (technical) movement, but in doing so they continued to work with fragments of real forms. "In cubofuturism, the totality of things is destroyed; it is shattered and fragmented. That was a step toward the destruction of objectivity. The cubofuturists gathered together all objects on the market square and shattered them into pieces, but they did not burn them. Too bad!"[8]

Malevich is interested in pure painting beyond given objects. Its elements are the basic forms, squares, circles, etc., and the primary colors, yellow, red, and blue. Suprematist painting knows no shadows, no atmosphere, no manner of objectivity, but only the relationship of color and form according to the egalitarian principle of the "equality of all elements."[9] It is painting without any support in reality, a free construction of a utopian world of color and form in nonperspectival space.

Duchamp's readymades comprise the polar opposite of Malevich's theory of art. The first readymades appeared simultaneously with suprematism, *The Bicycle Wheel* in 1913, *The Bottle Dryer* in 1914, and *The Fountain* in 1917. Looking back on his multifaceted body of work, Duchamp characterized the readymades as perhaps his most important idea.[10] The intention is related to that of Malevich: to escape the conventionality of the world of objects by means of the readymades, that is, by means of finished manufactured goods declared to be works of art solely by having been signed and displayed. Only the path is different: rather than doing away with the world of objects (or commodities), Duchamp uses them in the paradoxical intention of thereby

Marcel Duchamp, *The Bicycle Wheel*, 1913.

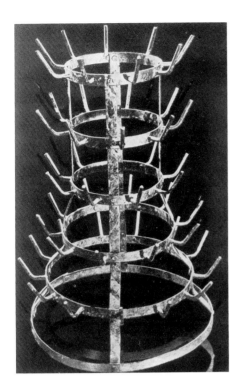

Marcel Duchamp, *The Bottle Dryer*, 1914.

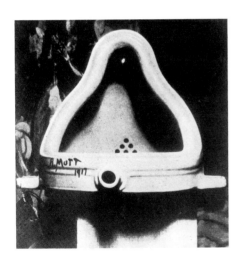

Marcel Duchamp, *The Fountain*, 1917.

eluding their commodity character (in this case, their exchange value as art) and their "aura."[11]

The Bottle Dryer in a museum is no longer a bottle dryer, since it has been withdrawn from the sphere of circulation. Nevertheless, it is not an artwork; it has not been created by an artist but is a commodity now located in a museum. But the commodity in the museum is not there as a commodity, as an object with an exchange and use value, but is there as an art object. It is not, however, exchangeable (without the signature) as an art object, because it is equally a commodity and arbitrarily reproducible without there being any difference between the original and reproductions. An exhibition of readymades is theoretically impossible, because, potentially infinite, the exhibition room cannot be subjected to bounds. In theory, a single readymade cannot but remain invisible, since the entire universe of commodities consists of readymades—an effect of which Duchamp makes use: "Until just a few years ago, I did not even exhibit them, with the exception of a single exhibit . . . in New York in 1916. I hung three of them on a clothes rack at the entrance, and no one noticed them—they thought it was just something someone had forgotten to take away. Which was a lot of fun."[12]

The selection (in either sense) of readymades is the negation of the autonomous artistic decision, a critique of the traditional meaning of art. With the urinal-fountain, Duchamp began with the notion of "selecting an object that had the least chance of being loved. A urinal bowl—there are only a few people who find that wonderful. For the danger is the artistic pleasing of the self."[13] To the sedimentation of habits and an artistic taste, Duchamp, unlike the purist Malevich, opposes complete indifference—thus his preference for mechanical drawings cleansed of all trace of an individual signature.

The readymades avoid the exaggerated elevation of the work of art into a "thing-in-itself"[14] by making into the work of art a thing, which, in turn, is not a "work" but an already existing object. An "objet trouvé" is also an existing object, as are the components of a surrealist collage; but where all of these enter into a relation of correspondence by virtue of the surprise of their having been met there, Duchamp's objects have no such meaning:

"My readymades have nothing to do with the 'objet trouvé' because the so-called 'found object' is completely guided by personal taste."[15] With this objectification Duchamp comes back to Malevich—both adopt extreme positions toward artistic material, which around 1915 was being rent in opposite directions: the correlate of objectlessness is pure objectivity.

NOTES

Whenever possible, previously published English-language translations have been used throughout this book. In all but a few cases, quotations from languages other than German have been translated from the original.

INTRODUCTION

1. Karl Kraus, *Die Fackel*, no. 457–461 (May 10, 1917), p. 39.

2. G. W. F. Hegel, *Sämtliche Werke*, vol. 20, *Jenenser Realphilosophie II: Die Vorlesungen von 1805/06*, ed. Johannes Hoffmeister (Leipzig, 1931), p. 254. Compare Karl Löwith, *From Hegel to Nietzsche*, trans. David E. Green (New York: Holt, Rinehart and Winston, 1964), pp. 265–266.

3. Hegel, *Sämtliche Werke*, vol. 19, *Jenenser Realphilosophie I: Die Vorlesungen von 1803/04*, ed. Johannes Hoffmeister (Leipzig, 1931), p. 239.

4. Hegel, *Jenenser Realphilosophie II*, p. 197.

5. Ibid., p. 256.

6. Paul Valéry, *Cahiers*, vol. 29 (Paris: CNRS, 1961), p. 118, quoted in Karl Löwith, *Paul Valéry* (Göttingen, 1971), p. 55.

7. Paul Valéry, "Address to the College of Surgeons," in *The Collected Works of Paul Valéry*, ed. Jackson Mathews, vol. 11, *Occasions*, trans. Roger Shattuck and Frederick Brown, Bollingen Series, vol. 45/11 (Princeton: Princeton University Press, 1970), pp. 144–145.

8. Friedrich Nietzsche, *Werke*, ed. Karl Schlechta (Munich: Ullstein, 1969), 3:515, 845.

9. Robert Musil, *The Man without Qualities*, trans. Eithne Wilkins and Ernest Kaiser (London: Picador, 1979), 2:435.

10. Walter Benjamin, *Gesammelte Schriften*, vol. 5, *Das Passagen-Werk*, ed. Rolf Tiedemann (Frankfurt: Suhrkamp, 1982), p. 962.

11. Musil, *The Man without Qualities* 2:435, 421, 420, 436.

12. Ibid. 1:175.

13. Novalis, *Schriften*, ed. Richard Samuel (Darmstadt, 1969), 3:449.

14. Karl Marx, *Capital: A Critique of Political Economy*, ed. Frederick Engels, trans. Samuel Moore and Edward Aveling (New York: International Publishers, 1975), 1:172.

15. Wilhelm Dilthey, *Das Leben Schleiermachers*, 2d ed., ed. Mulert (Berlin: W. de Gruyter, 1922), p. 341; quoted in Hans-Georg Gadamer, *Truth and Method* (New York: Crossroad, 1988), p. 58.

CHAPTER 1.   THE BODY, THE ECONOMY, AND THE WORLD OF THINGS

1. For a discussion of the concept of adequation, see Georges Bataille, *The Accursed Share*, trans. Robert Hurley (New York: Zone Books, 1988), pp. 129–137.

2. For an account of the theory of economic circulation in the eighteenth century, see Siegfried Giedion, *Mechanization Takes Command* (New York: Norton, 1969), pp. 136–137.

3. Benjamin Franklin, *Advice to a Young Tradesman*, in *The Works of Benjamin Franklin*, ed. Jared Sparks (Boston, 1836–1840), 2:87, quoted in Max Weber, *The Protestant Ethic and the Spirit of Capitalism*, trans. Talcott Parsons (New York: Scribners, 1958), p. 49.

4. Horst Kurnitzky, *Triebstruktur des Geldes* (Berlin, 1974), p. 122.

5. The Marquis de Sade, *The 120 Days of Sodom*, comp. and trans. Austryn Wainhouse and Richard Seaver (New York: Grove Press, 1966), p. 561. Compare Roland Barthes, *Sade, Fourier, Loyola*, trans. Richard Miller (New York: Hill and Wang, 1976), pp. 125, 152.

6. de Sade, *120 Days*, p. 218.

7. Ibid., p. 246.

8. Stéphane Mallarmé, "Vorwort" to *Vathek*, in William Beckford, *Vathek* (Frankfurt, 1964), p. 20.

9. William Beckford, *Vathek* (New York: John Day, 1928), p. 11. Subsequent references to *Vathek* are to this edition.

10. Ibid., pp. 20, 22.

11. Ibid., p. 12.

12. Ibid., p. 36.

13. Georg Simmel, *The Philosophy of Money*, trans. Tom Bottomore and David Frisby (London: Routledge & Kegan Paul, 1978), p. 506.

14. Beckford, *Vathek*, p. 33.

15. Karl Marx, *The Economic and Philosophic Manuscripts of 1844*, ed. Dirk Struik, trans. Martin Milligan (New York: International Publishers, 1964), p. 147.

16. Beckford, *Vathek*, p. 42.

17. Kurnitzky, *Triebstruktur*, p. 38.

18. Marx, *Economic and Philosophic Manuscripts*, p. 147.

19. Beckford, *Vathek*, p. 159. Compare p. 157.

20. Norbert Miller, *Archäologie des Traums* (Munich and Vienna, 1978), p. 381.

21. Mario Praz, *The Romantic Agony*, 2d ed., trans. Angus Davidson (London and New York: Oxford University Press, 1970), p. 284.

22. Quoted in Miller, *Archäologie*, p. 381.

23. Beckford, *Vathek*, p. 181.

24. Hans Sedlmayr, *Verlust der Mitte* (Frankfurt, Berlin, Vienna, 1973), p. 24.

25. Miller, *Archäologie*, p. 377.

26. Beckford, *Vathek*, p. 183.

27. Ibid., pp. 184, 195.

28. Quoted by Miller, *Archäologie*, p. 382.

29. Marx, *Capital* 1:87.

30. Beckford, *Vathek*, p. 186.

31. Ibid., p. 193.

32. Marx, *Capital* 1:51, 233, 132.

33. Adolf Max Vogt, *Russische und französische Revolutionsarchitektur 1917–1789* (Cologne, 1974), p. 183.

34. Quoted in *Die nützlichen Künste*, ed. Tilmann Buddensieg and Henning Rogge (Berlin, 1981), p. 151.

35. Novalis, *Schriften*, ed. Paul Kluckohn and Richard Samuel, vol. 3 (Stuttgart, 1977), p. 464.

36. Ibid., p. 378.

37. Novalis, *Heinrich von Ofterdingen*, in *Schriften*, ed. Kluckhohn and Samuel, vol. 1 (Stuttgart, 1977), p. 195.

38. Ibid., p. 244.

39. Novalis, *Die Christenheit oder Europa*, in *Werke und Briefe*, ed. A. Kelletat (Munich: Winkler-Verlag, 1968), p. 401.

40. Heinrich von Kleist, "Über das Marionettentheater," in *Kleists Werke*, vol. 1 (Berlin and Weimar, 1976), p. 314.

41. E. T. A. Hoffmann, "The Sandman," in *Tales of E. T. A. Hoffmann*, ed. and trans. Leonard J. Kent and Elizabeth C. Knight (Chicago: University of Chicago Press, 1969), p. 117.

42. Ibid., p. 115.

43. E. T. A. Hoffmann, *Späte Werke* (Munich, 1965), p. 122.

44. Ibid.

CHAPTER 2. FROM THE "EGO CRYSTAL FOREST" TO THE CRYSTAL PALACE

1. Ernst Bloch, *Geist der Utopie* (Frankfurt: Suhrkamp, 1971), p. 48.

2. Charles Baudelaire, "The Bad Glazier," in *Paris Spleen*, trans. Louise Varèse (New York: New Directions, 1970), p. 14.

3. Quoted in Aniela Jaffé, *Bilder und Symbole aus E. T. A. Hoffmanns Märchen "Der goldene Topf"* (Hildesheim, 1978), p. 62.

4. Novalis, *Heinrich von Ofterdingen*, p. 291.

5. E. T. A. Hoffmann, "The Mines of Falun," in *Tales of Hoffmann*, ed. and trans. Kent and Knight, p. 155.

6. Ibid., p. 156.

7. Hoffmann, *Tales of Hoffmann*, p. 14.

8. Ibid., pp. 18, 76.

9. Ibid., p. 76.

10. Ernst Bloch, *The Principle of Hope*, trans. Neville Plaice, Stephen Plaice, and Paul Knight (Cambridge, Mass.: MIT Press, 1986), 3:1133.

11. Ernst Bloch, *Atheismus im Christentum* (Frankfurt, 1980), p. 302.

12. G. W. F. Hegel, *Aesthetics: Lectures on Fine Arts*, vol. 2, trans. T. M. Knox (Oxford: Oxford University Press, 1975), pp. 662–663.

13. Bloch, *The Principle of Hope* 2:736.

14. Paul Scheerbart, *Glass Architecture*; Bruno Taut, *Alpine Architecture*, trans. James Palmer and Shirley Palmer, ed. with an introduction by Dennis Sharp (New York: Praeger, 1972), p. 14.

15. Julius Lessing, *Das halbe Jahrhundert der Weltausstellungen* (Berlin, 1900), pp. 6–10; quoted in Benjamin, *Das Passagen-Werk*, pp. 247–249.

16. A. G. Meyer, *Eisenbauten* (Esslingen, 1907), p. 65.

17. Bloch, *Principle of Hope* 2:725.

18. Kurt W. Forster, "Mies van der Rohes Seagram Building," in *Die nützlichen Künste*, p. 359.

19. Bruno Taut, *Frühlicht 1920–1922*, Bauwelt Fundamente, 8 (Berlin, Frankfurt, Vienna: Ullstein, 1963), p. 213.

20. Forster, "Mies van der Rohe," p. 368.

21. Lothar Bucher, *Kulturhistorische Skizze aus der Industrieausstellung aller Völker* (Frankfurt, 1851), quoted in Siegfried Giedion, *Space, Time and Architecture*, 5th ed. (Cambridge: Harvard University Press, 1982), p. 252.

22. Richard Lucae, "Über die Macht des Raumes in der Architektur," in *Zeitschrift für Bauwesen*, 19 (1861): 303; quoted in Wolfgang Schivelbusch, *The Railway Journey*, trans. Anselm Hollo (New York: Urizen, 1979), p. 53.

23. Hugh Walpole, *The Fortress* (Hamburg, Paris, Bologna, 1933), p. 306; quoted in Benjamin, *Das Passagen-Werk*, p. 255.

24. Marx, *Capital* 1:132.

CHAPTER 3. ECONOMY AND METAMORPHOSIS

1. Marx, *Capital* 1:52.

2. Ibid., p. 36.

3. Ibid., pp. 57, 67, 108, 183.

4. Ibid., p. 132.

5. Johann Wolfgang von Goethe, *Faust I and II*, ed. and trans. Stuart Atkins (Boston: Suhrkamp/Insel, 1984), p. 156.

6. Marx, *Economic and Philosophic Manuscripts*, pp. 165–166.

7. Pierre Klossowski, *Lebendes Geld* (Bremen, 1982), unpaged (final chapter, "Lebendes Geld").

8. Goethe, *Faust I and II*, p. 156.

9. Marx, *Capital* 1:154, 183, 589.

10. Johann Wolfgang von Goethe, *Conversations with Eckermann (1823–1832)*, trans. John Oxenford (San Francisco: North Point Press, 1984), February 14, 1830, pp. 283–284.

11. Compare *Die Memoiren des Herzogs von Saint-Simon*, vol. 4, *1715–1723*, ed. Sigrid von Massenbach (Frankfurt, Berlin, Vienna, 1977), p. 46.

12. Melchior Grimm, *Literarische Korrespondenz* (Munich, 1977), p. 406 (January 1779).

13. Marx, *Capital* 1:38.

14. Ibid., p. 103.

15. Ibid., p. 106.

16. Ibid., p. 72.

17. Ibid., p. 71.

18. Ibid., p. 13.

19. Gottfried Keller, *Der grüne Heinrich* (first version) (Frankfurt, 1978), p. 100.

20. Ibid.

21. Compare Aaron Gurewitsch, *Das Weltbild der mittelalterlichen Menschen* (Munich, 1980), p. 283.

22. Keller, *Der grüne Heinrich*, p. 103.

23. Ibid., pp. 104, 105.

24. Ibid., p. 110.

25. Adolf Muschg, *Gottfried Keller* (Frankfurt, 1980), p. 98.

26. Keller, *Der grüne Heinrich*, p. 120.

27. Marx, *Capital* 1:85.

28. Ibid., p. 87.

29. Ibid., p. 111.

30. Novalis, *Die Christenheit oder Europa*, p. 391.

31. Hans-Burkhard Schlichting, ed., *Die Phantasien des Grandville* (Darmstadt, 1976), p. 2.

32. Charles Baudelaire, "Some French Caricaturists," in Baudelaire, *Selected Writings on Art and Artists*, trans. P. E. Charvet (Cambridge: Cambridge University Press, 1981), p. 226.

33. Quoted in Gérald Schaeffer, "Die Ode an Charles Fourier und die esoterische Überlieferung," in André Breton, *Ode an Charles Fourier* (Berlin, 1982), p. 92.

34. Ralph Waldo Emerson, "Nature," in *Selected Writings of Emerson*, ed. Donald McQuade (New York: Modern Library, 1981), pp. 3–42.

35. Charles Baudelaire, "The Poem of Hashish," in *My Heart Laid Bare and Other Prose Writings*, trans. Norman Cameron, ed. with an introduction by Peter Quennell (London: Soho Book Co., 1986), p. 110.

36. Walter Benjamin, "On Some Motifs in Baudelaire," in *Illuminations*, ed. Hannah Arendt, trans. Harry Zohn (New York: Schocken, 1969), p. 182. Compare Susanne Ledanff, *Die Augenblicksmetapher* (Munich and Vienna, 1981), p. 123, for a discussion of the poetics of the correspondences.

37. Benjamin, "On Some Motifs in Baudelaire," p. 182.

38. Ibid., p. 181.

39. W. E. Richarz, "Über Henry David Thoreau," in *Über die Pflicht zum Ungehorsam gegen den Staat* (Zurich, 1973), p. 71.

40. Quoted in Benjamin, *Das Passagen-Werk*, p. 237.

41. Walter Benjamin, "Paris—The Capital of the Nineteenth Century," in *Charles Baudelaire: A Lyric Poet in the Era of High Capitalism*, trans. Harry Zohn (London: Verso, 1983), p. 166.

CHAPTER 4. ON THE PHYSIOGNOMY OF THE WORLD OF THE COMMODITY AND THE MACHINE

1. Honoré de Balzac, "Traité de la vie élégante," in *La comédie humaine*, vol. 12 (Paris: Gallimard, 1981), p. 212.

2. Marx, *Capital* 1:422.

3. Ibid., p. 419.

4. Samuel Butler, *Erewhon* (New York: Lancer Books, 1968), p. 268.

5. Ibid., pp. 104, 269–271.

6. Ibid.

7. Ernst Adolf Willkomm, *Weisse Sclaven; oder, Die Leiden des Volkes* (1845). The passage in question is reproduced in *Industrie und deutsche Literatur*, ed. Keith Bullivant and Hugh Ridley (Munich, 1976), pp. 115 ff.

8. Charles Dickens, *Hard Times* (London: Penguin, 1985), p. 65. Compare Marx, *Capital* 1:381.

9. Dickens, *Hard Times*, p. 102.

10. Honoré de Balzac, "Gaudissart II," in *The Works of Honoré de Balzac*, intro. George Saintsbury (Freeport, N.Y.: Books for Libraries Press, 1971), 17:1–10. The following quotations, unless otherwise indicated, are taken from this text.

11. E. T. A. Hoffmann, "Das Vetters Eckfenster," in *Späte Werke*, p. 611.

12. Ludwig Börne, *Lebens-Essenz: Schilderungen aus Paris, 1822–24*, in *Börnes Werke*, vol. 1 (Berlin and Weimar, 1976), p. 221.

13. Edgar Allen Poe, "The Man of the Crowd," in *Complete Stories and Poems of Edgar Allen Poe* (Garden City, N.Y.: Doubleday, 1966), p. 220.

14. Klaus Strohmeyer, *Warenhäuser* (Berlin, 1980), p. 181.

15. Giedion, *Mechanization Takes Command*, p. 3.

16. Karl Marx, *A Contribution to the Critique of Political Economy*, trans. S. W. Ryazanskaya, ed. Maurice Dobb (New York: International Publishers, 1970), p. 130.

17. Marx, *Capital* 1:153.

18. Ibid.

19. Ibid., p. 133.

20. Ibid., p. 592.

21. Ibid., p. 589.

22. Friedrich Nietzsche, *Daybreak: Thoughts on the Prejudices of Morality*, trans. R. J. Hollingdale (Cambridge: Cambridge University Press, 1982), p. 106 (no. 175).

23. Nietzsche, *Werke* 3:515.

24. Ibid., p. 514.

25. Ibid., p. 444.

26. Gustav René Hocke, *Die Welt als Labyrinth* (Hamburg, 1973), pp. 42, 151.

27. *The Characters of Jean de la Bruyère*, trans. Henri van Laun (London: George Routledge, 1929), pp. 380–381.

28. Honoré de Balzac, "The Wild Ass's Skin," in *Works of Honoré de Balzac* 1:14.

29. Ibid., p. 15.

30. Ibid., p. 16.

31. Ibid., p. 18.

32. Ibid., p. 21.

33. Marx, *Contribution to the Critique of Political Economy*, p. 129.

34. Jacques Derrida, *Of Grammatology*, trans. Gayatri Chakravorty Spivak (Baltimore: Johns Hopkins University Press, 1974), p. 41.

35. Honoré de Balzac, "Gobseck," in *Works of Honoré de Balzac* 6:60.

36. Nikolai Gogol, *Dead Souls*, trans. David Magarshack (Harmondsworth: Penguin, 1961), pt. 1, chap. 6.

37. Ibid., p. 126.

38. Ibid.

39. Theodor W. Adorno, "Reading Balzac," in *Notes to Literature*, ed. Rolf Tiedemann, trans. Shierry Weber Nicholsen (New York: Columbia University Press, 1991), pp. 121–136. Compare Honoré de Balzac, *Cousin Pons*, trans. Norman Cameron (London: Hamish Hamilton, 1950), p. 8.

40. Balzac, *Cousin Pons*, p. 10.

41. Ibid.

42. Charles Baudelaire, "The Salon of 1846," in *Art in Paris 1845–*

1862: Salons and Other Exhibitions Reviewed by Charles Baudelaire, trans. and ed. Jonathan Mayne (Oxford: Phaidon, 1965), p. 68.

43. Benjamin, *Das Passagen-Werk*, p. 279.

44. Benjamin, *Gesammelte Schriften*, vol. 3 (Frankfurt: Suhrkamp, 1981), p. 216.

CHAPTER 5.   CIRCULATION AS A

WAY OF LIFE

1. Thomas Hobbes, *Leviathan*, ed. C. B. Macpherson (Harmondsworth: Penguin, 1976), p. 261.

2. Marx, *Capital* 1:130.

3. The concept of a "way of life" (*Lebensform*) is discussed in Arno Borst, *Lebensformen im Mittelalter* (Frankfurt and Berlin, 1973), pp. 14 ff. On the history of movement, see Giedion, *Mechanization Takes Command*, p. 14.

4. Balzac, "The Girl with the Golden Eyes," in *History of the Thirteen*, trans. and intro. Herbert J. Hunt (Harmondsworth: Penguin, 1974), p. 309.

5. Ibid., p. 310.

6. Ibid.

7. Marx, *Capital* 1:85.

8. Balzac, "The Girl with the Golden Eyes," p. 315.

9. Marx, *Capital* 1:67.

10. Balzac, "The Girl with the Golden Eyes," p. 318.

11. Ibid., p. 323.

12. Giedion, *Space, Time and Architecture*, p. 739.

13. Victor Hugo, *Ninety-Three*, pt. 2, bk. 3, chap. 3, in *Works of Victor Hugo* (London and New York: The Chesterfield Society, 1900), 7:145.

14. *The Goncourt Journals 1851–1870*, ed. and trans. Lewis Galantière (New York: Doubleday, 1937), p. 93.

15. Giedion, *Space, Time and Architecture*, p. 740.

16. Ibid., p. 762.

17. Poe, "Man of the Crowd," p. 216.

18. Franz Kafka, "The Judgment," in *The Penal Colony*, trans. Willa and Edwin Muir (New York: Schocken, 1948), p. 63.

19. Walter Benjamin, "The Flâneur," in *Charles Baudelaire: A Lyric Poet in the Era of High Capitalism*, p. 45.

20. Joseph von Eichendorff, *Erlebtes: Autobiographische Schriften* (Leipzig, 1967), p. 5.

21. Paul Verlaine, "La bonne chanson," VII, in *Œuvres complètes de Paul Verlaine*, vol. 1 (Paris: Albert Messein, 1925), p. 117.

22. Charles Baudelaire, "Crowds," trans. Arthur Symons, in *Baudelaire, Rimbaud, Verlaine: Selected Verse and Prose Poems*, ed. Joseph M. Bernstein (New York: Citadel Press, 1947), p. 106.

23. Ibid.

24. Ibid.

25. Walter Benjamin, "Modernism," in *Charles Baudelaire: A Lyric Poet in the Era of High Capitalism*, p. 69.

26. Baudelaire, "Rockets," in *My Heart Laid Bare*, p. 169.

27. Ibid., p. 167.

28. Baudelaire, "The Poem of Hashish," p. 84.

29. Baudelaire, "Rockets," p. 155.

30. Charles Baudelaire, "Jewels," trans. David Paul, in *The Flowers of Evil*, ed. Marthiel and Jackson Mathews, rev. ed. (New York: New Directions, 1955), pp. 254 (original), 26–27.

31. Baudelaire, "The Cat," trans. Doreen Bell, and "The Dancing Serpent," trans. Barbara Gibbs, in *Flowers of Evil*, pp. 44, 36–37.

32. Baudelaire, "The Cat."

33. Baudelaire, "Spleen," in *Flowers of Evil*, p. 91.

34. Benjamin, *Das Passagen-Werk*, p. 562. Compare Benjamin, "The Flâneur," pp. 54–55.

35. Benjamin, *Das Passagen-Werk*, p. 562.

36. Letter to Louise Colet, December 23, 1853, in *The Letters of Gustave Flaubert 1830–1857*, selected, edited, and translated by Francis Steegmuller (Cambridge: Harvard University Press, 1979), p. 203.

37. Benjamin, *Das Passagen-Werk*, p. 867.

38. Ibid., pp. 966, 559.

39. *Metaphysica*, in *The Basic Works of Aristotle*, ed. and intro. Richard McKeon (New York: Random House, 1941), A:981, p. 689.

40. Benjamin, "On Some Motifs in Baudelaire," p. 176.

41. Ibid., p. 163.

42. F. Schleiermacher, *Über die Religion*, quoted in Gadamer, *Truth and Method*, p. 62.

43. Karl Heinz Bohrer, *Plötzlichkeit: Zum Augenblick des ästhetischen Scheins* (Frankfurt: Suhrkamp, 1981), p. 186.

44. Charles Baudelaire, "The Painter of Modern Life," in *The Painter of Modern Life and Other Essays*, trans. and ed. Jonathan Mayne (New York: Da Capo, 1986), p. 3.

45. Ibid., p. 5.

46. Ibid., p. 20.

47. Ibid., p. 8.

48. Ibid., p. 9.

49. Ibid.; Marx, *Capital* 1:152.

50. Baudelaire, "The Painter," p. 12.

51. Ibid., p. 16.

52. Benjamin, *Das Passagen-Werk*, p. 188.

53. Baudelaire, "The Swan," trans. Anthony Hecht, in *Flowers of Evil*, pp. 329–330 (original), 110.

54. "The Voyage," trans. Robert Lowell, in *Flowers of Evil*. For the concept of the new, see Theodor Adorno, *Minima Moralia*, trans. E. F. N. Jephcott (London: NLB, 1974), pp. 235–238.

CHAPTER 6.   IMPRESSIONISM

1. Paul Valéry, "The Triumph of Manet," in *The Collected Works of Paul Valéry*, ed. Jackson Mathews, vol. 12, *Degas, Manet, Morisot*, trans. David Paul, Bollingen Series, vol. 45/12 (New York: Pantheon Books, 1960), pp. 107–108.

2. Baudelaire, "The Ragpicker's Wine," trans. C. F. MacIntyre, in *Flowers of Evil*, p. 136, 354.

3. Theodore Reff, *Manet and Modern Paris* (Washington: National Gallery of Art, 1982), p. 182.

4. Ibid.

5. Compare Reff, *Manet and Modern Paris*, pp. 172 ff.

6. Erich Schild, *Zwischen Glaspalast und Palais des Illusions* (Braunschweig: Ullstein, 1983), p. 89.

7. Ernst Gombrich, *Aby Warburg: An Intellectual Biography* (Chicago: University of Chicago Press, 1986), p. 273.

8. John Rewald, *The History of Impressionism* (New York: Museum of Modern Art, 1961), p. 85.

9. Ibid.

10. Ibid., p. 86.

11. Gombrich, *Warburg*, p. 274.

12. Charles Baudelaire, "The Salon of 1846," in Baudelaire, *Selected Writings on Art and Artists*, p. 105.

13. Max von Boehm, *Die Mode 1843–1878* (Munich, 1908), p. 110.

14. Gombrich, *Warburg*, p. 275.

15. Friedrich Theodor Vischer, "Vernünftige Gedanken über die jetzige Mode," in *Kritische Gänge*, N.F., Heft 3 (Stuttgart: Cotta, 1861), p. 117; quoted in Benjamin, "Modernism," p. 77.

16. Compare Reff, *Manet and Modern Paris*, p. 24.

17. Charles Baudelaire, "Painters and Etchers," in *Art in Paris Salons*, p. 218.

18. Baudelaire, "The Widows," trans. Arthur Symons, in *Baudelaire, Rimbaud, Verlaine*, p. 111.

19. Compare Reff, *Manet and Modern Paris*, p. 236.

20. Baudelaire, "The Swan," p. 329 (original), 109.

21. *Rue Montorgueil*. Compare Reff, *Manet and Modern Paris*, p. 244 and illustration, p. 245.

22. Quoted in Rewald, *History of Impressionism*, p. 218.

23. Giedion, *Space, Time and Architecture*, p. 769.

24. Baudelaire, "The Eyes of the Poor," trans. Arthur Symons, in *Baudelaire, Rimbaud, Verlaine*, p. 132.

25. Compare Reff, *Manet and Modern Paris*, p. 72.

26. Valéry, *Degas, Manet, Morisot*, p. 11.

27. Ibid., p. 56.

28. *Lettres de Degas*, ed. M. Guerin (Paris, 1931), p. 52; quoted in Giorgio Giacomazzi, "Versuch über die Visualität in der Moderne: Benjamin, Degas und der Impressionismus," in *Affäre Stadt*, ed. Rudi Thiessen, Notizbuch, 7 (Berlin and Vienna: Medusa-Verlagsgesellschaft, 1982), p. 164.

29. Georg Simmel, "Sociology of the Senses: Visual Interaction," in *Introduction to the Science of Sociology*, ed. Robert E. Park and Ernest W. Burgess (Chicago: University of Chicago Press, 1921), p. 360.

30. Max Liebermann, *Die Phantasie in der Malerei* (Frankfurt, 1978), p. 73.

31. Antoine Terrasse, *Edgar Degas: Werkverzeichnis*, vol. 1 (Frankfurt, Berlin, Vienna: Ullstein, 1981), p. 8.

32. Quoted in Rewald, *History of Impressionism*, p. 60.

33. Terrasse, *Degas*, p. 3.

34. Aaron Scharf, *Art and Photography* (Harmondsworth: Penguin, 1974), pp. 181–209.

35. Liebermann, *Phantasie*, p. 72.

36. Baudelaire, "The Painter," p. 12.

37. Ibid., p. 16.

38. Quoted in Rewald, *History of Impressionism*, p. 380.

39. Valéry, *Degas, Manet, Morisot*, p. 39.

40. Baudelaire, "The Painter," p. 17.

41. Valéry, *Degas, Manet, Morisot*, p. 38.

42. Giedion, *Space, Time and Architecture*, p. 273.

43. Giedion, *Mechanization Takes Command*, p. 17.

44. Ibid., p. 20.

45. Ibid., p. 24.

46. Paul Valéry, *Briefe* (Wiesbaden, 1954), p. 171 (letter to Louis Séchan, August 1930).

47. Valéry, *Degas, Manet, Morisot*, p. 17.

48. Julius Meier-Graefe, *Manet und sein Kreis* (Berlin, 1902), p. 58.

49. Werner Haftmann, *Malerei im 20. Jahrhundert* (Munich, 1976), p. 41.

50. Rewald, *History of Impressionism*, p. 431.

51. Ibid., p. 316.

52. Reff, *Manet and Modern Paris*, p. 131.

53. Ibid., p. 64.

54. Ernst Mach, *The Analysis of Sensations*, trans. C. M. Williams (New York: Dover, 1959), pp. 6–7.

55. Quoted in Rewald, *History of Impressionism*, pp. 562–563.

56. Marcel Proust, *Swann's Way*, trans. C. K. Scott Moncrieff (New York: Vintage, 1970), p. 130. Compare Proust's letter to Geneviève Straus of December 28, 1907, in *Letters of Marcel Proust*, ed. and trans. Mina Curtis (New York: Random House, 1949), pp. 178–179.

57. Quoted in Rewald, *History of Impressionism*, p. 373.

58. Quoted in Wolfgang Schivelbusch, *Geschichte der Eisenbahnreise* (Frankfurt, Berlin, Vienna, 1979), p. 51. Translator's note: The English translation of this book (published as *The Railway Journey*) omits the quotation from Strindberg cited by Schivelbusch in the German edition; hence the reference here to the German, rather than the English, edition of the book.

59. Marcel Proust, *Within a Budding Grove*, trans. C. K. Scott Moncrieff (New York: Vintage, 1970), p. 77.

60. G. Chr. Lichtenberg, *Schriften und Briefe*, ed. Franz H. Mautner (Frankfurt, 1983), 4.1:154.

61. Hoffmann, *Späte Werke*, p. 599.

62. Benjamin, "On Some Motifs in Baudelaire," p. 197.

63. Quoted in Karl Riha, *Die Beschreibung der "Großen Stadt"* (Bad Homburg, Berlin, Zurich, 1970), p. 46.

64. Nikolai Gogol, "The Fair at Sorochintsi," in *Evenings Near the Village of Dikanka*, trans. Ovid Gorchakov (New York: Frederick Ungar Publishing Co., n.d.), p. 22.

65. Ibid., p. 18.

66. Quoted in Werner Hoffmann, *The Earthly Paradise: Art in the Nineteenth Century*, trans. Brian Battershaw (New York: George Braziller, 1961), p. 300.

67. Compare Elias Canetti, *Crowds and Power*, trans. Carol Stewart (New York: Seabury, 1978), p. 86.

68. Hoffmann, *Späte Werke*, p. 599.

69. Poe, "Man of the Crowd," p. 219.

70. Gogol, "The Fair at Sorochintsi," p. 22.

71. Günter Metken, in *Die Zeit*, May 27, 1983.

72. Ibid.

73. Arnold Hauser, *The Social History of Art*, trans. Stanley Godman, vol. 4 (New York: Vintage, 1958), p. 170.

74. Rewald, *History of Impressionism*, p. 514.

75. Theodor Adorno, *Prisms*, trans. Samuel and Shierry Weber (Cambridge, Mass.: MIT Press, 1981), p. 191.

76. Valéry, *Degas, Manet, Morisot*, p. 25.

77. Quoted in Rewald, *History of Impressionism*, pp. 149–150.

78. Ibid., p. 338.

79. Ibid.

80. Quoted ibid., p. 458.

81. Adorno, *Prisms*, p. 192.

82. Mach, *Analysis of Sensations*, pp. 23–24.

83. Ibid., pp. 8–9.

84. Max Raphael, *Von Monet zu Picasso* (Frankfurt and Paris, 1983), p. 91. Compare Theodor Adorno, *Aesthetic Theory*, trans. C. Leenhardt (London and New York: Routledge, 1984), p. 222.

CHAPTER 7.

COMMODITIES AND

THE EROTIC

1. Emile Zola, *The Ladies' Paradise* (Berkeley: University of California Press, 1992), pp. 205, 219.

2. Lothar Bucher, *Kulturhistorische Skizze aus der Industrieausstellung aller Völker* (Frankfurt, 1851), p. 174, quoted in Giedion, *Space, Time and Architecture*, p. 254.

3. Zola, *Ladies' Paradise*, p. 220.

4. Ibid., pp. 4, 214–215.

5. Ibid., p. 220.

6. Ibid., p. 205.

7. Giedion, *Space, Time and Architecture*, pp. 238–241.

8. Ibid.

9. Zola, *Ladies' Paradise*, p. 23.

10. Ibid., pp. 24, 376.

11. Compare Fritz Vögtle, *Edison* (Reinbek, 1982), p. 47.

12. Zola, *Ladies' Paradise*, p. 376.

13. Benjamin, *Das Passagen-Werk*, p. 236.

14. Villiers de L'Isle-Adam, "Celestial Publicity," in *Cruel Tales*, trans. Robert Baldick (London: Oxford University Press, 1963), p. 41.

15. Ibid., 43.

16. Zola, *Ladies' Paradise*, p. 63.

17. Ibid., p. 4.

18. Ibid., pp. 3, 214, 220.

19. Ibid., pp. 314, 378.

20. Ibid., p. 25.

21. Ibid., p. 3.

22. Ibid., p. 4.

23. Benjamin, *Das Passagen-Werk*, p. 267.

24. Zola, *Ladies' Paradise*, pp. 89, 212.

25. Ibid., quotation from p. 224; cf. p. 372.

26. Ibid., p. 41.

27. Ibid., p. 232.

28. Ibid., p. 63.

29. Ibid., p. 13.

30. Ibid., p. 64.

31. Ibid., pp. 206, 13.

32. Ibid., p. 206.

33. Canetti, *Crowds and Power*, p. 15.

34. Ibid., p. 17.

35. Alfred Jarry, *The Supermale*, trans. Barbara Wright (London: Jonathan Cape, 1968), p. 46.

36. Marx, *Capital* 1:383.

37. *Die nützlichen Künste*, ed. Buddensieg and Rogge, p. 374.

38. J. K. Huysmans, *Là-bas (Down There)*, trans. Keene Wallace [i.e., Wallis] (New York: Dover, 1972), p. 183.

39. C. S. Ford and F. A. Beach, *Formen der Sexualität* (Hamburg, 1968), p. 28. For the notion of "de-organization," see Bloch, *Principle of Hope* 2:661.

40. J. K. Huysmans, *Against Nature*, trans. Robert Baldick (Harmondsworth: Penguin, 1959), p. 37.

41. Günter Metken, in *Les machines célibataires* (Paris, 1976), p. 52.

42. Gerhart Hauptmann, *Bahnwärter Thiel* (Stuttgart, 1970), p. 19.

43. Ibid., p. 28.

44. Ibid., p. 16.

45. Ibid., pp. 14, 19.

46. Emile Zola, *La bête humaine*, trans. Leonard Tancock (Harmondsworth: Penguin, 1977), p. 68.

47. Ibid., p. 190.

48. Sigmund Freud, *Three Essays on the Theory of Sexuality*, trans. and rev. James Strachey (New York: Basic Books, 1962), p. 68. Compare Paul Virilio, *Fahren, fahren, fahren . . .* (Berlin: Merve, 1978), p. 36.

49. Metken, in *Les machines célibataires*, p. 58.

50. Kurt Grobecker, *Gleich Vogeln durch die Luft zu schweben* (Hamburg, 1980), p. 30. Compare illustration on p. 38 and *Les machines célibataires*, pp. 1, 107.

51. Compare Helmuth Poll, "Ausflug nach Utopia: Der Einzelne und sein Fahrrad," *Aufriss: Zeitschrift des Centrum Industriekultur Nürnberg* 1, no. 2 (1982): 58.

52. Jarry, *The Supermale*, p. 49.

53. Illustration in *Les machines célibataires*, p. 58.

54. Illustration in ibid., p. 58, and Grobecker, *Gleich Vogeln*, pp. 24, 28.

55. Illustration in *Les machines célibataires*, pp. 133, 135, and 137.

56. Illustrations in ibid., pp. 123, 179. Compare Jean Tinguely, "*Méta*," text by K. G. Pontus Hultén (Berlin, Frankfurt, Vienna: Propyläen-Verlag, 1972), p. 153.

57. *Les machines célibataires*, p. 197.

58. Arnold Gehlen, *Man in the Age of Technology*, trans. Peter Lipscomb (New York: Columbia University Press, 1980), pp. 14–15.

CHAPTER 8. THE DECAY OF THE WORLD OF THINGS AND ITS RESTORATION IN ART

1. Johann Wolfgang von Goethe, *Wilhelm Meister's Journeyman Years; or, The Renunciants*, trans. Krishna Winston, ed. Jane K. Brown (New York: Suhrkamp, 1989), p. 144.

2. Rainer Maria Rilke, *Letters on Cézanne*, trans. Joel Agee (New York: Fromm, 1985), p. 18.

3. Quoted in Werner Haftmann, *Der Mensch und seine Bilder* (Cologne, 1980), p. 29.

4. Martin Heidegger, "The Origin of the Work of Art," in *Poetry, Language, Thought*, trans. Albert Hofstadter (New York: Harper and Row, 1965), p. 33.

5. Ibid., p. 29.

6. Ibid., p. 33.

7. Ibid.

8. Ibid., p. 35.

9. Ibid., p. 34.

10. Ibid., p. 37.

11. Musil, *The Man without Qualities* 3:101; 2:256.

12. Letter 520 to Theo van Gogh, in Vincent van Gogh, *Complete Letters* (Greenwich, Conn.: New York Graphic Society, [1958]), 3:6.

13. Letter 418 to Theo van Gogh, ibid. 2:401.

14. Letter 528 to Theo van Gogh, ibid. 3:21.

15. Letter 130 to Theo van Gogh, ibid. 1:189. Compare Cézanne: "Whoever wishes to create an artistic work must follow Bacon, who defined the artist as *homo additus naturae*." Quoted in Walter Hess, *Dokumente zum Verständnis der modernen Malerei* (Hamburg, 1980), p. 17.

16. Hess, *Dokumente*, p. 27.

17. Letter 531 to Theo van Gogh, in van Gogh, *Complete Letters* 3:25.

18. Odilon Redon, *To Myself: Notes on Life, Art and Artists*, trans. Mira Jacob and Jeanne L. Wasserman (New York: George Braziller, 1986), p. 135.

19. Stéphane Mallarmé, *Mallarmé: Selected Prose Poems, Essays, and Letters*, trans. Bradford Cook (Baltimore: Johns Hopkins University Press, 1956), p. 21.

20. Huysmans, *Against Nature*, p. 73.

21. Ibid., pp. 14–15.

22. Huysmans, *Against Nature*, pp. 67–68. Illustration appears in Hans H. Hofstätter, *Moreau* (Cologne, 1978), illustration 36.

23. Quoted in Hofstätter, *Moreau*, p. 163.

24. Roland Barthes, *Mythologies*, trans. Annette Lavers (New York: Hill and Wang, 1972), p. 85.

25. Hofstätter, *Moreau*, p. 163.

26. Ibid., p. 170.

CHAPTER 9. THE *INTERIEUR*, OR

THINGS IN THE

EVERYDAY LIFE

OF THE BOURGEOISIE

1. Friedrich Nietzsche, *Human, All Too Human*, trans. R. J. Hollingdale, introd. Erich Heller (Cambridge: Cambridge University Press, 1986), p. 381.

2. Norbert Elias, *The Court Society*, trans. Edmund Jephcott (New York: Pantheon, 1984), p. 51.

3. Jürgen Habermas, *The Structural Transformation of the Public Sphere*, trans. Thomas Burger with the assistance of Frederick Lawrence (Cambridge, Mass.: MIT Press, 1989), p. 44.

4. W. H. Riehl, *Die Familie*, 10th ed. (Stuttgart, 1889), pp. 174, 179; quoted in Habermas, *The Structural Transformation of the Public Sphere*.

5. Giedion, *Mechanization Takes Command*, p. 364.

6. Ibid., p. 372.

7. Ibid., pp. 334, 371.

8. Ibid., pp. 364–388.

9. Ibid.

10. Balzac, "The Girl with the Golden Eyes," p. 364.

11. Giedion, *Mechanization Takes Command*, p. 346.

12. Gottfried Semper, *Der Stil in den technischen und tektonischen Künsten*, 2d ed., vol. 1 (Munich: F. Bruckmann, 1878), p. 105.

13. Ibid., p. 107.

14. Nikolaus Pevsner, *Pioneers of Modern Design: From William Morris to Walter Gropius* (Harmondsworth: Penguin, 1960), p. 41.

15. Compare Edgar Allan Poe, "The Philosophy of Furniture," in *The Unabridged Edgar Allan Poe* (Philadelphia: Running Press, 1983), p. 643.

16. Giedion, *Mechanization Takes Command*, p. 320.

17. Guy de Maupassant, *Mont Oriol; or, A Romance of Auvergne*, in *The Life Work of Henry René Guy de Maupassant*, pref. by Paul Bourget, intro. Robert Arnot (New York and London: M. Walter Dunne, 1903), p. 184.

18. Giedion, *Mechanization Takes Command*, p. 672.

19. Cornelius Gurlitt, *Im Bürgerhause* (Dresden, 1888), p. 166; quoted

in Dolf Sternberger, *Panorama of the Nineteenth Century*, trans. Joachim Neugroschel (New York: Urizen, 1977), p. 145.

20. Robert Musil, *Der Mann ohne Eigenschaften* (Aus dem Nachlaβ) (Reinbek: Rowohlt, 1978), pp. 1049, 1069.

21. Semper, *Der Stil*, p. 160.

22. Georg Hirth, *Das deutsche Zimmer der Renaissance* (Munich, 1880); quoted in Sternberger, *Panorama*, pp. 139–140.

23. Hoffmann R. Hays, *Mythos Frau* (Frankfurt, 1978), p. 290.

24. Giedion, *Mechanization Takes Command*, p. 349.

25. Egon Friedell, *A Cultural History of the Modern Age*, trans. Charles Francis Atkinson (New York: Knopf, 1953–1954), 3:300.

26. Sternberger, *Panorama*, p. 140.

27. Quoted in Giedion, *Mechanization Takes Command*, p. 363.

28. Hirth, *Das deutsche Zimmer der Renaissance*, p. 2; quoted in Sternberger, *Panorama*, p. 155.

29. Hermann Glaser, *Maschinenwelt und Alltagsleben* (Frankfurt, 1981), p. 78.

30. Sedlmayr, *Verlust der Mitte*, p. 32.

31. Letter from Ch. A. H. Clodius to Elisa von der Recke (December 2, 1811), in *Deutsche Menschen*, ed. Walter Benjamin, in Benjamin, *Gesammelte Schriften*, vol. 4 (Frankfurt: Suhrkamp, 1981), p. 183.

32. Adalbert Stifter, *Der Nachsommer* (Frankfurt, 1982), p. 9.

33. Ibid., p. 10.

34. Ibid., p. 11. Compare Jean-Paul Sartre, *The Words*, trans. Bernard Frechtman (Greenwich, Conn.: Fawcett, 1964), p. 55: "House and field reflect back to the young heir a stable image of himself. He touches himself on *his* gravel, on the diamond-shaped panes of *his* veranda, and makes of their inertia the deathless substance of his soul. . . . *I was not* substantial or permanent, *I was not* the future continuer of my father's work. . . . In short, I had no soul."

35. Stifter, *Nachsommer*, p. 13.

36. Ibid., p. 15.

37. Simmel, *Philosophy of Money*, p. 460.

38. Ibid.

39. Friedrich Theodor Vischer, *Auch Einer* (Stuttgart and Leipzig, 1910), p. 17.

40. Benjamin, *Charles Baudelaire*, p. 46.

41. Ibid., p. 168.

42. Huysmans, *Against Nature*, pp. 30–31.

43. Ibid., p. 26.

44. Ibid., pp. 33, 35.

45. Ibid., pp. 36, 38.

46. Ibid., p. 118.

47. Ibid., p. 128.

48. Anton Chekhov, "The Man in a Case," in *Stories of Russian Life*, trans. Marian Fell (New York: Charles Scribner's Sons, 1914), pp. 77–78.

49. Adolf Behne, *Neues Wohnen, neues Bauen* (Leipzig, 1927), pp. 59–65. Compare illustration on p. 65. I owe this reference to Behne to Benjamin's *Passagen-Werk*.

50. Simmel, *Philosophy of Money*, p. 508.

51. Behne, *Neues Wohnen*, pp. 43–47.

52. Compare Adorno, *Minima Moralia*, p. 238.

53. Semper, *Der Stil*, p. 213.

54. Benjamin, *Das Passagen-Werk*, p. 286.

55. Thomas Mann, "Das Eisenbahnunglück," in *Sämtliche Erzählungen* (Frankfurt, 1979), pp. 331, 333, 337.

CHAPTER 10.   THE PRODUCTION OF

"HOMOGENEOUS AND

EMPTY TIME"

1. Jorge Luis Borges, "Swedenborg's Angel," in *The Book of Imaginary Beings,* rev., enl., and trans. Norman Thomas di Giovanni (Harmondsworth: Penguin Books, 1974), p. 137.

2. Musil, *Man without Qualities* 1:207.

3. Heinrich Heine, *Sämtliche Schriften*, ed. Klaus Briegleb, Reihe Hanser, 220 (Munich and Vienna: Hanser, 1976), 11:649.

4. Kazimierz Piesowicz, "Lebensrhythmus und Zeitrechnung in der vorindustriellen und in der industriellen Gesellschaft," *Geschichte in Wissenschaft und Unterricht* 8 (1980): 478.

5. Ibid., p. 466.

6. Lewis Mumford, *The Myth of the Machine* (New York: Harcourt, Brace and World, 1966), p. 286.

7. Jacques Le Goff, "Zeit der Kirche und Zeit des Händlers im Mittelalter," in *Schrift und Materie der Geschichte*, ed. M. Bloch, F. Braudel, L. Febvre (Frankfurt, 1977), p. 393.

8. William of Auxerre, *Summa Aurea*, II, 21, fol. 225v; quoted in Le Goff, "Zeit der Kirche," p. 410.

9. Franklin, "Advice to a Young Tradesman," p. 48.

10. Mumford, *Myth of the Machine*, p. 286.

11. Marx, *Capital* 1:403; see also pp. 422–423.

12. Ibid., p. 408.

13. Ibid., pp. 552–553.

14. Règlement de la fabrique de Saint-Maur, Art. 1, B.N. MS Coll. Delamare, Manufactures III; quoted in Michel Foucault, *Discipline and Punish*, trans. Alan Sheridan (New York: Pantheon, 1977), p. 149.

15. Projet de règlement pour la fabrique d'Amboise, Art. 4; quoted in Foucault, *Discipline and Punish*, p. 150.

16. J. A. de Guibert, *Essai général de tactique*, vol. 1 (1772); quoted in Foucault, *Discipline and Punish,*, p. 155.

17. Giedion, *Mechanization Takes Command*, p. 115.

18. Heine, *Sämtliche Schriften* 9:448. Compare Schivelbusch, *Railway Journey*, pp. 41–50.

19. Gustav Schmoller, "Über den Einfluß der heutigen Verkehrsmittel," *Preussische Jahrbücher*, ed. H. von Treitschke and W. Wehrenpfennig, 31, no. 4 (1873): 422.

20. Ibid., p. 423.

21. Ibid.

22. Piesowicz, "Lebensrhythmus," p. 479; Schivelbusch, *Railway Journey*, p. 50; R. R. Rosenberg, *Geschichte der Eisenbahn* (Künzelsau, 1977), p. 493.

23. Charles Dickens (1848), quoted in *Die Welt der Bahnhöfe* (exhibition catalog), Centre Pompidou, Paris, and Staatliche Kunsthalle, Berlin, 1980 (Berlin: Elefanten-Press-Verlag, 1980), p. 68.

24. Schmoller, "Über den Einfluß," p. 424.

25. Ibid., p. 426.

26. Ibid.

27. Ibid., p. 427.

28. Ibid., p. 424.

29. Ibid., p. 426.

30. Foucault, *Discipline and Punish*, p. 161.

31. Compare Walter Benjamin, "Theses on the Philosophy of History," in *Illuminations*, pp. 253–264.

32. Compare Thorstein Veblen, *Theory of the Leisure Class* (New York: Funk and Wagnalls, n.d.), pp. 33–35.

33. Gadamer, *Truth and Method*, p. 110; Benjamin, "On Some Motifs in Baudelaire," pp. 112–113.

CHAPTER 11. NERVES AND

ELECTRICITY

1. Johann Wolfgang von Goethe, *Goethes Sämtliche Werke: Jubiläums-Ausgabe*, vol. 40 (Stuttgart and Berlin: Cotta, 1907), p. 333.

2. Novalis, *Enzyklopädie, II, Mathematik und Naturwissenschaften*, in Novalis, *Werke und Briefe*, ed. A. Kelletat (Munich: Winkler-Verlag, 1968), p. 483, no. 378.

3. Ricarda Huch, *Die Romantik* (Tübingen, 1979), p. 596.

4. Ibid., p. 607.

5. Johann Wolfgang von Goethe, Letter to J. F. Krafft of December 11, 1778, in *Briefe*, ed. Karl Robert Mandelkow and Bodo Morawe, vol. 1 (Hamburg: Wegner, n.d.), p. 256.

6. Mary Shelley, *Frankenstein; or, The Modern Prometheus* (Berkeley, Los Angeles, London: University of California Press, 1984), p. 51.

7. Marx, *Economic and Philosophic Manuscripts of 1844*, p. 167.

8. For the prehistory, compare M. Heidelberger and S. Thiessen, *Natur und Erfahrung* (Hamburg, 1981), pp. 98 and, esp., 108.

9. Will and Ariel Durant, *The Story of Civilization*, vol. 9, *The Age of Voltaire* (New York: Simon and Schuster, 1965), p. 519.

10. Quoted in Friedell, *Cultural History of the Modern Age* 2:183.

11. Franz Blei, *Ungewöhnliche Menschen und Schicksale* (Berlin, 1929), p. 147.

12. E. T. A. Hoffmann, "Der Magnetiseur," in *Fantasiestücke*, p. 214.

13. Ibid.

14. Goethe, *Conversations with Eckermann [1823–1832]*, trans. Oxenford, October 7, 1827, p. 190.

15. G. W. F. Hegel, *Phenomenology of Spirit*, trans. A. V. Miller (New York: Oxford, 1977), p. 153.

16. Kleist, *Werke* 1:310.

17. Compare Bohrer, *Plötzlichkeit*.

18. Balzac, *The Rise and Fall of César Birotteau*, trans. Ellen Marriage (New York: Carroll and Graf, 1989), p. 2.

19. Lewis Carroll, *Through the Looking-Glass, and What Alice Found There* (Berkeley, Los Angeles, London: University of California Press, 1983), p. 28.

20. Count Gustav von Schlabrendorf in Paris on events and people of the time, in Carl Gustav Jochmann, *Reliquien aus seinen nachgelassenen Papieren*, ed. Heinrich Zschokke (Hechingen, 1836), p. 146; quoted in Benjamin, *Das Passagen-Werk*, p. 741.

21. Bloch, *Principle of Hope* 1:434.

22. Hans Christian Andersen, "The Galoshes of Fortune," in *Stories for the Household* (London: G. Routledge; New York: E. P. Dutton [1888?]), p. 72.

23. Heine, *Sämtliche Schriften* 9:533.

24. Johann Wolfgang von Goethe, *Werke*, ed. Erich Trunz, vol. 6 (Munich, 1977), p. 621.

25. Friedrich Schlegel, *Schriften zur Literatur*, ed. Wolfdietrich Rasch (Munich, 1972), pp. 47, 77.

26. Ibid., p. 77.

27. Novalis, *Die Enzyklopädie, III, Medizin, Psychologie*, in Novalis, *Werke und Briefe*, ed. A. Kelletat, p. 493, no. 423.

28. Quoted in Gottfried von Haeseler, "Der Erfinder-Unternehmer Thomas A. Edison," *Aufriss: Zeitschrift des Centrum Industriekultur, Nürnberg* 1, no. 2 (1982): 71.

29. Wolfgang Schivelbusch, *Disenchanted Night*, trans. Angela Davies (Berkeley, Los Angeles, London: University of California Press, 1988), p. 71.

30. Zola, *The Ladies' Paradise*, p. 376.

31. Proust, *Swann's Way*, p. 206.

32. Schivelbusch, *Disenchanted Night*, p. 153.

33. Ibid., p. 55.

34. Bachelard, *La flamme d'une chandelle*, quoted in Schivelbusch, *Disenchanted Night*, p. 178.

35. Wilhelm Hausenstein, *Licht unter dem Horizont: Tagebücher von 1942 bis 1946* (Munich, 1967), p. 273; quoted in Schivelbusch, *Disenchanted Night*, p. 178.

36. Veblen, *Theory of the Leisure Class*, p. 121.

37. Redon, *To Myself*, p. 135.

38. Schivelbusch, *Disenchanted Night*, p. 71.

39. Villiers de L'Isle-Adam, *Tomorrow's Eve*, trans. with an introduction by Robert Martin Adams (Urbana: University of Illinois Press, 1982), p. 194.

40. Jarry, *The Supermale*, p. 117.

41. Maurice Maeterlinck, "Im Automobil," in *Der doppelte Garten* (Jena, 1904), p. 35.

42. *Les machines célibataires*, p. 35.

43. Jarry, *The Supermale*, p. 118.

44. Schivelbusch, *Disenchanted Night*, p. 70.

45. Huysmans, *Là-bas*, p. 99.

46. Anson Rabinbach, "The Age of Exhaustion: Energy and Fatigue in the Late Nineteenth Century" (unpublished manuscript), p. 38; quoted in Schivelbusch, *Disenchanted Night*, p. 71.

47. Baudelaire, "Her Hair," trans. Doreen Bell, in *Flowers of Evil*, pp. 259 (original), 32–33.

48. Dolf Sternberger, *Über Jugendstil* (Frankfurt: Suhrkamp, 1977), p. 37.

49. Eduard von Hartmann, *Philosophie des Unbewußten, Versuch einer Weltanschauung* (Berlin, 1872), p. 63; quoted in Sternberger, *Panorama*, pp. 25–26.

50. Hartmann, *Philosophie*, p. 152; quoted in Sternberger, *Panorama*, p. 192.

51. Hartmann, *Philosophie*, p. 63; quoted in Sternberger, *Panorama*, p. 26.

52. Peter Altenberg, "Was der Tag mir zuträgt" (1901), in *Ausgewählte Werke* (Munich: Hanser, 1979), 1:82.

53. Thomas Mann, *Das Altenbergbuch*, ed. E. Friedell (Leipzig and Vienna, 1922), p. 70.

54. Theodor Fontane, *Der Stechlin* (Zurich, 1983), p. 27.

55. Peter Altenberg, "Neues Altes," in *Ausgewählte Werke* 1:214.

56. Prentice Mulford, *Your Forces and How To Use Them* (1887), quoted in Bloch, *Principle of Hope* 2:681.

57. Maurice Maeterlinck, "Der Ölzweig," quoted in Bloch, *Principle of Hope* 2:681.

58. Georg Simmel, *Fragmente und Aufsätze* (Munich: Drei Masken Verlag, 1923), p. 174.

59. Musil, *The Man without Qualities* 1:124.

60. Ibid. 2:250; 1:217.

61. Novalis, *Werke und Briefe*, p. 457.

62. Thomas Mann, *Confessions of Felix Krull, Confidence Man*, trans. Dever Lindley (Harmondsworth: Penguin, 1958), p. 105.

63. Mach, *Analysis of Sensations*, pp. 6–7.

64. Ibid.

65. Ibid., p. 24.

66. Nietzsche, *Werke* 3:312.

67. Mach, *Analysis of Sensations*, pp. 26–27.

68. Ibid., p. 27.

69. In *Die Wiener Moderne*, ed. G. Wundberg (Stuttgart, 1981), p. 204.

70. Ibid., p. 225.

71. Ibid., p. 257.

72. W. Erb, *Über die wachsende Nervosität unserer Zeit* (1893), quoted in Sigmund Freud, " 'Civilized' Sexual Morality and Modern Nervousness," in *Collected Papers*, authorized translation under the supervision of Joan Riviere, vol. 2 (New York: Basic Books, 1959), p. 78.

73. Marx, *Capital* 1:85.

74. "Neurasthenia," in J. Laplanche and J. B. Pontalis, *The Language of Psychoanalysis*, trans. Donald Nicholson-Smith (New York: Norton, 1973), pp. 265–266.

75. Maupassant, "Mad?" in *The Complete Short Stories of Guy de Maupassant* (Garden City, N.Y.: Hanover House, 1955), pp. 261–262.

76. August Strindberg, *Legende*, in *Inferno-Legende*, trans. Emil Schering (Munich and Leipzig: Georg Müller, 1910), p. 287.

77. Simmel, "Sociology of the Senses," p. 360.

78. Strindberg, *Inferno-Legende*, p. 97.

79. Ibid., p. 180; cf. p. 225.

80. August Strindberg, *Entzweit*, quoted in Karl Jaspers, *Strindberg*

and van Gogh, trans. Oskar Grunow and David Woloshin (Tucson: University of Arizona Press, 1977), p. 49.

81. Strindberg, *Inferno-Legende*, p. 371.

82. August Strindberg, *Berichte*, quoted in Jaspers, *Strindberg and van Gogh*.

83. Strindberg, *Inferno-Legende*, p. 105.

84. Ibid., p. 115; cf. pp. 100 f., 181.

85. Ibid., pp. 107, 377.

<table>
<tr><td>CHAPTER 12. THE CONSTITUTION OF PERCEPTION FROM 1900 TO 1914</td><td>

1. Henri Bergson, *Matter and Memory*, trans. Nancy Margaret Paul and W. Scott Palmer (London: George Allen and Co.; New York: The Macmillan Co., 1911), p. 278.

2. Simmel, *Philosophy of Money*, p. 61.

3. Ibid., p. 55.

4. On the relationship between Mach and Hofmannsthal, see G. Wunberg, *Der frühe Hofmannsthal* (Stuttgart, Berlin, Cologne, Mainz, 1965), p. 30.

5. Hugo von Hofmannsthal, "Balzac," in *Selected Prose*, trans. Mary Hottinger and Tania and James Stern, intro. Hermann Broch (New York: Pantheon, 1952), p. 278.

6. Werner Volke, *Hofmannsthal* (Reinbek: Rowohlt, 1976), p. 108.

7. Simmel, *Philosophy of Money*, p. 78.

8. Ibid., p. 449.

9. Fritz Mauthner, "Wissen und Worte," in *Beiträge zu einer Kritik der Sprache* (Stuttgart: Cotta, 1901–1902), 3:547.

10. Maurice Maeterlinck, "Das Schweigen," in *Der Schatz der Armen* (Leipzig, 1898), p. 7.

11. Simmel, *Philosophy of Money*, p. 80.

12. Hugo von Hofmannsthal, *Der Schwierige*, act 1, scene 8 (Frankfurt, 1976), p. 26.

13. Ibid., act 1, scene 12, p. 33.

14. Hugo von Hofmannsthal, *Ferdinand von Saar, "Schloss Kostinitz"* (1882), in *Reden und Aufsätze* (Leipzig: Insel-Verlag, 1921), p. 480.

15. Hofmannsthal, *Eine Monographie* (1895), in *Rede und Aufsätze*, p. 480.

16. Ibid., p. 479.

17. Hofmannsthal, *Die unvergebliche Tänzerin* (1906), in *Reden und Aufsätze*, p. 499.

18. Hofmannsthal, "Über die Pantomime" (1911), in *Reden und Aufsätze*, p. 505.

19. Bloch, *Principle of Hope* 1:406–409.

</td></tr>
</table>

20. Hofmannsthal, "Die Menschen in Ibsens Dramen" (1892), in *Reden und Aufsätze*, p. 150.

21. Hofmannsthal, "Eleonora Duse" (1892), in *Reden und Aufsätze*, p. 471.

22. Hofmannsthal, "Der Dichter und diese Zeit" (1906), in *Reden und Aufsätze*, p. 67.

23. Ibid.

24. Ibid.

25. Musil, *The Man without Qualities* 1:118.

26. Compare Frisé's documentation in Robert Musil, *Tagebücher*, ed. Adolf Frisé (Reinbek: Rowohlt, 1983), 2:394–401.

27. Musil, *The Man without Qualities* 2:247; compare 1:214.

28. Ibid. 2:104; compare 1:125.

29. Ibid. 2:95.

30. Hofmannsthal, "Ansprache gehalten am Abend des 10. Mai (1902) in Hause des Grafen Karl Lanckoronski," in *Reden und Aufsätze*, p. 22.

31. Ibid., p. 20.

32. Hofmannsthal, "Der Dichter und diese Zeit," p. 70.

33. Robert Musil, "Address at the Memorial Service for Rilke in Berlin," in *Precision and Soul: Essays and Addresses*, ed. and trans. Burton Pike and David S. Luft (Chicago: University of Chicago Press, 1990), p. 246.

34. Robert Musil, " 'Nation' as Ideal and as Reality," in *Precision and Soul*, p. 109.

35. Musil, *The Man without Qualities* 1:8. Compare 2:231–232, 3:65, 420–421, and Robert Musil, *Gesammelte Werke*, ed. Adolf Frisé (Reinbek, 1978), 2:737.

36. Henry van de Velde, "Das neue Ornament" (1901), in *Kunst und Alltag um 1900*, ed. Eckhard Siepman, Werkbund-Archiv, vol. 3 (Gießen: Anabas, 1978), p. 353.

37. Ibid., p. 359.

38. Ibid., p. 362.

39. Siegfried Kracauer, *The Mass Ornament*, trans. Thomas Levin (Cambridge: Harvard University Press, 1994).

40. Adolf Loos, "Ornament und Verbrechen," in *Kunst und Alltag um 1900*, p. 373.

41. Compare Theodor Adorno, "Funktionalismus heute," in *Ohne Leitbild, Parva Aesthetica* (Frankfurt: Suhrkamp, 1973), pp. 104, esp. p. 111.

42. Carl E. Schorske, *Fin-de-siècle Vienna: Politics and Culture* (New York, 1981), pp. 270–271, pls. 4–6.

43. Sternberger, *Über Jugendstil*, p. 33.

44. Walter Benjamin, *Über Haschisch*, ed. Tillman Rexroth (Frankfurt: Suhrkamp, 1972), pp. 57, 120. Compare pp. 58, 109.

45. Letter of August 8, 1903, to Lou Andreas-Salomé, *Letters of Rainer Maria Rilke*, trans. Jane Bannard Greene and M. D. Herter Norton (New York: Norton, 1945), p. 122.

46. Rainer Maria Rilke, *Das Buch der Bilder* (1902) (Frankfurt, 1980), p. 18.

47. Ibid., p. 41.

48. Ibid., pp. 94 f.

49. Rainer Maria Rilke, "On the Verge of Night," in *Translations from the Poetry of Rainer Maria Rilke*, ed. and trans. M. D. Herter Norton (New York: Norton, 1938), p. 76 (original), 77.

50. Rainer Maria Rilke, "Evening in Skane," in *Selected Poems*, trans. Robert Bly (New York: Harper and Row, 1981), p. 98 (original), 99.

51. "The Man Watching," in *Selected Poems*, p. 104 (original), 105.

52. "Gebet," in *Das Buch der Bilder*, p. 41.

53. Rilke, *Das Buch der Bilder*, p. 101.

54. Rilke, *Ausgesetzt auf den Bergen des Herzens* (Frankfurt, 1980), "Waldteich, weicher, in sich eingekehrter," p. 76; cf. "Wendung," ibid., pp. 77 ff.

55. Rilke, *Das Buch der Bilder*, "Die Konfirmanden," p. 26.

56. Ibid., "Fragmente aus verlorenen Tagen," p. 83.

57. Ibid., "Aus einer Sturmnacht 3," p. 98.

58. Rilke, "Die Irren," *Neue Gedichte* (1907–1908) (Frankfurt, 1981), p. 110.

59. Benjamin, *Charles Baudelaire*, pp. 168–169.

60. Johann Wolfgang von Goethe, *Maximen und Reflexionen*, ed. Max Hecker (Frankfurt, 1980), no. 565.

61. Rilke, "Erlebnis," in *Über den jungen Dichter* (Frankfurt, 1978), p. 69.

62. Simmel, *Philosophy of Money*, pp. 97, 477–478.

63. Freud, *Totem and Taboo*, trans. James Strachey (New York and London: Norton, 1950), p. 85.

64. Ibid., p. 86.

65. Ibid., pp. 85, 89.

66. Veblen, *Theory of the Leisure Class*, p. 204.

67. Musil, *The Man without Qualities* 1:28–29.

68. Walter Benjamin, "On Some Motifs in Baudelaire," p. 198; Baudelaire, "Le jeu," in *Flowers of Evil*, pp. 121–122. See also Werner Sombart, *Luxury and Capitalism*, trans. W. R. Dittmar (Ann Arbor: University of Michigan Press, 1967), pp. 87–89.

69. Sartre, *The Words*, p. 79.

70. Ibid.

71. Georg Lukács, "Thoughts on an Aesthetic for the Cinema," trans. Barrie Ellis-Jones, *Framework* 14 (Spring 1981): 3–4.

72. Sartre, *The Words*, p. 78.

73. Hofmannsthal, "Ansprache gehalten am Abend des 10. Mai (1902) im Hause des Grafen Karl Lanckoronski," p. 21.

74. Ibid.

75. Béla Balász, "Der sichtbare Mensch oder die Kultur des Films" (1924), in *Schriften zum Film* (Budapest and Munich, 1982), 1:66.

76. Musil, *Gesammelte Schriften* 2:1817.

77. Ibid., p. 1141.

78. Hofmannsthal, "Über die Pantomime" (1911), p. 503.

79. "Kino und Buchhandel," statement by Max Bruns in *Kino-Debatte 1909–1929*, ed. Anton Kaes (Tübingen: Max Niemeyer Verlag, 1978), p. 86; Hugo von Hofmannsthal, "Der Ersatz für die Träume," in *Kino-Debatte*, p. 149.

80. Bloch, *Principle of Hope* 1:406.

81. Egon Friedell, "Prolog vor dem Film," in *Kino-Debatte*, p. 45. Compare Simmel, "Sociology of the Senses."

82. Henri Bergson, "Laughter," in *Comedy*, intro. and app. by Wylie Sypher (Garden City, N.Y.: Doubleday, 1956), p. 79.

83. Walter Benjamin, "The Work of Art in the Age of Mechanical Reproduction," in *Illuminations*, p. 228.

84. Robert Musil, "Binoculars," in *Posthumous Papers of a Living Author*, trans. Peter Wortsman (Hygiene, Colo.: Eriadnos Press, 1987), pp. 82–83.

85. Benjamin, "The Work of Art," p. 235.

86. Ibid., p. 238.

87. Karl Joël, *Seele und Welt* (1912), p. 3, quoted in Richard Hamann and Jost Hermand, *Impressionismus*, 2d ed. (Munich, 1974), p. 88.

88. Quoted in Hamann and Hermand, *Impressionismus*, p. 89. Compare p. 85.

89. Robert Musil, *Young Torless*, trans. Eithne Wilkins and Ernst Kaiser (New York: Pantheon, 1955), p. 210.

90. Ibid.

91. Ibid.

92. Robert Musil, "[On the Essay]," in *Precision and Soul*, p. 48.

93. Ibid., p. 49.

94. Ibid, p. 50. See Musil, *The Man without Qualities* 1:300–301, and *Der Mann ohne Eigenschaften* (Aus dem Nachlaß), p. 1914; and Georg Lukács, "On the Nature and Form of the Essay," in *Soul and Form*,

trans. Anna Bostock (Cambridge, Mass.: MIT Press, 1984), p. 8. For a discussion of Musil's inspiration by Ralph Waldo Emerson, see " 'Lebende Gedanken' und Emersons Kreise," in *Robert Musil: Untersuchungen*, ed. Uwe Baur and Elisabeth Castex (Königstein: Athenaeum, 1980), p. 139, and Musil, *Tagebücher* 2:849.

95. Wilhelm Worringer, *Abstraction and Empathy*, trans. Michael Bullock (London: Routledge & Kegan Paul, 1953), p. 15.

96. Eberhard Freitag, *Schönberg* (Reinbek: Rowohlt, 1974), p. 66.

97. Wassily Kandinsky, *Concerning the Spiritual in Art*, trans. M. T. H. Sadler (New York: Dover, 1977), pp. 29–32.

98. Ibid., p. 35.

99. Ibid., p. 49. The passage concerning the "spiritual eye" does not appear in the English translation of Kandinsky's work. It may be found in the German edition, *Über das Geistige in der Kunst*, 4th ed., intro. Max Bill (Bern-Bümpliz: Benteli-Verlag, 1952), p. 120.

100. Kandinsky, *Über das Geistige in der Kunst*, p. 123.

101. Ibid., p. 129.

102. Kandinsky, "Rückblicke," quoted in Max Bill, "Introduction," in Kandinsky, *Über das Geistige in der Kunst*, p. 11.

103. Kandinsky, *Über das Geistige in der Kunst*, p. 46.

104. Musil, "Wiener Kunstaustellungen," in *Gesammelte Werke* 2:1643.

105. Hugo von Hofmannsthal, *The Lord Chandos Letter*, trans. Russell Stockman (Marlboro, Vt.: Marlboro Press, 1986), pp. 16–17.

106. Compare Theodor Lipps, *Ästhetik: Psychologie de Schönen und der Kunst* (Hamburg and Leipzig: Voss, 1903–1906).

107. Hofmannsthal, *Letter*, p. 17.

108. Quoted in Max Scheler, *Die Transzendentale und Psychologische Methode* (Leipzig, 1900), p. 148.

109. Hofmannsthal, *Letter*, p. 17.

110. Alfred Kubin, *Die andere Seite* (Munich, 1975), p. 9.

111. Ibid., p. 187.

112. Hofmannsthal, *Letter*, 21.

113. Goethe, *Wilhelm Meister's Journeyman Years*, p. 179.

114. Simmel, *Philosophy of Money*, pp. 449, 457.

115. Hofmannsthal, *Letter*, p. 17.

116. Ibid., pp. 26, 28.

117. Ibid., p. 23.

118. Ibid., p. 24.

119. Rainer Maria Rilke, *The Notebooks of Malte Laurids Brigge*, trans. M. D. Herter Norton (New York: Norton, 1949), pp. 14, 48.

120. Hofmannsthal, *Letter*, p. 25.

121. Ibid., pp. 29, 31.

122. Ibid., p. 32.

EPILOGUE

1. Hugo Ball, *Flight Out of Time*, ed. John Elderfield, trans. Ann Raimes (New York, 1974), pp. 12, 18.

2. Ibid., p. 55.

3. Ibid., p. 57.

4. Henry van de Velde and Paul Klee, quoted in Carola Giedion-Wecker, *Klee* (Reinbek: Rowohlt, 1982), p. 77.

5. Ball, *Flight Out of Time*, p. 22.

6. Ibid., p. 68.

7. Kasimir Malevich, "Vom Kubismus zum Suprematismus in der Kunst, zum neuen Realismus in der Malerei, als der absoluten Schöpfung," in *Sieg über die Sonne,* Schriftenreihe der Akademie der Künste, vol. 15 (Berlin, 1983), p. 134.

8. Ibid., pp. 136 f.

9. Kasimir Malevich, *Suprematismus—Die gegendstandlose Welt* (Cologne, 1962), p. 164.

10. Marcel Duchamp, *Ready Made*, ed. Serge Stauffer (Zurich, 1973), p. 52.

11. Ibid.

12. Ibid.

13. Ibid., p. 49.

14. Ibid.

15. Ibid., p. 51. Compare Pierre Cabanne, *Dialogues with Marcel Duchamp*, trans. Ron Padgett (New York: Viking Press, 1971), pp. 47–48.

Designer: Steve Renick
Compositor: Impressions, *a division of* Edwards Brothers
Text: 11/15 Adobe Garamond
Display: Syntax
Printer: Malloy Lithographing Inc.
Binder: John H. Dekker & Sons